COLLINS

W9-BBL-690

PHRASE BOOK & DICTIONARY

German

HarperCollins*Publishers*

Food section by Edite Vieira Phillips

Other languages in the *Collins Phrase Book & Dictionary* series:

FRENCH
GREEK
ITALIAN
JAPANESE
PORTUGUESE
RUSSIAN
SPANISH

These titles are also published in a language pack containing
60-minute cassette and phrase book

First published 1998
Copyright © HarperCollins*Publishers*
Reprint 10 9 8 7 6 5 4 3 2 1 0
Printed in Italy by Amadeus SpA

ISBN 0 00-472073 3

INTRODUCTION

Your *Collins Phrase Book & Dictionary* is a handy, quick-reference guide that will help you make the most of your stay abroad. Its clear layout will save you valuable time when you need that crucial word or phrase.

There are three main sections in this book:

Practical topics arranged thematically with an opening section **KEY TALK** containing vital phrases that should stand you in good stead in most situations.

PHRASES

Short easy phrases that can be adapted for your situation

practical tips are highlighted in yellow boxes

SIGNS ARE IN GREEN BOXES

replies you might hear are highlighted in red

FOOD SECTION

Phrases for ordering drinks and food
A description of German and Austrian food and drink with a short section on Swiss food
Drinks reader
Menu reader

DICTIONARY

English-German   **German-English** signs highlighted

---

and finally, a short **GRAMMAR** section explaining how the language works.

So, just flick through the pages to find the information you need. Why not start with a look at pronouncing German on page 6. From there on the going is easy with your *Collins Phrase Book & Dictionary*.

CONTENTS

PRONOUNCING GERMAN 6

KEY TALK 7-11

MONEY
  CHANGING 12
  SPENDING 13

GETTING AROUND
  AIRPORT 14
  CUSTOMS & PASSPORTS 15
  ASKING THE WAY 16
  BUS 18
  UNDERGROUND 19
  TRAIN 20
  TAXI 22
  BOAT 23

CAR
  DRIVING/PARKING 24
  PETROL STATION 25
  PROBLEMS/BREAKDOWN 26
  HIRE 27

SHOPPING
  HOLIDAY 28
  CLOTHES 29
  FOOD 30

DAYLIFE
  SIGHTSEEING 32
  BEACH 33
  SPORT 34
  SKIING 35

NIGHTLIFE
  POPULAR 36
  CULTURAL 37

ACCOMMODATION
  HOTEL 38
  SELF-CATERING 40
  CAMPING & CARAVANNING 41

CHILDREN 42
SPECIAL NEEDS 43
EXCHANGE VISITORS 44

DIFFICULTIES
  PROBLEMS 46
  COMPLAINTS 47
  EMERGENCIES 48

HEALTH 50

BUSINESS
  GENERAL 52
  PHONING 54
  FAXING/E-MAIL 55

REFERENCE
  NUMBERS 56
  DAYS & MONTHS 57
  TIME 58

FOOD SECTION 60-90
ORDERING DRINKS & FOOD 60-61
GERMAN/AUSTRIAN/SWISS FOOD
DRINKS 78-79
MENU READER 80-90

DICTIONARY 92-187

GRAMMAR 188-192

PRONOUNCING GERMAN

We've tried to make the pronunciation under the phrases as clear as possible. We've split up words to make them easy to read, but don't pause too long between the syllables. German is not all that hard to pronounce and once you get the hang of unfamiliar letters or letter combinations, you should find yourself reading straight from the German.

You'll notice some differences in the way the language is written. The most obvious is that all nouns begin with capital letters. There is also a letter which doesn't exist in English – **ß** – which is like **ss**.

Most letters are pronounced in much the same way as their English equivalents. However, when they appear at the end of a word **b** is pronounced like **p**, **d** like **t**, and **g** like **k**; and **v** is pronounced like **f**, and **w** like **v**. **S** is pronounced like **sh** in **shock** before **p** and **t** when they are at the beginning of a word, and when it is combined with **ch**.

The umlaut ¨ often appears over German vowels and makes a difference to the pronunciation. Two sounds, **ö** and **ü**, are rather different from anything in English. We show **ö** as **ur'** because the nearest sound to it is in English words like hurt, but don't roll the **r**! The sound of **ü** can be made if you purse your lips and try to say **ee**. We give this sound as **oo** in the pronunciation.

A final **e** is always pronounced, and sounds like **a** in sof**a** or **e** in Porsch**e**. So German 'bitte' sounds like English 'bitter'.

The syllable to be stressed is the one in **heavy type**.

Here are a few other rules to be aware of:

german	sounds like	example	pronunciation
au	ow	**Auto**	owto
äu	oy	**Säule**	zoy-le
ch	kh	**ich**	ikh
ei	'eye'	**ein**	ine
ie	ee	**sie**	zee
eu	oy	**neun**	noyn

Among friends you will hear **hi!** and **tschüs! (bye)** but you should avoid these unless you know the person well. In southern Germany and Austria you often hear the greeting **Grüß Gott** for **hello**. In Switzerland you will hear **Grüezi** for **hello** and **Ade** for **goodbye**. To catch someone's attention use **Entschuldigung!**

yes	**no**	**that's fine**
ja	nein	das ist gut so
ya	*nine*	*das ist goot zoh*

please	**thank you**	**bitte!**
bitte	danke	***bi*-te**
***bi*-te**	***dang*-ke**	a pleasure!

hello	**goodbye**	**goodnight**
guten Tag	auf Wiedersehen	gute Nacht
***goo*ten tahk**	*owf **vee**der-zayn*	***goo*te nakht**

excuse me	**sorry**	**pardon?**
Entschuldigung	Verzeihung	wie bitte?
*ent**shool**-digoong*	*fer-**tsy**-oong*	*vee **bi**-te*

Here is an easy way to ask for something... just add **bitte**

a...	**a coffee**	**2 coffees**
einen... ('der' words)	einen Kaffee	zwei Kaffee
ine-en...	*ine-en ka**fay***	*tsvy ka**fay***
	a bottle	**2 bottles**
eine... ('die' words)	eine Flasche	zwei Flaschen
ine-e...	*ine-e **fla**-she*	*tsvy **fla**-shen*
	a Pils	**2 Pils**
ein... ('das' words)	ein Pils	zwei Pils
ine...	*ine pilz*	*tsvy pilz*

a coffee and two Pils, please
einen Kaffee und zwei Pils, bitte
*ine-en ka**fay** oont tsvy pilz **bi**-te*

KEY TALK

| I'd like...
| ich möchte...
| *ikh **mur'kh**-te...*

we'd like...
wir möchten...
*veer **mur'kh**-ten...*

I'd like an ice cream
ich möchte ein Eis
*ikh **mur'kh**-te ine ice*

we'd like to visit Potsdam
wir möchten Potsdam besuchen
*veer **mur'kh**-ten **pots**-dam be**zoo**khen*

| do you have ...?
| haben Sie...?
| ***hah**-ben zee...*

do you have any milk?
haben Sie Milch?
***hah**-ben zee milkh*

do you have stamps?
haben Sie Briefmarken?
***hah**-ben zee **breef**-marken*

do you have a map?
haben Sie eine Landkarte?
***hah**-ben zee i**ne**-e **lant**-kar-te*

do you have salami?
haben Sie Salami?
hah**-ben zee sala**mee

| how much is...?
| was kostet...?
| *vas **kos**tet...*

how much is it?
was kostet das?
*vas **kos**tet das*

how much is the cheese?
was kostet der Käse?
*vas **kos**tet der **kay**-ze*

how much is the room?
was kostet das Zimmer?
*vas **kos**tet das **tsim**mer*

how much is a kilo?
was kostet ein Kilo?
*vas **kos**tet ine **kee**lo*

how much is it each?
was kostet es pro Stück?
*vas **kos**tet es pro shtook*

TOMATEN..................KG 2,99 DM	TOMATOES PER KILO
BIRNEN ....KG 4,99 DM	PEARS PER KILO
ORANGEN ....STÜCK 0,59 DM	ORANGES EACH

where is...?	**where are...?**
wo ist...?	wo sind...?
voh ist...	*voh zint...*

where is the station?
wo ist der Bahnhof?
*voh ist der **bahn**-hof*

where are the toilets?
wo sind die Toiletten?
*voh zint dee twa-**le**-ten*

DAMEN LADIES	**FREI** FREE	**EINGANG** ENTRANCE
HERREN GENTS	**BESETZT** OCCUPIED	**AUSGANG** EXIT

is there/are there ...?
gibt es ...?
gipt es...

is there a restaurant?
gibt es ein Restaurant?
*gipt es ine restoh-**rong***

where's there a chemist?
wo gibt es eine Apotheke?
*voh gipt es ine-e apoh-**tay**-ke*

are there reductions?
gibt es Ermäßigung?
*gipt es er-**may**-sigoong*

is there a golf course?
gibt es einen Golfplatz?
*gipt es ine-en **golf**-plats*

there is no...
es gibt kein *(das)*/keinen *(der)*/keine *(die & plural)*...
*es gipt **ki**ne/**ki**ne-en/**ki**ne-e...*

there is no hot water
es gibt kein heißes Wasser
*es gipt kine **hy**-ses **vas**ser*

there are no towels
es gibt keine Handtücher
*es gipt **ki**ne-e **hant**-tookher*

I need...
ich brauche...
*ikh **brow**-khe...*

I need help
ich brauche Hilfe
*ikh **brow**-khe **hil**-fe*

I need a receipt
ich brauche eine Quittung
*ikh **brow**-khe ine-e **kvi**-toong*

KEY TALK

can I...
kann ich...
kan ikh...

can I phone?
kann ich telefonieren?
*kan ikh taylay-fo-**nee**ren*

can I book a ticket?
kann ich ein Ticket buchen?
*voh kan ikh ine **ti**cket **boo**-khen*

where can I...?
wo kann ich...?
voh kan ikh...

where can I buy tickets?
wo kann ich Karten kaufen?
*voh kan ikh **kar**-ten **kow**fen*

where can I hire a bike?
wo kann ich ein Fahrrad leihen?
*voh kan ikh ine **fah**-rat **lye**-en*

Karten können Sie am Kiosk kaufen
*kar-ten **kur'**-nen zee am **ki**osk **kow**fen*
you can buy tickets at the kiosk

when?
wann?
van

when is breakfast?
wann gibt es Frühstück?
*van gipt es **froo**-shtook*

when is lunch?
wann gibt es Mittagessen?
*van gipt es **mi**tahk-essen*

when does it open?
wann ist geöffnet?
*van ist ge-**ur'f**net*

when does it close?
wann wird geschlossen?
*van virt ge**shlo**ssen*

yesterday	**today**	**tomorrow**
gestern	heute	morgen
***ges**tern*	***hoy**-te*	***mor**gen*

this morning	**this afternoon**	**this evening**
heute morgen	heute nachmittag	heute abend
***hoy**-te **mor**gen*	***hoy**-te **nakh**-mitahk*	***hoy**-te **ah**bent*

10

| ÖFFNUNGSZEITEN | BUSINESS HOURS |
| UHR BIS ___UHR | FROM... UNTIL... |

MO.	MON
DI.	TUE
MI.	WED
DO.	THU
FR.	FRI
SA.	SAT
SO.	SUN

is it open?
ist es geöffnet?
*ist es ge-**ur'f**net*

is it closed?
ist es geschlossen?
*ist es ge**shlo**ssen*

TÄGLICH DAILY

DAUER DURATION

| **2 STUNDEN** | 2 HOURS |
| **3 STUNDEN** | 3 HOURS |

RUHETAG RESTDAY

es macht um 9 auf
es makht oom noyn owf
it opens at 9

das Museum ist sonntags geschossen
*das moo-**zay**-oom ist **zonn**taks ge**shlo**ssen*
the museum is closed on Sunday

GETTING TO KNOW PEOPLE

The equivalent to Mr is Herr, Mrs or Ms is Frau. The word for Miss Fräulein is not used very much.

how are you?
wie geht es Ihnen?
*vee gayt es **ee**-nen*

fine, thanks. And you?
danke, gut. Und Ihnen?
***dang**-ke goot. oont **ee**-nen*

my name is...
mein Name ist...
*mine **nah**-me ist...*

what is your name?
wie ist Ihr Name?
*vee ist eer **nah**-me*

I don't understand
ich verstehe nicht
*ikh fer-**shtay**-e nikht*

do you speak English?
sprechen Sie Englisch?
***shpre**-khen zee **eng**-lish*

MONEY – changing

| GELDWECHSEL | BUREAU DE CHANGE |
| GELDAUTOMAT | CASH DISPENSER |

Eurocheque card cash dispensers are widely available in Germany. It is often much more reasonable to change money using these rather than changing cash and paying the commission.

where can I change money?
wo kann ich Geld wechseln?
*voh kan ikh gelt **vek**-seln*

where is the bank?
wo ist die Bank?
voh ist dee bank

where is the bureau de change?
wo ist der Geldwechsel?
*voh ist der **gelt**-veksel*

when does the bank open?
wann macht die Bank auf?
van makht dee bank owf

when does the bank close?
wann macht die Bank zu?
van makht dee bank tsoo

I want to cash these traveller's cheques
ich möchte gern diese Reiseschecks einlösen
*ikh **mu'rkh**-te gern **dee**-ze **ry**-ze-sheks **ine**-lur'-zen*

what's the rate...?
wie ist der Kurs...?
vee ist der koors...

for pounds
für Pfund Sterling
*foor pfoont **ster**-ling*

for dollars
für Dollars
*foor **do**llars*

I want to change £50
ich möchte fünfzig Pfund wechseln
*ikh **mur'kh**-te **foonf**-tsikh pfoont **vek**-seln*

what's the commission?
wie hoch ist die Gebühr?
*vee hohkh ist dee ge-**boohr***

can I use my credit card to get Marks?
kann ich hier mit meiner Kreditkarte D-Mark bekommen?
*kan ikh heer mit **mi**ne-er kre**deet**-kar-te **da**y-mark be-**kom**men*

I'd like small notes
ich möchte kleine Scheine
*ikh **mur'kh**-te **kli**ne-e **shi**ne-e*

KASSE	CASH DESK
MWST (MEHRWERTSTEUER)	VAT

how much is it?
was kostet das?
*vas **kost**et das*

how much will it be?
was wird das kosten?
*vas virt das **kost**en*

I want to pay
zahlen, bitte
***tsah**-len **bi**-te*

we want to pay separately
wir möchten einzeln bezahlen
*veer **mur'kh**-ten **ine**-tseln be**tsah**-len*

can I pay by credit card?
kann ich mit Kreditkarte bezahlen?
*kan ikh mit kre**deet**-kar-te be**tsah**-len*

do you accept traveller's cheques?
nehmen Sie Reiseschecks?
***nay**men zee **ry**-ze-sheks*

how much is it...?	**per person**	**per night**	**per kilo**
was kostet das...?	pro Person	pro Nacht	pro Kilo
*vas **kost**et das...*	*pro per-**zon***	*pro nakht*	*pro **kee**-lo*

are service and VAT included?
sind Bedienung und Mehrwertsteuer inbegriffen?
*zint be-**dee**noong oont **mayr**-vayrt-shtoy-er **in**-be-griffen*

put it on my bill
setzen Sie es auf meine Rechnung
***zet**-sen zee es owf **mine**-e **rekh**-noong*

I need a receipt
ich brauche eine Quittung
*ikh **brow**-khe **ine**-e **kvi**-toong*

do you require a deposit?
nehmen Sie eine Kaution?
nay**men zee **ine**-e kow-**tsyohn

I've nothing smaller
ich habe es nicht kleiner
*ikh **hah**-be es nikht **kli**ne-er*

keep the change
stimmt so
shtimt zoh

AIRPORT

ANKUNFT / ABFLUG	ARRIVALS / DEPARTURES
GEPÄCKAUSGABE	BAGGAGE RECLAIM
FLUGHAFENBUS	AIRPORT BUS
VERSPÄTUNG	DELAY
ABFERTIGUNG	CHECK-IN

to the airport, please
zum Flughafen, bitte
*tsoom **flook**-hafen **bi**-te*

how can I get into town?
wie komme ich in die Stadt?
*vee **kom**me ikh in dee shtat*

where do I get the bus to the town centre?
wo fährt der Bus zum Stadtzentrum ab?
*voh fayrt der boos tsoom **shtat**-tsentroom ap*

how much is it...?
was kostet die Fahrt...?
*vas **kos**tet dee fahrt...*

to the town centre
ins Stadtzentrum
*ins **shtat**-tsentroom*

to the airport
zum Flughafen
*tsoom **flook**-hafen*

where do I check in for...?
wo ist der Check-in für...?
*voh ist der **check**-in foor...*

which gate for the flight to...?
welches Gate hat der Flug nach...?
***vel**-khes gate hat der flook nakh...*

Sie steigen von Gate Nummer ... ein
*zee **shty**-gen fon gate noomer ... ine*
boarding will take place at gate number...

gehen Sie sofort zu Gate Nummer...
***gay**en zee zo-**fort** tsoo gate noomer...*
go immediately to gate number...

Ihr Flug hat Verspätung
*eer flook hat fer-**shpay**-toong*
your flight is delayed

CUSTOMS & PASSPORTS

ZOLL	CUSTOMS CONTROL
PASSKONTROLLE	PASSPORT CONTROL

With the single European market, EU (European Union) citizens are subject to only highly selective spot checks and they can go through the blue customs channel (unless they have goods to declare). There is no restriction by quantity or value, on goods purchased by travellers in another EU country provided they are for their own personal use (guidelines have been published). If unsure, check with customs officials.

I have nothing to declare
ich habe nichts zu verzollen
*ikh **hah**-be nikhts tsoo fer-**tsoll**en*

here is...	**my passport**	**my green card**
hier ist...	mein Paß	meine grüne Versicherungskarte
heer ist...	*mine pass*	*mine-e **groo**-ne fer-**zikh**-e-roongz-kar-te*

do I have to pay duty on this?
muß ich das verzollen?
*moos ikh das fer-**tsoll**en*

it's for my own personal use
es ist für meinen persönlichen Gebrauch
*es ist foor **mine**-en per-**zur'n**-likhen ge-**browkh***

we're on our way to...
wir sind auf der Durchreise nach...
*veer zint owf der **doorkh**-ry-ze nakh...*

the children are on this passport
die Kinder stehen in diesem Paß
*dee **kin**der **shtay**-en in **dee**-zem pass*

I'm...	**British** (m/f)	**Australian** (m/f)
Ich bin...	Brite/Britin	Australier/Australierin
ikh bin...	***bree**-te/**bree**-tin*	*ow**strah**lee-er/ow**strah**lee-er-in*

ASKING THE WAY – questions

excuse me, please
entschuldigen Sie, bitte
*ent**shool**-digen zee **bi**-te*

where is the nearest...?
wo ist der/die/das nächste...?
*voh ist der/dee/das **naykh**-ste...*

how do I get to...?
wie komme ich zum/zur/nach...?
*vee **komm**e ikh tsoom/tsoor/nakh...*

is this the right way to...?
bin ich hier richtig zum/zur/nach...?
*bin ikh heer **rikh**tikh tsoom/tsoor/nakh...*

the...	**is it far?**
der/die/das...	ist es weit?
der/dee/das...	*ist es vite*

can I walk there?
kann ich dahin laufen?
*kan ikh da**hin low**fen*

is there a bus that goes there?
fährt ein Bus dahin?
*fayrt ine boos da**hin***

we're looking for...
wir suchen...
*veer **zoo**khen...*

we're lost (on foot)
wir haben uns verlaufen
*veer **hah**-ben oons fer-**low**fen*

where is...?
wo ist...?
voh ist...

where are the toilets?
wo sind die Toiletten?
*voh zint dee twa-**le**-ten*

---

zum/zur/nach = to

to the station
zum Bahnhof (der/das nouns)
*tsoom **bahn**-hohf*

to the castle
zur Burg (die nouns)
tsoor boork

to Bonn
nach Bonn (with place names)
nakh bon

---

we're lost (in car)
wir haben uns verfahren
*veer **hah**-ben oons fer-**fah**ren*

can you show me on the map?
können Sie mir das auf der Karte zeigen?
***kur**'-nen zee meer das owf der **kar**-te **tsy**-gen*

answers – ASKING THE WAY

It's no use being able to ask the way if you're not going to understand the directions you get. We've tried to anticipate the likely answers, so listen carefully for these key phrases.

gehen Sie immer geradeaus weiter
*gay-en zee immer ge-**rah**-de-ows **vye**-ter*
keep going straight ahead

kehren Sie um
kehr-ren zee oom
you have to turn round

biegen Sie...	**rechts ab**	**links ab**
bee-gen zee...	*rekhts ap*	*links ap*
turn...	right	left
gehen Sie...	**in Richtung...**	**bis zu...**
gay-en zee...	*in **rikh**-toong...*	*bis tsoo...*
you go... (on foot)	towards...	as far as...
fahren Sie...	**nach rechts**	**nach links**
***fah**-ren zee...*	*nakh rekhts*	*nakh links*
you go... (driving)	right	left
nehmen Sie...	**die erste Straße rechts**	
***nay**-men zee...*	*dee **ers**-te **shtrah**-se rekhts*	
take...	the first road on the right	

die zweite Straße links
*dee **tsvye**-te **shtrah**-se links*
the second road on the left

die Straße nach...
*dee **shtrah**-se nakh...*
the road to...

folgen Sie den Schildern nach...
***fol**-gen zee den **shil**-dern nakh...*
follow the signs for...

BUS

Most cities have a pay-as-you-enter system, with a standard fare for all journeys. Otherwise bus and tram tickets can be purchased from slot machines or tobacconists and stamped on board the bus/tram/underground.

where is the bus station?
wo ist der Busbahnhof?
*voh ist der **boos**-bahn-hohf*

where is the tram stop?
wo ist die Straßenbahnhaltestelle?
*voh ist dee **shtrah**senbahn-**hal**-te-shtel-le*

I want to go...
ich möchte...
*ikh **mur'kh**-te...*

to the station
zum Bahnhof *(m)*
*tsoom **bahn**-hohf*

to the museum
zum Museum *(nt)*
*zum moo-**zay**-oom*

to the art gallery
zur Kunsthalle *(f)*
*tsoor **koonst**-hal-le*

to Bonn
nach Bonn
nakh bon

does a bus go there?
fährt ein Bus dahin?
*fayrt ine boos da**hin***

which bus do I take to get there?
mit welchem Bus komme ich dahin?
*mit **vel**-khem boos **kom**me ikh da**hin***

where does the bus go from?
wo fährt der Bus ab?
voh fayrt der boos ap

how often are the buses?
wie oft fahren die Busse?
*vee oft **fah**-ren dee **boo**-se*

when is the last bus?
wann geht der letzte Bus?
*van gayt der **let**-ste boos*

please tell me when to get off
sagen Sie mir bitte, wann ich aussteigen muß
***zah**gen zee meer **bi**-te van ikh **ows**-shtygen moos*

UNDERGROUND

U-BAHN	UNDERGROUND
EINGANG / AUSGANG	ENTRANCE / EXIT

*In many cities you can get **eine Touristenkarte** (which covers all public transport), or **eine Familienkarte** (2 adults, 2 children). Ask for **spezielle Fahrkarten**. Usually there is a zone system and you will be asked if you want a card for **die Innenstadt** (inner city) or **das gesamte Stadtgebiet** (all zones).*

where is the nearest underground station?
wo ist die nächste U-Bahn-Haltestelle?
*voh ist dee **naykh**-ste **oo**bahn-**hal**-te-shtel-le*

what special tickets are there?
welche speziellen Fahrkarten gibt es?
*vel-khe shpe-tsee-**el**-len **fahr**-kar-ten gipt es*

a tourist ticket, please
eine Touristenkarte, bitte
*ine-e too**ris**ten-karte **bi**-te*

inner zones
die Innenstadt
*dee **in**-nen-shtat*

all zones
alle Zonen
*al-le **tsoh**-nen*

do you have a map of the metro?
gibt es eine Karte mit allen U-Bahn-Linien?
*gipt es ine-e **kar**-te mit **al**-len **oo**-bahn-**lee**-nee-en*

I want to go to...
ich möchte zum/zur/nach...
*ikh **mur'kh**-te tsoom/tsoor/nakh...*

can I go by underground?
kann ich mit der U-Bahn fahren?
*kan ikh mit der **oo**bahn **fah**-ren*

do I have to change?
muß ich umsteigen?
*moos ikh **oom**-shtygen*

where?
wo?
voh

which line is it for...?
welche Linie fährt nach...?
***vel**-khe **lee**-nee-e fayrt nakh...*

what is the next stop?
was ist der nächste Halt?
*vas ist der **naykh**-ste halt*

welche Zonen?
***vel**-khe **tsoh**-nen*
which zones?

für die Innenstadt oder für alle Zonen?
*foor dee **in**nen-shtat **oh**der foor **al**-le **tsoh**-nen*
for the inner city or all zones?

TRAIN

ICE (InterCity Express)	SPECIAL FARE APPLIES
EC / IC (EuroCity / InterCity)	SUPPLEMENT PAYABLE
REISEZENTRUM	TICKETS AND INFORMATION
ABFAHRT	DEPARTURES
ANKUNFT	ARRIVALS
BAHNSTEIG	PLATFORM
S-BAHN	LOCAL RAIL NETWORK
SPEISEWAGEN	RESTAURANT CAR
SCHLAFWAGEN	SLEEPER

*Check if a supplement, **ein Zuschlag**, is required before you board the train. It costs less if you buy it with your ticket. In Germany children under 10 pay half fare, and those under 4 travel free. If you plan to travel in Switzerland by train, a number of passes are available which must be purchased from Switzerland Tourism in your own country before departing for Switzerland.*

where is the station?
wo ist der Bahnhof?
*voh ist der **bahn**-hohf*

to the station, please
zum Bahnhof, bitte
*tsoom **bahn**-hohf bi-te*

a single to...
einmal einfach nach...
***ine**-mal **ine**-fakh nakh...*

2 singles to...
zweimal einfach nach...
***tsvy**-mal **ine**-fakh nakh...*

a return to...
eine Rückfahrkarte nach...
*ine-e **rook**-fahr-kar-te nakh...*

2 returns to...
zweimal hin und zurück nach...
***tsvy**-mal hin oont tsoo-**rook** nakh...*

a child's return to...
eine Kinderrückfahrkarte nach...
*ine-e kinder-**rook**-fahr-kar-te nakh...*

lst class	**2nd class**	**Smoking**	**Non smoking**
erster Klasse	zweiter Klasse	Raucher	Nichtraucher
*er-ster **kla**-se*	*tsvy-ter **kla**-se*	***row**-kher*	***nikht**-row-kher*

do I have to pay a supplement?
muß ich einen Zuschlag zahlen?
*moos ikh ine-en **tsoo**shlak **tsah**len*

is my pass valid on this train?
ist mein Paß für diesen Zug gültig?
*ist mine pass foor **dee**zen tsook **gool**tikh*

I want to book...	**a seat**	**a couchette**
ich möchte ... buchen	einen Platz	einen Liegewagenplatz
*ikh **mur'kh**-te ... **boo**-khen*	*ine-en plats*	*ine-en **lee**-ge-vahgen-plats*

do you have a timetable?
haben Sie einen Fahrplan?
***hah**-ben zee ine-en **fahr**-plahn*

do I need to change?
muß ich umsteigen?
*moos ikh **oom**-shty-gen*

where?
wo?
voh

which platform does it leave from?
von welchem Bahnsteig fährt er ab?
*fon **vel**-khem **bahn**-shtike fayrt er ap*

does the train to ... leave from here?
fährt hier der Zug nach ... ab?
fayrt heer der tsook nakh ... ap

is this the train for...?
ist das der Zug nach...?
ist das der tsook nakh...

where is the left-luggage?
wo ist die Gepäckaufbewahrung?
*voh ist dee ge**pek**-owf-bevahroong*

is this seat free?
ist hier noch frei?
ist heer nokh fry

TAXI

In Germany to take a taxi you have to find a taxi rank, **Taxistand**, or phone for one. You can often find adverts for taxi firms in public phone boxes and you must give your name and the address of the phone box which will be written under the word **Standort**.

to the airport, please
zum Flughafen, bitte
tsoom **flook**-hafen **bi**-te

to the station, please
zum Bahnhof, bitte
tsoom **bahn**-hohf **bi**-te

to this address, please
zu dieser Adresse bitte
tsoo **dee**zer a-**dre**-se **bi**-te

to hotel...
zum Hotel...
tsoom ho**tel**...

how much will it cost?
was wird das kosten?
vas virt das **kos**ten

why is it so much?
warum ist das so teuer?
vah**room** ist das zoh **toy**-er

how much is to the centre?
was kostet die Fahrt ins Zentrum?
vas **kos**tet dee fahrt ins **tsen**troom

where can I get a taxi?
wo bekomme ich hier ein Taxi?
voh be-**kom**me ikh heer ine **ta**xi

please order me a taxi
bitte bestellen Sie mir ein Taxi
bi-te be-**shtel**len zee meer ine **ta**xi

straightaway
sofort
zo-**fort**

for ...
für ... Uhr
foor ... oor

I need a receipt
ich brauche eine Quittung
ikh **brow**-khe **i**ne-e **kvi**-toong

I've nothing smaller
ich habe es nicht kleiner
ikh **hah**-be es nikht **kli**ne-er

keep the change
stimmt so
shtimt zoh

BOAT

The Swiss travel pass allows you reduced travel on the Swiss Lakes. Check with Swtizerland Tourism before your holiday to find out what is available. Passes have to be purchased in your own country before arriving in Switzerland.

1 ticket	**2 tickets**	**single**	**round trip**
einmal	zweimal	einfach	eine Rundfahrt
ine-mal	*tsvy-mal*	*ine-fakh*	*ine-e roont-fahrt*

is there a tourist ticket?
gibt es eine Touristenkarte?
gipt es ine-e tooristen-kar-te

are there any boat trips?
gibt es Schiffsfahrten?
gipt es shifs-fahr-ten

how long is the trip?
wie lange dauert die Fahrt?
vee lang-e dow-ert dee fahrt

when is the next boat?
wann geht das nächste Schiff?
van gayt das naykh-ste shif

when is the next ferry?
wann geht die nächste Fähre?
van gayt dee naykh-ste fair-re

when is the first boat?
wann geht das erste Schiff?
van gayt das er-ste shif

when is the last boat?
wann geht das letzte Schiff?
van gayt das lets-te shif

is there a time table?
gibt es einen Fahrplan?
gipt es ine-en fahr-plahn

can we eat on board?
können wir an Bord essen?
kur'-nen veer an board es-sen

can we hire a boat?
können wir ein Boot mieten?
kur'-nen veer ine boat mee-ten

CAR – driving/parking

ALLE RICHTUNGEN	ALL ROUTES
AUSFAHRT	EXIT
AUTOBAHN	MOTORWAY
MAUT	TOLL
PARKEN VERBOTEN	NO PARKING
STADTZENTRUM	CITY CENTRE

Motorway tax is payable in Switzerland and Austria. The Swiss tax is valid for one year and runs from 1 Dec to 31 Jan. It can be purchased at the border. Once attached to the windscreen you will be unable to remove it without destroying it. For Austria there are stickers valid for one week or 2 months.

can I park here?
kann ich hier parken?
*kan ikh heer **par**ken*

do I need a parking disk?
brauche ich eine Parkscheibe?
***brow**-khe ikh ine-e **park**-shy-be*

where can I park?
wo kann ich parken?
*voh kan ikh **par**-ken*

is there a car park?
gibt es einen Parkplatz?
*gipt es ine-en **park**-plats*

where can I get a parking disk?
wo kann ich eine Parkscheibe bekommen?
*voh kan ikh ine-e **park**-shy-be be-**kom**men*

how long can I park here?
wie lange kann ich hier parken?
*vee **lang**-e kan ikh heer **par**ken*

we're going to....
wir fahren nach...
*veer **fah**-ren nakh...*

what's the best route?
was ist der beste Weg?
*vas ist der **bes**-te vayk*

is the pass open?
ist der Paß offen?
*ist der pass **of**fen*

do I need snow chains?
brauche ich Schneeketten?
***brow**-khe ikh **shnay**-ketten*

petrol station – CAR

SUPER	4 STAR
BLEIFREI	UNLEADED
DIESEL	DIESEL
BENZIN	PETROL
SELBSTBEDIENUNG	SELF-SERVICE

Note that leaded petrol is no longer available in Germany. If your car runs on leaded petrol, an additive is available that allows your car to run on lead-free petrol.

is there a petrol station near here?
ist hier in der Nähe eine Tankstelle?
*ist heer in der **nay**-e **i**ne-e **tank**-shte-le*

fill it up, please
volltanken, bitte
***fol**-tang-ken **bi**-te*

50 DM worth of unleaded petrol
für fünfzig DM bleifrei bitte
*foor **foonf**-tsikh day-mark **bly**-fry **bi**-te*

I need additive
Ich brauche Bleiersatz-Additiv
*ikh **brow**-khe bly-er**sats**-ahditeef*

pump number...
Säule Nummer...
***zoy**-le **noo**mer...*

where is the air line?
wo ist die Druckluft?
*voh ist dee **drook**-looft*

where is the water?
wo ist das Wasser?
*voh ist das **vas**ser*

please check...
bitte überprüfen Sie...
***bi**-te oober-**proo**fen zee...*

the tyre pressure
den Reifendruck
*den **ry**fen-drook*

the oil	**the water**
das Öl	das Wasser
das ur'l	*das **vas**ser*

welche Säule?
***vel**-khe **zoy**-le*
which pump?

25

CAR – problems/breakdown

If you break down on the motorway in Germany you can call the roadside services from one of the emergency phones. Assistance is free, though any parts must be paid for.

the street police, please
die Straßenwacht, bitte
*dee **shtra**sen-vakht **bi**-te*

I'm on my own
ich bin allein
*ikh bin **al**-line*

where is the nearest garage?
wo ist die nächste Werkstatt?
*voh ist dee **naykh**-ste **verk**-shtat*

is it serious?
ist es etwas Ernstes?
*ist es **et**vas **ern**-stes*

when will it be ready?
wann wird es fertig sein?
*van virt es **fer**-tikh zine*

the car won't start
das Auto springt nicht an
*das **ow**to shpringt nikht an*

the engine is overheating
der Motor wird zu heiß
*der **moh**tor virt tsoo hice*

have you the parts?
haben Sie Ersatzteile?
***hah**-ben zee er**zats**-tile-e*

I've broken down
ich habe eine Panne
*ikh **hah**-be **i**ne-e **pa**-ne*

I have children in the car
ich habe Kinder dabei
*ikh **hah**-be **kin**der da-**by***

the ... is leaking
der/die/das ... ist leck
der/dee/das ... ist leck

can you repair it?
können Sie es reparieren?
***kur'n**-en zee es raypa-**ree**ren*

how much will it cost?
was wird das kosten?
*vas virt das **kos**ten*

I have a flat tyre
ich habe einen Platten
*ikh **hah**-be **i**ne-en **pla**-ten*

the battery is flat
meine Batterie ist leer
***mi**ne-e ba-te**ree** ist layr*

something is wrong with...
es stimmt etwas nicht mit...
*es shtimt **et**vas nikht mit...*

can you put in a new windscreen?
können Sie eine neue Windschutzscheibe einsetzen?
***kur'**-nen zee **i**ne-e **noy**-e **vint**shoots-shy-be **i**ne-zetsen*

AUTOVERMIETUNG   CAR HIRE

Remember, a credit card is very useful for car hire companies that require a deposit.

I want to hire a car
ich möchte ein Auto mieten
*ikh **mur'kh**-te ine **ow**to **mee**ten*

for one day
für einen Tag
foor ine-en tahk

for ... days
für ... Tage
*foor ... **tah**-ge*

how much is it?
was kostet es?
*vas **kos**tet es*

is fully comprehensive insurance included?
ist eine Vollkaskoversicherung inbegriffen?
*ist ine-e **fol**-kasko-fer-**zikh**eroong **in**-be-griffen*

do you have...?
haben Sie...?
***hah**-ben zee...*

a larger car
ein größeres Auto
*ine **grur'**-ser-es **ow**to*

a smaller car
ein kleineres Auto
*ine **kli**ne-e-res **ow**to*

a cheaper car
ein billigeres Auto
*ine **bil**-ig-er-es **ow**to*

an automatic
eines mit Automatik
*ine-es mit owto-**mah**-tik*

what do we do if we break down?
was tun wir bei einem Unfall?
*vas toon veer by ine-em **oon**fal*

must I return the car here?
muß ich das Auto hierher zurückbringen?
*moos ikh das **ow**to **heer**-her tsoo**rook**-bringen*

by what time?
bis wann?
bis van

I'd like to leave it in...
ich würde es gern in ... abgeben
*ikh **voor**-de es gern in ... **ap**-gayben*

please show me the controls
bitte erklären Sie mir die Schalter
***bi**-te er-**klay**-ren zee meer dee **shal**-ter*

where are the documents?
wo sind die Papiere?
*voh zint dee pa**pee**re*

bitte bringen Sie das Auto vollgetankt zurück
***bi**-te bringen zee das **ow**to **fol**-ge-tankt tsoo**rook**
please return the car with a full tank

SHOPPING – holiday

GEÖFFNET OPEN | **KASSE** CASH DESK
GESCHLOSSEN CLOSED | **AUSVERKAUF** SALE

Most large shops in Germany are open all day approx. 9am-8pm Mon-Fri. On Thursdays they stay open until 9pm. On Saturdays they are open until 4pm. Shops shut on Sundays.

do you sell...?
verkaufen Sie...?
*fer-**kow**fen zee...*

stamps
Briefmarken
***breef**-mar-ken*

batteries for this camera
Batterien für diese Kamera
*ba-te**ree**-en foor **dee**-ze **ka**mera*

where can I buy...?
wo bekomme ich...?
*voh be-**kom**me ikh...*

stamps
Briefmarken
***breef**-marken*

films
Filme
***fil**me*

10 stamps
zehn Briefmarken
*tsayn **breef**-marken*

for postcards
für Postkarten
*foor **post**-kar-ten*

to Britain
nach England
*nakh **eng**-lant*

a colour film
einen Farbfilm
*ine-en **farp**-film*

a tape for this video camera
ein Videoband für diese Videokamera
*ine **vee**day-o-bant foor **dee**-ze **vee**day-o-kamera*

I'm looking for a present
ich suche ein Geschenk
*ikh **zoo**khe ine ge**shenk***

have you anything else?
haben Sie noch etwas anderes?
***hah**-ben zee nokh **et**vas **an**-de-res*

it's a gift
es ist ein Geschenk
*es ist ine ge**shenk***

please wrap it up
bitte verpacken Sie es
***bi**-te fer-**pak**-en zee es*

is there a market?
gibt es einen Markt?
*gipt es **i**ne-en markt*

when?
wann?
van

clothes – SHOPPING

WOMEN		MEN		SHOES			
UK	EU	**UK**	EU	**UK**	EU	**UK**	EU
10	36	**36**	46	**2**	35	**7**	41
12	38	**38**	48	**3**	36	**8**	42
14	40	**40**	50	**4**	37	**9**	43
16	42	**42**	52	**5**	38	**10**	44
18	44	**44**	54	**6**	39	**11**	45
20	46	**46**	56	**7**	41	**12**	46

can I try this on?
kann ich das anprobieren?
*kan ikh das **an**proh-beeren*

it's too big
es ist zu groß
es ist tsoo grohs

it's too small
es ist zu klein
es ist tsoo kline

it's too expensive
es ist zu teuer
*es ist tsoo **toy**-er*

I'm just looking
ich schaue mich nur um
*ikh **show**-e mikh noor oom*

I take size ... shoe
ich habe Schuhgröße...
*ikh **hah**-be **shoo**-grur'-se...*

where are the changing rooms?
wo sind die Umkleidekabinen?
*voh zint dee **oom**-kly-de-ka-**bee**nen*

have you anything smaller?
haben Sie etwas Kleineres?
***hah**-ben zee **et**vas **kli**ne-er-es*

have you anything larger?
haben Sie etwas Größeres?
***hah**-ben zee **et**vas **grur'**-ser-es*

have you anything cheaper?
haben Sie etwas Billigeres?
***hah**-ben zee **et**vas **bil**-ig-er-es*

I'll take this one
ich nehme das hier
*ikh **nay**-me das heer*

---

welche Größe haben Sie?
***vel**-khe **grur'**-se **hah**-ben zee*
what size are you?

paßt es?
past es
does it fit?

29

SHOPPING – food

BÄCKEREI BAKER		**SUPERMARKT** SUPERMARKET	
FLEISCHEREI BUTCHER		**OBST** FRUIT	
FISCHHANDLUNG FISHMONGER		**FEINKOST** DELICATESSEN	
LEBENSMITTEL GROCERIES		**KONDITOREI** CAKE SHOP	

where can I buy...?   **fruit**
wo kann ich ... kaufen?   Obst
*voh kan ikh ... **kow**fen*   *ohbst*

bread   **milk**
Brot   Milch
broht   *milkh*

where is the supermarket?
wo ist der Supermarkt?
*voh ist der **su**per-markt*

where is the baker's?
wo ist die Bäckerei?
*voh ist dee be-ke-**rye***

where is the market?
wo ist der Markt?
voh ist der markt

when is the market?
wann ist Markt?
van ist markt

it's my turn next
ich bin dran
ikh bin dran

that's enough
das reicht
das rykht

a litre of ...	**milk**	**water**	**beer**
einen Liter...	Milch	Wasser	Bier
*i*ne-en **lee**ter...	*milkh*	***vas**ser*	*beer*
a bottle of...	**water**	**wine**	**sparkling wine**
eine Flasche...	Wasser	Wein	Sekt
*i*ne-e **fla**-she...	***vas**ser*	*vine*	*sekt*
a can of...	**coke**	**beer**	**tonic water**
eine Dose...	Cola	Bier	Tonic
*i*ne-e **doh**-ze...	***co**la*	*beer*	***to**nic*
a carton of...	**orange juice**	**apple juice**	**milk**
einen Karton...	Orangensaft	Apfelsaft	Milch
*i*ne-en kar-**tong**...	*o**ron**jen-saft*	***ap**fel-saft*	*milkh*

food – SHOPPING

4 oz of...
hundert Gramm...
hoondert gram...

cheese
Käse
kay-ze

ham
Schinken
shin-ken

half a pound of...
ein halbes Pfund...
ine hal-bes pfoont...

minced pork
Schweinehack
shvy-nehak

liver sausage
Leberwurst
leh-ber-voorst

a kilo of...
ein Kilo...
ine keelo...

potatoes
Kartoffeln
kar-tofeln

apples
Äpfel
epfel

8 slices of...
acht Scheiben...
akht shy-ben...

ham
Schinken
shin-ken

salami
Salami
salamee

a portion of...
eine Portion...
ine-e por-tsyohn...

sauerkraut
Sauerkraut
sauerkraut

salad
Salat
zalaht

a dozen eggs
ein Dutzend Eier
ine doo-tsent eye-er

a packet of...
ein Päckchen...
ine pek-khen...

biscuits
Kekse
kayk-se

pumpernickel bread
Pumpernickel
poomper-nickel

a tin of...
eine Dose...
ine-e doh-ze...

tomatoes
Tomaten
tomah-ten

stew
Eintopf
ine-topf

a jar of...
ein Glas...
ine glahs...

jam
Marmelade
mar-melah-de

olives
Oliven
oleeven

gherkins
Gurken
goorken

---

kann ich Ihnen helfen?
kan ikh ee-nen helfen
can I help you?

darf es sonst noch etwas sein?
darf es zonst nokh etvas zine
would you like anything else?

SIGHTSEEING

FREMDENVERKEHRSBÜRO TOURIST OFFICE

Many motorway service stations in Germany, Austria and Switzerland have tourist information.

where is the tourist office?
wo ist die Touristeninformation?
*voh ist dee too**ris**ten-infor-matsy**ohn***

we want to visit...
wir möchten ... besuchen
*veer **mur'kh**-ten ... be**zoo**khen*

when can we visit...?
wann können wir ... besichtigen?
*van **kur'**-nen veer ... be**zikh**-tigen*

what day does it close?
an welchem Tag ist es zu?
*an **vel**-khem tahk ist es tsoo*

we'd like to go go to...
wir möchten nach...
*veer **mur'kh**-ten nakh...*

when does it leave?
wann ist die Abfahrt?
*van ist dee **ap**-fahrt*

how much is the entrance?
was kostet der Eintritt?
*vas **kos**tet der **ine**-trit*

have you any leaflets?
haben Sie Broschüren?
***hah**-ben zee bro-**shoo**ren*

are there any excursions?
gibt es Ausflugsfahrten?
*gipt es **ows**-flooks-fahrten*

where does it leave from?
wo ist die Abfahrt?
*voh ist dee **ap**-fahrt*

are there reductions for...?
gibt es Ermäßigung für...?
*gipt es er-**may**-sigoong foor...*

children	**senior citizens**
Kinder	Rentner
***kin**der*	***rent**ner*

students	**unemployed**
Studenten	Arbeitslose
*shtoo-**den**ten*	***ar**-bites-loh-ze*

BADEN VERBOTEN	NO SWIMMING
TAUCHEN VERBOTEN	NO DIVING
GEFAHR	DANGER
GEFÄHRLICHE STRÖMUNG	DANGEROUS CURRENTS

If you are swimming in the Baltic, a red ball on top of a pole indicates that it is too dangerous to swim in the sea. If the ball is halfway down the pole, then it means that it is dangerous for children to swim but ok for adult swimmers.

which is a good beach?
welcher Strand ist gut?
vel-kher shtrahnt ist goot

how do I get there?
wie komme ich dahin?
vee komme ikh dahin

is there a swimming pool near here?
gibt es ein Hallenbad in der Nähe?
gipt es ine hallen-baht in der nay-e

can we swim in the lake?
können wir im See baden?
kur'-nen veer im zeh bah-den

is the water clean?
ist das Wasser sauber?
ist das vasser zow-ber

is the water deep?
ist das Wasser tief?
ist das vasser teef

is the water cold?
ist das Wasser kalt?
ist das vasser kalt

is it safe for children?
ist es sicher für Kinder?
ist es zikher foor kinder

are there currents?
gibt es Strömungen?
gipt es shtrur'-moong-en

where can we...?
wo können wir...?
voh kur'-nen veer...

windsurf
Windsurfen
wint-surfen

waterski
Wasserski fahren
vasser-shee fah-ren

can we hire...?
können wir ... mieten?
kur'-nen veer ... mee-ten

a jetski
einen Jetski
ine-en jetski

a deck chair
einen Liegestuhl
ine-en lee-ge-shtool

SPORT

Most tourist offices will have details of local sports facilities. If you plan to fish in Germany you will require a fishing licence and local fishing permit. Enquire at the tourist office.

where can we...?
wo können wir...?
*voh **kur'**-nen veer...*

play tennis
Tennis spielen
*ten**nis shpee**len*

play golf
Golf spielen
*golf **shpee**len*

go swimming
baden
***bah**-den*

hire bikes
Fahrräder leihen
***fah**-rehder **lye**-en*

go fishing
angeln
***angel**n*

go riding
reiten
***ry**-ten*

how much is it...?
was kostet es...?
*vas **kost**et es...*

per hour
pro Stunde
*pro **shtoon**-de*

per day
pro Tag
pro tahk

how do I book a court?
wie reserviere ich einen Platz?
*vee ray-zer-**vee**-re ikh **in**e-en plats*

can we hire rackets?
kann man Schläger leihen?
*kan man **shlay**-ger **lye**-en*

do I need a fishing permit?
brauche ich einen Angelschein?
***brow**-khe ikh **in**e-en **angel**-shine*

where can I get one?
wo bekomme ich einen?
*voh be**komm**e ikh **in**e-en*

is there a guide to local walks?
gibt es einen Wanderführer von dieser Gegend?
*gipt es **in**e-en **van**der-foorer fon **dee**zer **gay**gent*

do I need walking boots?
brauche ich Wanderstiefel?
***brow**-khe ikh **van**der-shteefel*

where is the nearest sports shop?
wo ist das nächste Sportgeschäft?
*voh ist das **naykh**-ste **shport**-gesheft*

can I hire skis?
kann ich Skier leihen?
*kan ikh **shee**-er **lye**-en*

how much is a pass?
was kostet ein Paß?
*vas **kos**tet ine pass*

I'm a beginner
ich bin Anfänger
*ikh bin **an**-fenger*

which is an easy run?
welche Abfahrt ist einfach?
***vel**-khe **ap**-fahrt ist **ine**-fakh*

is it safe to ski today?
ist das Skifahren heute ungefährlich?
*ist das **shee**-fahren **hoy**-te **oon**-gefayrlikh*

what is the snow like?
wie ist der Schnee?
vee ist der shnay

is there a map of the ski runs?
gibt es eine Pistenkarte?
*gipt es **ine**-e **pis**ten-kar-te*

my skis are...	**too long**	**too short**
meine Skier sind...	zu lang	zu kurz
***mine**-e **shee**-er zint...*	*tsoo lang*	*tsoo koorts*

my bindings are...	**too loose**	**too tight**
meine Bindungen sind...	zu locker	zu fest
***mine**-e **bin**-doong-en zint...*	*tsoo **lo**cker*	*tsoo fest*

where can we go cross-country skiing?
wo können wir Skilanglauf treiben?
*voh **kur'**-nen veer shee-**lang**-lowf **try**-ben*

---

welche Länge brauchen Sie?
***vel**-khe leng-e **brow**-khen zee*
what length skis do you want?

welche Schuhgröße haben Sie?
***vel**-khe **shoo**-grur'-se **hah**-ben zee*
what is your shoe size?

es besteht Lawinengefahr
*es be**shtayt** la**vee**-nen-gefahr*
there is danger of avalanches

diese Piste ist gesperrt
*dee-ze pis-te ist ge**shpert***
this run is closed off

NIGHTLIFE – popular

Bars and discos in Germany are open till late. You have to be over 18 years to drink alcohol. Student clubs are often lively places to go and are open to the public at a slightly higher charge.

what is there to do at night?
was kann man abends machen?
*vas kan man **ah**bents **ma**khen*

which is a good bar?
welche Bar ist gut?
***vel**-khe bar ist goot*

which is a good disco?
welche Disko ist gut?
***vel**-khe **dis**co ist goot*

where can we hear live music?
wo gibt es Live-Musik?
*voh gipt es **live**-moo-zeek*

is it expensive?
ist es teuer?
*ist es **toy**-er*

is there a student club?
gibt es hier einen Studentenklub?
*gipt es heer **i**ne-en shtoo-**den**ten-klup*

where do local people go at night?
wo gehen die Einheimischen abends hin?
*voh **gay**-en dee **ine**-hime-mee-shen **ah**bents hin*

is it a safe area?
ist die Gegend sicher?
*ist dee **gay**gent **zi**kher*

are there any concerts?
gibt es Konzerte?
*gipt es kon-**tser**te*

möchten Sie mit mir tanzen?
*mur'kh-ten zee mit meer **tan**tsen*
do you want to dance with me?

möchten Sie morgen abend mit mir ausgehen?
*mur'kh-ten zee **mor**gen **ah**bent mit meer **ows**-gay-en*
would you like to go out tomorrow night?

36

A list of cultural events should be available from tourist offices or listed in the local paper.

is there a list of cultural events?
gibt es einen Veranstaltungskalender?
gipt es ine-en fehr-anshtaltoongs-kalender

are there any festivals?
gibt es hier Festivals?
gipt es heer festivals

we'd like to go...	**to the theatre**	**to the opera**
wir möchten ... gehen	ins Theater	in die Oper
veer mur'kh-ten ... gay-en	*ins tay-ahter*	*in dee oh-per*
	to the ballet	**to a concert**
	ins Ballett	in ein Konzert
	ins bahl-let	*in ine kon-tsert*

what's on?
was wird gespielt?
vas virt geshpeelt

do I need to book?
muß ich reservieren?
moos ikh ray-zer-vee-ren

how much are the tickets?
was kosten die Karten?
vas kosten dee kar-ten

2 tickets...	**for tonight**	**for tomorrow night**
zwei Karten...	für heute abend	für morgen abend
tsvy kar-ten...	*foor hoy-te ahbent*	*foor morgen ahbent*
	for 5th August	
	für den fünften August	
	foor den foonf-ten owgoost	

when does the performance end?
wann ist die Vorstellung zu Ende?
van ist dee for-shtelloong tsoo en-de

HOTEL

ZIMMER FREI   VACANCIES (B & B)

Tourist information offices will be able to provide a list of all the different kinds of accommodation available.

have you a room for tonight?
haben Sie ein Zimmer für heute nacht?
*hah-ben zee ine **tsim**mer foor **hoy**-te nakht*

a single room	**a double room**	**a family room**
ein Einzelzimmer	ein Doppelzimmer	ein Familienzimmer
*ine **ine**-tsel-tsimmer*	*ine **dopp**el-tsimmer*	*ine fa**mee**lee-en-tsimmer*

with bath	**with shower**
mit Bad	mit Dusche
mit baht	*mit **doo**-she*

how much is it per night?	**is breakfast included?**
wieviel kostet es pro Nacht?	ist das Frühstück inbegriffen?
*vee**feel kos**tet es pro nakht*	*ist das **froo**-shtook **in**-be-griffen*

I booked a room	**my name is...**
ich habe ein Zimmer reserviert	mein Name ist...
*ikh **hah**-be ine **tsim**mer ray-zer-**veert***	*mine **nah**-me ist...*

I'd like to see the room
ich möchte das Zimmer gern ansehen
*ikh **mur'kh**-te das **tsim**mer gern an-**zay**en*

have you anything cheaper?
haben Sie etwas Billigeres?
*hah-ben zee **et**vas **bil**i-ge-res*

what time is...?	**breakfast**	**dinner**
wann gibt es...?	Frühstück	Abendessen
van gipt es...	*froo-shtook*	*ahbent-essen*

we'll be back late tonight
wir kommen heute abend spät zurück
*veer **kom**men **hoy**-te **ah**bent shpayt tsoo**rook***

the key, please
den Schlüssel, bitte
den **shloo**-sel **bi**-te

room number...
Zimmer *(number)*...
tsimmer...

are there any messages for me?
sind Nachrichten für mich da?
zint **nahkh**-rikhten foor mikh dah

come in!
herein!
he-**rine**

please come back later
bitte kommen Sie später noch einmal
bi-te **kom**men zee **shpay**ter nokh **ine**-mal

I'd like breakfast in my room
ich möchte gern Frühstück auf meinem Zimmer
ikh **mur'kh**-te gern **froo**-shtook owf **mine**-em **tsim**mer

please bring...
bitte bringen Sie...
bi-te **bring**en zee...

toilet paper
Toilettenpapier
twa-**le**-ten-pa**peer**

soap
Seife
zye-fe

clean towels
saubere Handtücher
zow-be-re **hant**-tookher

a glass
ein Glas
ine glahs

please clean...
bitte machen Sie ... sauber
bi-te **ma**khen zee ... **zow**-ber

my room
mein Zimmer
mine **tsim**mer

the bath
das Bad
das baht

I need an alarm call
ich brauche eine Weckruf
ikh **brow**-khe **ine**-en **vek**-roof

at 7 o'clock
um sieben Uhr
oom **zee**ben oor

is there a laundry service?
gibt es einen Wäschereiservice?
gipt es **ine**-en veshe-**rye**-service

can I borrow an iron?
kann ich ein Bügeleisen haben?
kan ikh ine **boo**gel-ize-en **hah**-ben

I'm leaving tomorrow
ich reise morgen ab
ikh **ry**-ze **mor**gen ap

please prepare the bill
machen Sie bitte die Rechnung fertig
makhen zee **bi**-te dee **rekh**-noong **fer**tikh

SELF-CATERING

Germany, Austria and Switzerland all use 220 volts. If you plan to take any electrical appliances such as hairdryers, irons or kettles, you should make sure you have an adaptor.

which is the key for this door?
welcher Schlüssel ist für diese Tür?
vel-kher shloo-sel ist foor dee-ze toor

where are the fuses?
wo sind die Sicherungen?
voh zint dee zikh-eroong-en

please show us how this works
bitte zeigen Sie uns, wie das funktioniert
bi-te tsy-gen zee oons vee das foonk-tsyoh-neert

how does ... work?	**the dryer**	**the waterheater**
wie funktioniert...?	der Wäschetrockner	der Wasserboiler
vee foonk-tsyoh-neert...	*der veshe-trok-ner*	*der vasser-boy-ler*
	the washing machine	**the cooker**
	die Waschmaschine	der Herd
	die vash-mah-shee-ne	*der hert*

whom do I contact if there are any problems?
wen spreche ich bei Problemen an?
vehn shprekhe ikh by prohblehmen an

we need extra...	**keys**	**cutlery**	**sheets**
wir brauchen extra...	Schlüssel	Besteck	Bettwäsche
veer brow-khen ekstra...	*shloo-sel*	*beshtek*	*bet-ve-she*

the gas has run out
das Gas ist alle
das gahs ist al-le

what do I do?
was muß ich tun?
vas moos ikh toon

CAMPING & CARAVANNING

In Germany and Switzerland the speed of a car towing a caravan must not exceed 50 kph in built-up areas and 80 kph on other roads and motorways (Austria up to 100 kph on motorways).

have you a list of campsites?
haben Sie eine Liste von Campingplätzen?
hah-ben zee ine-e lis-te fon kamping-pletsen

have you any vacancies?
haben Sie noch Plätze frei?
hah-ben zee nokh plet-se fry

how much is it per night?
was kostet die Nacht?
vas kostet dee nakht

we'd like to stay for ... nights
wir möchten ... Nächte bleiben
veer mur'kh-ten ... nekh-te bly-ben

is the campsite sheltered?
liegt der Campingplatz geschützt?
leegt der kamping-plats ge-shootst

can we have a more sheltered site?
könnten wir eine besser geschützte Stelle haben?
kur'n-ten veer ine-e be-ser ge-shoots-te shte-le hah-ben

this site is very muddy
der Platz ist sehr schlammig
der plats ist zehr shla-mikh

is there a restaurant?
gibt es ein Restaurant?
gipt es ine restoh-rong

is there a shop?
gibt es einen Laden?
gipt es ine-en lah-den

can we park our caravan here overnight?
können wir unseren Wohnwagen hier über Nacht parken?
kur'-nen veer oonseren vohn-vahgen heer oober nakht parken

can we camp here overnight? *(for tent)*
können wir über Nacht hier zelten?
kur'-nen veer oober nakht heer tsel-ten

CHILDREN

In Germany children up to 4 years must have their own special car seat and those up to 12 must have booster seats. In Austria and Switzerland children must travel in the back with seatbelts.

a child's ticket
eine Kinderkarte
*ine-e **kin**der-kar-te*

he/she is ... years old
er/sie ist...
er/zee ist...

is there a reduction for children?
gibt es Ermäßigung für Kinder?
*gipt es er-**may**-sigoong foor **kin**der*

do you have a children's menu?
haben Sie eine Kinderkarte?
*hah-ben zee ine-e **kin**der-kar-te*

do you have...?
haben Sie...?
hah-ben zee...

a high chair
einen Kinderstuhl
*ine-en **kin**der-shtool*

a cot
ein Kinderbett
*ine **kin**der-bet*

is it ok to bring children here?
können wir die Kinder mitbringen?
***kur'**-nen veer dee **kin**der **mit**-bringen*

what's there for children to do?
was können die Kinder hier unternehmen?
*vas **kur'**-nen dee **kin**der heer oonter-**nay**men*

is it safe for children?
ist es für Kinder ungefährlich?
*ist es foor **kin**der **oon**-gefayrlikh*

I have two children
ich habe zwei Kinder
*ikh **hah**-be tsvy **kin**der*

Sarah is 10
Sarah ist zehn
***sa**rah ist tsayn*

Tom is 4
Tom ist vier
tom ist feer

do you have children?
haben Sie Kinder?
*hah-ben zee **kin**der*

SPECIAL NEEDS

On all Intercity and on most Eurocity and fast trains, special wheelchair compartments are now available in second class. A wheelchair sign indicates facilities for the disabled.

is it possible to visit ... with a wheelchair?
kann man ... auch im Rollstuhl besuchen?
*kan man ... aukh im **rol**-shtool be**zoo**khen*

do you have toilets for the disabled?
haben Sie Toiletten für Behinderte?
***hah**-ben zee twa-**le**-ten foor be-**hin**-der-te*

I need a bedroom on the ground floor
ich brauche ein Zimmer im Erdgeschoß
*ikh **brow**-khe ine **tsim**mer im **ert**-geshos*

is there a lift?
gibt es einen Aufzug?
*gipt es ine-en **owf**tsook*

where is the lift?
wo ist der Aufzug?
*voh ist der **owf**tsook*

I can't walk far
ich kann nicht weit laufen
*ikh kan nikht vite **low**-fen*

do you have wheelchairs?
haben Sie Rollstühle?
***hah**-ben zee **rol**-shtoo-le*

are there many steps?
sind es viele Stufen?
*zint es **fee**le **shtoo**fen*

is there an entrance for wheelchairs?
gibt es einen Eingang für Rollstuhlfahrer?
*gipt es ine-en **ine**-gang foor **rol**-shtool-fahrer*

can I travel on this train with a wheelchair?
kann ich als Rollstuhlfahrer in diesem Zug mitfahren?
*kan ikh als **rol**-shtool-fahrer in **dee**zem tsook **mit**-fahren*

is there a reduction for the disabled?
gibt es Ermäßigung für Behinderte?
*gipt es er-**may**-sigoong foor be-**hin**-der-te*

EXCHANGE VISITORS

These phrases are intended for families hosting German-speaking visitors.

what would you like for breakfast?
was möchten Sie zum Frühstück?
vas mur'kh-ten zee tsoom froo-shtook

what would you like to eat?
was möchten Sie essen?
vas mur'kh-ten zee es-sen

did you sleep well?
haben Sie gut geschlafen?
hah-ben zee goot geshlahfen

what would you like to do today?
was möchten Sie heute unternehmen?
vas mur'kh-ten zee hoy-te oonter-naymen

I will pick you up at...
ich hole Sie um ... ab
ikh hoh-le zee oom ... ap

did you enjoy yourself?
hat es Ihnen gefallen?
haht es eenen gefallen

take care
passen Sie auf sich auf
passen zee owf zikh owf

please be back no later than...
bitte seien Sie bis spätestens ... zurück
bi-te zy-en zee bis shpay-testens ... tsoorook

we'll be in bed when you get back
wir werden schon schlafen, wenn Sie zurückkommen
veer vehr-den shohn shlahfen ven zee tsoorook-kommen

do you eat...?
essen Sie...?
es-sen zee...

EXCHANGE VISITORS

These phrases are intended for those people staying with German-speaking families.

I like...
ich mag...
ikh makh...

I don't like...
ich mag ... nicht
ikh makh ... nikht

that was delicious
das war sehr gut
das vahr zehr goot

thank you very much
vielen Dank
***fee**-len dank*

may I phone home?
darf ich nach Hause telefonieren?
*darf ikh nakh **how**-ze taylay-fo-**nee**ren*

may I make a local call?
darf ich im Ort anrufen?
*darf ikh im ohrt **an**roofen*

can I have a key?
kann ich einen Schlüssel bekommen?
*kan ikh **i**ne-en **shloo**-sel be-**kom**men*

can I borrow...?
kann ich ... borgen?
*kan ikh ... **bohr**-gen*

an iron
ein Bügeleisen
*ine boogel-**ize**-en*

a hairdryer
einen Fön
***i**ne-en fur'n*

can you take me by car?
können Sie mich mit dem Auto hinbringen?
***kur'**-nen zee mikh mit dem **ow**to **hin**'-bringen*

what time do you get up?
wann stehen Sie auf?
*van **shtay**en zee owf*

I'm staying with...
ich wohne bei...
*ikh **voh**-ne by...*

whom are you staying with?
bei wem wohnen Sie?
*by vehm **voh**-nen zee*

I've had a great time
es hat mir sehr gut gefallen
*es haht meer zehr goot ge**fal**len*

PROBLEMS

can you help me?
können Sie mir helfen?
*kur'-nen zee meer **helf**en*

do you speak English?
sprechen Sie Englisch?
***shpre**khen zee **eng**-lish*

I'm lost
ich habe mich verlaufen
*ikh **hah**-be mikh fer-**low**fen*

I'm late
ich habe mich verspätet
*ikh **hah**-be mikh ver**shpay**-tet*

I've missed...
ich habe ... verpaßt
*ikh **hah**-be ... fer-**past***

I've lost...
ich habe ... verloren
*ikh **hah**-be ... fer-**loh**ren*

I don't speak German
ich spreche kein Deutsch
*ikh **shpre**-khe kine doytch*

does anyone speak English?
spricht jemand Englisch?
*shprikht **yay**mant **eng**-lish*

how do I get to...?
wie komme ich zum/zur/nach...?
*vee **komm**e ikh tsoom/tsoor/nakh...*

I need to get to...
ich muß zum/zur/nach...
ikh moos tsoom/tsoor/nakh...

my plane
mein Flugzeug
*mine **flook**-tsoyk*

my money
mein Geld
mine gelt

my camera
meine Kamera
*mine-e **ka**mera*

my connection
meinen Anschluß
***mine**-en **an**-shloos*

my passport
meinen Paß
***mine**-en pass*

my key
meinen Schlüssel
***mine**-en **shloo**-sel*

my suitcase...
mein Koffer...
*mine **ko**fer...*

is damaged
wurde beschädigt
***voor**-de be-**shay**-dikht*

is missing
ging verloren
*geeng fer-**loh**ren*

is there a lost property office?
gibt es hier ein Fundbüro?
*gipt es heer ine **foont**-booroh*

leave me alone!
lassen Sie mich in Ruhe!
***las**sen zee mikh in **roo**-e*

go away!
hau ab!
how ap

COMPLAINTS

the light
das Licht
das likht

the lock
das Schloß
das shlos

... doesn't work
... funktioniert nicht
*... foonk-tsyoh-**neert** nikht*

the toilet
die Toilette
*dee twa-**le**-te*

the heating
die Heizung
*dee **hyt**-soong*

the room is ...
das Zimmer ist...
*das **tsim**mer ist...*

dirty
schmutzig
***shmoo**tsik*

too hot
zu warm
tsoo varm

too cold
zu kalt
tsoo kalt

too noisy
zu laut
tsoo lowt

too small
zu klein
tsoo kline

this isn't what I ordered
das habe ich nicht bestellt
*das **hah**-be ikh nikht be**shtelt***

I want to complain
ich möchte mich beschweren
*ikh **mur'kh**-te mikh be**shveh**ren*

I want my money back
ich möchte mein Geld zurück
*ikh **mur'kh**-te mine gelt tsoo**rook***

we've been waiting for a very long time
wir warten schon sehr lange
*veer **var**-ten shohn zehr **lang**-e*

the bill is not correct
die Rechnung stimmt nicht
*dee **rekh**-noong shtimt nikht*

this is broken
das ist kaputt
*das ist ka**poot***

can you repair it?
können Sie das reparieren?
***kur'**-nen zee das raypa-**ree**ren*

EMERGENCIES

POLIZEI	POLICE
FEUERWEHR	FIRE BRIGADE
UNFALLSTATION	ACCIDENT AND EMERGENCY DEPT

	Germany	Austria	Switzerland
POLICE	110	133	117
AMBULANCE	(check locally)	144	144
FIRE	112	122	118

In Germany, if you don't have time to check in the local telephone directory for the emergency ambulance service, the fire brigade also has an ambulance service.

help!
Hilfe!
hil-fe

can you help me?
können Sie mir helfen?
kur'n-en zee meer hel-fen

there's been an accident
ein Unfall ist passiert
ine oonfal ist paseert

someone is injured
es ist jemand verletzt worden
es ist yaymant ferletst vorden

please call...
bitte rufen Sie...
bi-te roofen zee...

the police
die Polizei
dee poli-tsye

the fire brigade
die Feuerwehr
dee foy-er-vehr

an ambulance
einen Krankenwagen
ine-en kranken-vahgen

where's the police station?
wo ist die Polizeiwache?
voh ist dee poli-tsy-va-khe

EMERGENCIES

I want to report a theft
ich möchte einen Diebstahl melden
*ikh **mur'kh**-te **i**ne-en **deep**-shtahl **mel**den*

my car has been stolen
mein Auto ist gestohlen worden
*mine **ow**to ist ge**shtoh**-len **vor**den*

my car has been broken into
mein Auto ist aufgebrochen worden
*mine **ow**to ist **owf**-gebro-khen **vor**den*

I've been robbed
ich bin beraubt worden
*ikh bin be-**rowpt vor**den*

I've been attacked
ich bin überfallen worden
*ikh bin oober-**fa**llen **vor**den*

I've been raped
ich bin vergewaltigt worden
*ikh bin fer-ge**val**-tikht **vor**den*

I need a report for my insurance
ich brauche einen Bericht für meine Versicherung
*ikh **brow**-khe **i**ne-en be**rikht** foor **mi**ne-e fer**zikh**-eroong*

how much is the fine?
wieviel Strafe muß ich zahlen?
***vee**feel **shtrah**-fe moos ikh **tsah**-len*

where do I pay it?
wo kann ich das bezahlen?
*voh kan ikh das be-**tsah**len*

I would like to phone my embassy
ich möchte mit meiner Botschaft telefonieren
*ikh **mur'kh**-te mit **mi**ne-er **boht**shaft taylay-fo-**nee**ren*

---

wir sind unterwegs zu Ihnen
*veer zint oonter-**veks** tsoo **ee**-nen*
we're on our way

HEALTH

APOTHEKE	PHARMACY
KRANKENHAUS	HOSPITAL
UNFALLSTATION	ACCIDENT AND EMERGENCY DEPT

Pharmacies will be able to provide advice on any health matters and deal with minor problems.

have you something for...?
haben Sie etwas gegen...?
hah-ben zee etvas gay-gen...

car sickness
Reisekrankheit
ry-ze-krank-hite

diarrhoea
Durchfall
doorkh-fal

is it safe to give children?
kann man es bedenkenlos auch Kindern geben?
kan man es be-deng-ken-lohs owkh kindern gayben

I'm ill
ich bin krank
ikh bin krank

I need a doctor
ich brauche einen Arzt
ikh brow-khe ine-en artst

my son/my daughter has a high temperature
mein Sohn/meine Tochter hat hohes Fieber
mine zohn / mine-e tokhter hat hoh-es feeber

I'm on this medication
ich nehme dieses Medikament
ikh nay-me deezes medeekament

I have high blood pressure
ich habe hohen Blutdruck
ikh hah-be hoh-en bloot-drook

I'm diabetic
ich habe Zucker
ikh hah-be tsooker

I'm pregnant
ich bin schwanger
ikh bin shvanger

I'm on the pill
ich nehme die Pille
ikh nay-me dee pi-le

I'm allergic to penicillin
ich bin allergisch gegen Penizillin
ikh bin a-ler-gish gay-gen peni-tsileen

my blood group is...
meine Blutgruppe ist...
mine-e blootgroo-pe ist...

I'm breastfeeding
ich stille mein Baby
*ikh **shtil**le mine **ba**by*

is it safe to take?
kann man das bedenkenlos einnehmen?
*kan man das be-**deng**-ken-lohs **ine**-naymen*

will I / he / she have to go to hospital?
muß ich / er / sie ins Krankenhaus?
*moos ikh / er / zee ins **kran**ken-hows*

I need to go to casualty
ich muß zur Notaufnahme
ikh moos tsoor noht-owf-nahme

where is the hospital?
wo ist das Krankenhaus?
*voh ist das **kran**ken-hows*

when are visiting hours?
wann ist die Besuchszeit?
*van ist dee be**zookhs**-tsite*

which ward?
welche Station?
vel**-khe shtah-tsee-**ohn

I need a dentist
ich brauche einen Zahnarzt
*ikh **brow**-khe ine-en **tsahn**artst*

he / she has toothache
er / sie hat Zahnschmerzen
*er / zee hat **tsahn**-shmer-tsen*

can you do a temporary filling?
können Sie mir eine provisorische Plombe machen?
***kur'**-nen zee meer ine-e provi-**zo**rish-e **plom**-be **ma**khen*

I have an abscess
ich habe einen Abszeß
*ikh **hah**-be ine-en apst**sess***

it hurts
das tut weh
das toot vay

can you repair my dentures?
können Sie mein Gebiß reparieren?
***kur'**-nen zee mine ge**biss** raypa-**ree**ren*

do I have to pay now?
muß ich das gleich bezahlen?
*moos ikh das **glykh** be**tsah**-len*

how much will it be?
wie teuer wird es?
*vee **toy**-er virt es*

I need a receipt for my insurance
ich brauche eine Quittung für meine Krankenkasse
*ikh **brow**-khe ine-e **kvi**-toong foor **mi**ne-e **kran**ken-ka-se*

BUSINESS

my name is...
mein Name ist...
*mine **nah**-me ist...*

here's my card
hier ist meine Karte
*heer ist **mi**ne-e **kar**-te*

I work for...
ich arbeite für...
*ikh **ar**by-te foor...*

I'd like to arrange a meeting
ich möchte eine Besprechung ausmachen
*ikh **mur'kh**-te **i**ne-e be-**shpre**-khoong **ows**-makhen*

on April 4th at 11 o'clock
am vierten April um elf Uhr
*am **feer**-ten a**pril** oom elf oor*

can we meet for lunch?
können wir uns bei einem Mittagessen treffen?
***kur'**-nen veer oons by **i**ne-em **mi**tahk-essen **tref**fen*

I will send a fax to confirm
ich schicke ein Fax zur Bestätigung
*ikh **shi**-ke ine fax tsoor be-**shtay**-tigoong*

I'm staying at Hotel...
ich wohne im Hotel...
*ikh **voh**-ne im ho**tel**...*

how do I get to your office?
wie komme ich zu Ihrem Büro?
*vee **kom**me ikh tsoo **ee**-rem boo**roh***

here is some information about my company
hier sind einige Informationen über meine Firma
*heer zint **i**ne-nee-ge infor-matsy**ohn**-en **oo**ber **mi**ne-e **feer**-ma*

I have an appointment with...
ich habe einen Termin mit...
*ikh **hah**-be **i**ne-en ter-**meen** mit...*

at ... o'clock
um ... Uhr
oom ... oor

I'm delighted to meet you at last
schön, daß wir uns endlich persönlich kennenlernen
*shur'n das veer oons **ent**-likh per-**sur'n**-likh **ken**nen-layr-nen*

my German isn't very good
mein Deutsch ist nicht sehr gut
mine doytch ist nikht zehr goot

please speak slowly
bitte sprechen Sie langsam
*bi-te **shpre**-khen zee **lang**-zahm*

what is the name of the managing director?
wie ist der Name des Geschäftsführers?
*vee ist der **nah**-me des ge**shefts**-foorers*

I'd like some information about the company
ich möchte einige Informationen über die Firma
*ikh **mur'kh**-te ine-neege infor-matsy**ohn**-en **oo**ber dee **feer**-ma*

do you have a press office?
haben Sie eine Presseabteilung?
***hah**-ben zee ine-e **pres**-se-ap-tye-loong*

I need an interpreter
ich brauche einen Dolmetscher
*ikh **brow**-khe ine-en **dol**-met-sher*

can you copy this for me?
können Sie das für mich kopieren?
***kur'**-nen zee das foor mikh ko**pee**-ren*

is there a business centre?
gibt es hier ein Business-Center?
*gipt es heer ine **bus**iness centre*

haben Sie einen Termin?
hah**-ben zee ine-en ter-**meen
do you have an appointment?

...ist im Augenblick nicht im Büro
*...ist im **ow**gen-blik nikht im boo**roh***
...isn't in the office at the moment

er/sie kommt in ein paar Minuten wieder
*er/zee kommt in ein pahr mi**noo**-ten **vee**der*
he/she will be back in a few minutes

PHONING

Dialling codes from the UK:
Germany 00 49   Switzerland 00 41   Austria 00 43
Dialling code to the UK: 00 44

a phonecard, please
eine Telefonkarte, bitte
*ine-e taylay-**fon**-kar-te **bi**-te*

I want to make a phone call
ich möchte telefonieren
*ikh **mur'kh**-te taylay-fo-**nee**ren*

Herr Braun, please
Herr Braun, bitte
*hayr brown **bi**-te*

extension ..., please
Apparat ..., bitte
*apa-**raht** ... **bi**-te*

can I speak to ...?
kann ich mit ... sprechen?
*kan ikh mit ... **shpre**-khen*

this is Jim Brown
hier ist Jim Brown
heer ist jim brown

I'll call back later
ich rufe später wieder an
*ikh **roo**-fe **shpay**ter **vee**der an*

I'll call back tomorrow
ich rufe morgen wieder an
*ikh **roo**-fe **mor**gen **vee**der an*

an outside line, please
eine Amtsleitung, bitte
*ine-e **amts**-lye-toong **bi**-te*

I can't get through
ich komme nicht durch
*ikh **kom**me nikht doorkh*

hallo
*ha**lo***
hello

wer spricht, bitte?
*ver shprikht **bi**-te*
who is calling?

Augenblick, ich verbinde
*ow**gen**-blik ikh fer**bin**-de*
just a moment, I'm trying to connect you

es ist besetzt
*es ist be**zetst***
it's engaged

bitte rufen Sie später wieder an
***bi**-te **roo**fen zee **shpay**ter veeder an*
please try again later

FAXING/E-MAIL

I want to send a fax
ich möchte ein Fax schicken
*ikh **mur'kh**-te ine fax **shi**-ken*

what's your fax number?
wie ist Ihre Faxnummer?
*vee ist **ee**-re **fax**-noomer*

please resend your fax
bitte schicken Sie Ihr Fax noch einmal
***bi**-te **shi**-ken zee eer fax nokh **ine**-mal*

your fax is constantly engaged
Ihr Fax ist immer besetzt
*eer fax ist **im**mer be**zetst***

can I send a fax from here?
kann ich von hier ein Fax schicken?
*kan ikh fon heer ine fax **shi**-ken*

I want to send an e-mail
ich möchte eine E-Mail schicken
*ikh **mur'kh**-te ine-e **e**-mail **shi**-ken*

what's your e-mail address?
wie ist Ihre E-Mail-Adresse?
*vee ist **ee**-re **e**-mail-a-**dre**-se*

did you get my fax?
haben Sie mein Fax bekommen?
***hah**-ben zee mine fax be-**kom**men*

did you get my e-mail?
haben Sie meine E-Mail bekommen?
***hah**-ben zee **mi**ne-e **e**-mail be-**kom**men*

do you have a fax?
haben Sie ein Fax?
***hah**-ben zee ine fax*

I can't read it
ich kann es nicht lesen
*ikh kan es nikht **lay**-zen*

NUMBERS

0	**null** *nool*	
1	**eins** *ines*	
2	**zwei** *tsvy*	
3	**drei** *dry*	
4	**vier** *feer*	
5	**fünf** *foonf*	
6	**sechs** *zekhs*	
7	**sieben** *zee*ben	
8	**acht** *akht*	
9	**neun** *noyn*	
10	**zehn** *tsayn*	
11	**elf** *elf*	
12	**zwölf** *tsvur'lf*	
13	**dreizehn** *dry*-tsayn	
14	**vierzehn** *feer*-tsayn	
15	**fünfzehn** *foonf*-tsayn	
16	**sechzehn** *zekh*-tsayn	
17	**siebzehn** *zeep*-tsayn	
18	**achtzehn** *akh*-tsayn	
19	**neunzehn** *noyn*-tsayn	
20	**zwanzig** *tsvan*-tsikh	
21	**einundzwanzig** *ine*-oont-tsvan-tsikh	
22	**zweiundzwanzig** *tsvy*-oont-tsvan-tsikh	
30	**dreißig** *dry*-sikh	
40	**vierzig** *feer*-tsikh	
50	**fünfzig** *foonf*-tsikh	
60	**sechzig** *zekh*-tsikh	
70	**siebzig** *zeep*-tsikh	
80	**achtzig** *akh*-tsikh	
90	**neunzig** *noyn*-tsikh	
100	**hundert** *hoon*dert	
101	**hunderteins** *hoon*dert-ines	
200	**zweihundert** *tsvy*-hoondert	
1,000	**tausend** *tow*zent	
1 million	**eine Million** *ine*-e mil**yohn**	

1st	**erste** *er*-ste	
2nd	**zweite** *tsvy*-te	
3rd	**dritte** *drit*-te	
4th	**vierte** *feer*-te	
5th	**fünfte** *foonf*-te	
6th	**sechste** *zehks*-te	
7th	**siebte** *zeep*-te	
8th	**achte** *akh*-te	
9th	**neunte** *noyn*-te	
10th	**zehnte** *tsayn*-te	

DAYS & MONTHS

JANUAR	JANUARY	**MONTAG**	MONDAY
FEBRUAR	FEBRUARY	**DIENSTAG**	TUESDAY
MÄRZ	MARCH	**MITTWOCH**	WEDNESDAY
APRIL	APRIL	**DONNERSTAG**	THURSDAY
MAI	MAY	**FREITAG**	FRIDAY
JUNI	JUNE	**SAMSTAG**	SATURDAY
JULI	JULY	**SONNTAG**	SUNDAY
AUGUST	AUGUST		
SEPTEMBER	SEPTEMBER		
OKTOBER	OCTOBER		
NOVEMBER	NOVEMBER		
DEZEMBER	DECEMBER		

what's the date?
der wievielte ist heute?
der vee-feel-te ist hoy-te

which day?
welcher Tag?
vel-kher tahk

which month?
welcher Monat?
vel-kher mohnat

it's the 5th of March 1998
heute ist der fünfte März neunzehnhundertachtundneunzig
hoy-te ist der foonf-te merts noyntsayn-hoondert-akht-oont-noyn-tsikh

on Saturday
am Samstag
am zamstahk

on Saturdays
samstags
zamstahks

every Saturday
jeden Samstag
yay-den zamstahk

this Saturday
diesen Samstag
deezen zamstahk

next Saturday
nächsten Samstag
naykh-sten zamstahk

last Saturday
letzten Samstag
lets-ten zamstahk

please can you confirm the date?
können Sie bitte das Datum bestätigen?
kur'-nen zee bi-te das dahtoom beshtay-teegen

TIME

Note that throughout Europe the 24-hour clock is used much more widely than in the UK.

what time is it, please?
wie spät ist es, bitte?
*vee shpayt ist es **bi**-te*

am
morgens
***mor**gens*

pm
abends
***ah**bents*

it's 2 o'clock
es ist zwei Uhr
es ist tsvy oor

it's 3 o'clock
es ist drei Uhr
es ist dry oor

it's 6 o'clock
es ist sechs Uhr
es ist zekhs oor

In German the half hour is expressed by referring forwards to the next full hour as opposed to backwards to the last full hour as in English. You will also hear in Austria and eastern Germany **viertel** (quarter) **acht** meaning 'a quarter past 7' and **dreiviertel** (three quarters) **acht** meaning 'a quarter to 8'.

it's half past 8
es ist halb neun
es ist halp noyn

it's half past 10
es ist halb elf
es ist halp elf

an hour
eine Stunde
*ine-e **shtoon**-de*

half an hour
eine halbe Stunde
*ine-e **hal**-be **shtoon**-de*

a quarter of an hour
eine Viertelstunde
*ine-e **feer**tel-**shtoon**-de*

three quarters of an hour
eine Dreiviertelstunde
*ine-e **dry**-feertel-**shtoon**-de*

until 8 o'clock
bis acht Uhr
bis akht oor

it's half past 9
es ist halb zehn
es ist halp tsayn

at 10 am
um 10 Uhr morgens
*oom tsayn oor **mor**gens*

at 4 pm
um 16 Uhr
*oom **zekh**-tsayn oor*

FOOD

ORDERING DRINKS

Remember, the easiest way to ask for something is to ask for a... einen (der) /eine (die) /ein (das) and add bitte.

a black coffee
einen schwarzen Kaffee
ine-en shvar-tsen kafay

a white coffee
einen Kaffee mit Sahne
ine-en kafay mit zah-ne

a tea
einen Tee
ine-en tay

with milk	**with lemon**
mit Frischmilch	mit Zitrone
mit frish-milkh	*mit tsitroh-ne*

a lager
ein helles Bier
ine he-les beer

a bitter
ein Altbier
ine alt-beer

a half pint
ein Kleines
ine kline-es

a pint
ein Großes
ine groh-ses

a bottle of mineral water
eine Flasche Mineralwasser
ine-e fla-she mi-nerahl-vasser

sparkling	**still**
mit Kohlensäure	still
mit kohlen-zoy-re	*shtill*

would you like a drink?
möchten Sie etwas trinken?
mur'kh-ten zee etvas trinken

what will you have?
was möchten Sie?
vas mur'kh-ten zee

the wine list, please
die Weinkarte, bitte
dee vinekar-te bi-te

a bottle of house wine
eine Flasche Hauswein
ine-e fla-she howsvine

a glass of white wine/red wine
ein Glas Weißwein / Rotwein
ine glahs vicevine / rohtvine

a bottle of red wine
eine Flasche Rotwein
ine-e fla-she rohtvine

a bottle of white wine
eine Flasche Weißwein
ine-e fla-she vicevine

ORDERING FOOD

can you recommend a good restaurant?
können Sie ein gutes Restaurant empfehlen?
kur'-nen zee ine **goo**-tes restoh-**rong** emp-**fay**len

I'd like to book a table
ich möchte einen Tisch reservieren
ikh **mur'kh**-te *i*ne-en tish ray-zer-**vee**ren

for ... people
für ... Personen
*foor ... per-***zoh**nen

for tonight
für heute abend
foor **hoy**-te **ah**bent

at 8 pm
um acht Uhr
oom akht oor

the menu, please
die Speisekarte, bitte
dee **shpy**-ze-kar-te **bi**-te

is there a dish of the day?
gibt es ein Tagesgericht?
gipt es ine **tah**ges-gerikht

have you a set-price menu?
haben Sie eine Tageskarte?
hah-ben zee *i*ne-e **tah**ges-kar-te?

I'll have this
ich nehme das
ikh **nay**-me das

are there any vegetarian restaurants here?
gibt es hier vegetarische Restaurants?
*gipt es heer vaygay-***ta***rish-e restoh-***rongs**

what do you recommend?
was können Sie empfehlen?
vas **kur'**-nen zee emp-**fay**len

I don't eat meat
ich esse kein Fleisch
ikh **es**-se kine flysh

do you have any vegetarian dishes?
haben Sie vegetarische Gerichte?
hah-ben zee vaygay-***ta***rish-e ge-**rikh**-te

excuse me!
Entschuldigung!
*ent***shool**-digoong

more bread
noch Brot
nokh broht

more water
noch Wasser
nokh **vas**ser

the bill, please
zahlen, bitte
tsah-len **bi**-te

GERMAN FOOD

German food is hearty and warming, geared to satisfying large appetites. It is also the kind of food best enjoyed with beer: a happy circumstance, as beers in Germany are both good and extremely varied. There are also, of course, excellent wines.

Germans take everything to do with food or drink with the utmost seriousness, and as a result all the products are handled very carefully, in order to meet with the highest standards of hygiene and quality control. Care and pride are taken in the preparation of meals, however humble, at home or elsewhere. This is a firm tradition handed down from the distant past, when the very first laws in the world on food and drink were passed. For example, the rules for the production of beer, the **Reinheitsgebot**, date from 1516 and are still applied.

Industrial development notwithstanding, Germany is still a thriving agricultural and food-processing country. Meat has always been, and still is, the favourite food. This is not surprising, considering that in global terms Germany holds third place as a pork producer, occupying the same place regarding dairy products and fourth as a (general) meat producer. Pork is the favoured meat, followed by beef, lamb and poultry. The famous sausages, although made mainly from pork meat, can also include other kinds of meat.

In early times, meals were very plain, based on meat and accompanied by large amounts of mead, a fermented drink made with honey and water. Later, with the influence of the occupying Romans, things began to change, but after the Romans left the people reverted to their old ways, keeping cattle and eating meat, cheese and milk. However, a more stable Europe and the flowering of the Renaissance meant increasing sophistication, the start of wine and beer production, the introduction of spices, and an interest in the culinary art of the surrounding neighbours, particularly the French. This period laid the foudation for the development of German cuisine. This was further reinforced by the gradual introduction of other products in Europe, such as potatoes, sugar, coffee and rice, although the love for simple food has remained throughout.

One of the surprising elements in German food is the combination of sweet and sour flavours, given by fruit served together with meat (such as **Rippenbraten mit Backpflaumen**, spareribs with prunes). There are even soups made solely with fruit. Another unusual combination is meat and fish in the same dish, served in the northern coastal area, for example **Labskaus** (sailor's stew), a stew of cured beef with mashed potato, pickled beetroot and fish.

German farmers grow a great variety of green and root vegetables, used for accompanying meat and fish dishes, and for salads. Apples are an important crop and a great deal of apple juice is produced.

Regional specialities which have become popular all over Germany still tend to keep the name of the town where they originated, as is the case with **Wiener** (Viennese) which in English are called frankfurters. But you will find scores of others, such as **Westfälischer Schinken** (Westphalian ham), **Leipziger Allerlei** (a mixed vegetable dish) or **Allgäuer Käsespätzle** (cheese noodles from the Allgäu).

Sauerkraut is a national institution, and **Brot** (bread), of which there are many excellent varieties, is a staple food. Cakes and biscuits are also very important. Some of them are influenced by France, others by Austria. There are many delicious fruit tarts and cream cakes of a very high standard, as well as creamy fruit desserts, like **rote Grütze** (raspberry, red currant and wine jelly served with fresh cream).

For the purposes of food characteristics, the provinces of Germany can be grouped into three main regions – northern, western and southern.

The northern region is the only one with a coastline and therefore fish, especially herring, appears on the menu here more often than elsewhere. Try **Krabbensalat**, shrimp salad, and don't miss **Matjeshering** (salted herring) especially in June when the new season starts and the herring is at its freshest. Fish is also used for canning. However, meat is still the most important item on the menu here, as it is in the rest of the country. The northern region offers robust dishes based on meat and root vegetables, such as potatoes. There is evidence of a strong influence from Polish and Scandinavian cuisines. It is in this region that the sweet and sour dishes are most popular.

The western region comprises the areas on both sides of the river Rhine and its famous valley. In this part of the country one can detect a greater French influence, although everything that is good in the northern and

GERMAN FOOD

southern regions is present here too. The western region is more food conscious in the sense of innovation and refinement, and it is said that the best German restaurants are to be found here. Some very local specialities involve the use of frogs' legs (**Froschschenkel**) and snails (**Schnecke**). Venison, asparagus and artichokes are the main ingredients of excellent local specialities. The delicious **Schwarzwälder Schinken** (Black Forest ham) must not be missed.

The southern region of Germany is dominated by Bavaria, where meat-eating reaches its highest level. Here veal is popular, and the main speciality is **Kalbshaxe** (knuckles of veal). A pork speciality is **Eisbein** (knuckle of pork), and the favourite sausage is one made from pork, beef and seasonings (**Leberkäse**). People love to eat pasta, in various dishes, especially in Swabia where **Spätzle** (noodles) are poplular. In the South, potatoes are more often than not served as dumplings, and cereals are used more than in other parts of Germany. **Sauerkraut** is also a favourite, served with pork. Embracing the Alps, this region is rich in dairy products. Try also the **Kaiserschmarren** (pancakes with a rich filling) and **Strudel**, normally filled with apples.

SAUSAGES AND OTHER PORK PRODUCTS

Germany is renowned for its sausages. No wonder, when there are about 1500 different kinds of them in the country – or so they say. Many, of course, will be very similar, with just a little variation depending on where they come from. There is great respect for the place of origin and each town has specialist shops and manufacturers of all sizes, busily producing this national addiction. Sausages are served at all times of day, from breakfast onwards. It must be noted that German sausages are by law made with one hundred per cent meat (no bread fillers or anything like that here), with only the permitted seasonings added. Sausages (**Wurst**) are such a part of German culture that when thinking of German food, one automatically thinks of sausages. The most famous one, at least internationally, is the frankfurter, which the Germans also call **Wiener** (Viennese), a thin sausage made only with pork and spices. There are however similar ones, like the **Knackwurst** and the **Bockwurst**, the latter having some beef in them. Another very popular sausage is **Bratwurst**, which can be made from pork or veal. **Cervelat** is made from beef and pork and looks more like a salami, albeit finer. There are many kinds of liver sausage (**Leberwurst**). **Bierwurst** is a sausage with a strong garlic flavour. Other sausages are the popular **Schinkenwurst** and **Bierschinken**, both made with ham. **Brühwurst** are fresh sausages, made from minced meat (pork and beef or just pork) but occasionally they also contain larger pieces of meat.

Hams are varied and delicious, the best being the Westphalian ham and the Black Forest ham. **Kasseler** is pork which is smoked after being salted and pickled in brine. Whatever you see looking like bacon is in fact **Katenspeck**, which is different in taste and is already cooked, so it can be consumed as it is or used in cooking. There are many kinds of cooked ham of high quality, all very lean. The salamis are tempting too and original, like **Apfelsalami** (with apple), **Käsesalami** (with cheese) and **Zwiebelsalami** (with onion).

BREAD

Brot (bread) in Germany is generally dense and dark. It lasts for a very long time although it does not contain preservatives. The difference in colour and texture is due to this bread being made with rye flour, not wheat. Rye is really too hard to be ground as it is, needing a period of soaking, which imparts a moist quality to the bread.

There are many varieties of **Brot**, but the main ones are **Vollkornbrot** and **Schwarzbrot**, made from wholemeal rye and less dark and the lighter **Landbrot** or **Mischbrot**. All of them are magnificent with cheese, sausages and other cured meats. There is linseed bread, **Leinsamenbrot**, which, because of the oil contained in the seeds, is very digestible and again ideal to team up with cheese and sausages (especially the liver ones). Another variety is **Pumpernickel**, a very dark bread (cooked for hours in special steam ovens) made with wholemeal coarse rye flour.

Other breads to look out for are **Kraftbrot**, made with wheatgerm; **Fünfkornbrot**, made with five different cereals; and **Sonnenblumenbrot**, made with full grain rye and a high percentage of sunflower seeds.

These breads are served at the breakfast table, to go with cold meats and cheeses, and also with the cold table (evening meal), known as **Abendbrot**.

GERMAN FOOD

At breakfast you will be likely to have **Brötchen**, the German variety of breadrolls. The ordinary white roll is made from wheat flour, but there are endless variations such as **Käsebrötchen** (topped with cheese) and **Mehrkornbrötchen** (made of dark flour with several kinds of cereal in it).

SAUERKRAUT

This typically German way of preparing cabbage is a very welcome change from ordinary cabbage and a real delicacy when served with pork and sausages. You will find **Sauerkraut** canned or packed in jars or bags or even straight from the barrel, for this is not homemade fare. **Sauerkraut** consists of fermented cabbage with salt, and a range of other seasonings, which can include peppercorns, juniper berries, onion, wine and even apples. Try **Kasseler Rippe mit Sauerkraut** (smoked saddle of pork with sauerkraut), a typical dish from Berlin. Red cabbage, also popular in Germany, is generally cooked with apple, not fermented.

DAIRY PRODUCTS

Dairy products, especially cheese, are another very important part of German food. Like everything else in the country, these products are of the highest quality. Cheese has been produced in Germany for many centuries but it was in the nineteenth century that the industry actually started in earnest, in Bavaria. This is the province where most of the cheese is still produced, as a true local speciality.

Many cheeses are processed, for convenient use in sandwiches and salads. Their generic name is **Schmelzkäse**, meaning that they have been melted. There are many kinds of **Schmelzkäse**, including the smoked varieties, which can also be used for cooking, such as **Räucherkäse mit Walnüssen** (with walnuts), **Räucherkäse mit Schinken** (with ham) and **Pfefferkäse mit Schinken** (ham and pepper log). Other types of cheese spreads contain nuts, spices, herbs and sausages. One of the best hard cheeses (**Hartkäse**) is **Allgäuer Emmentaler**, from the Alps in Bavaria. Another Alpine cheese is **Bergkäse**. Interestingly enough, Germany produces excellent Camembert and Brie and even sells them to France. A mild, buttery cheese is the **Damenkäse** (ladies' cheese), so called because of its delicate flavour and texture. As for stronger cheeses, two good examples are **Blauschimmelkäse**, a blue cheese, and **Limburger**, which is spicy and smooth.

GERMAN FOOD

A popular low-fat cheese is **Quark** which looks like thick yoghurt. There are several varieties, from virtually fat-free up to a creamy 40% fat. You can buy pure **Quark** or a delicious piquant sort such as **Liptauer Quark** (with various herbs) or even a sweet mixture. It can be eaten on its own but normally it is used for mixing with various ingredients and served as a dip or as a topping on bread. **Quark** is good for desserts, instead of cream, and for cheesecakes.

FESTIVE FOOD

Christmas is essentially a family affair in Germany to the extent that not even Christmas cards are sent out except to very close friends. However, tourists can enjoy the famous Christmas markets, the best known of which takes place in Nuremburg. Here you can buy all sorts of Christmas decorations, and sample the **Lebkuchen** (gingerbread cookies) with a glass of delicious **Glühwein** (mulled wine). The Christmas celebration itself is normally confined to a festive dinner (on Christmas Eve) and a special lunch on Christmas Day, so do not expect to find shops open during the afternoon of Christmas Eve.

Great importance is given to soup in Germany, so any soup served for Christmas (generally a light, clear soup on this occasion) will be garnished with a careful choice of small dumplings or thin pancakes rolled up and cut into strips. The soup is preceded by delicate savoury tit-bits, which can be bought ready-made at delicatessens. They include little rounds of bread or cucumber topped with cold meats, cheeses and seafood. A rich herring salad is also part of the Christmas spread. For the meat course goose (**Gans**) is the most popular, with a delicious stuffing of chestnuts or prunes and apples. Dessert includes **Stollen**, the typically German spiced loaf with candied peel, which is normally bought ready-baked, although in the past it used to be made at home.

Easter means a holiday from work, without any special sign of festivity except perhaps for the chocolate Easter eggs, Easter rabbits and so on, enjoyed by adults and children alike. On Good Friday, people traditionally eat fish, especially carp.

GERMAN FOOD

EATING PLACES AND TYPES OF FOOD SERVED

In Germany the main meal of the day is usually **Mittagessen**, lunch. It starts with soup, followed by the main dish (meat and vegetables or salad, normally) and an optional dessert or fruit.

Dinner (**Abendessen**) consists of platters of cold meats and cheeses. On occasions Germans also have a hot meal, but not very heavy.

Breakfast (**Frühstück**) generally consists of a variety of cold meats and cheeses, with different kinds of bread and jam and freshly brewed coffee.

Baker's shops open their doors at 7am and are excellent places to eat breakfast, in the eating area (**Stehcafé**).

Café is a snack bar with excellent coffee, chocolates and rich cakes.

In butcher's shops there is often an area for a quick meal such as **Bockwurst** or **Buletten mit Kartoffelsalat** (meatballs with potato salad).

Imbiß or **Imbißstube** are shops serving cheap snacks for eating in or taking out, like a snack bar. They have soups and various dishes which can be prepared quickly, including hamburgers, sausages, barbecued chicken and fried potatoes. Most of these establishments serve beer.

A **Markt** (market) is also a good place to buy snacks.

As a rule, eating places (including restaurants) have a menu with prices outside, so you will be prepared for the cost before going in.

If you see a sign saying **durchgehend warme Küche**, it means there will be hot meals all day.

One of the unusual places where one can eat in Germany (and eat well) is the town hall (**Rathaus**), which normally has a restaurant open to the public, called the **Ratskeller** (town hall cellar).

Restaurants (restaurants) usually offer set-price meals.

Gaststätte is a cross between a restaurant and a pub, where the food is accompanied by beer.

Weinstube is a wine bar, where there is often a buffet.

Beisel (in Austria) is a bar/bistro serving simple Austrian dishes.

Konditorei is a cake shop with a selection of mouth-watering pastries.

GERMAN FOOD

DRINKS

Germany is a coffee-drinking nation, with fresh coffee served at breakfast and all hours. Apart from drinking coffee in restaurants, the Germans frequent **Stehcafé**, a kind of shop where they serve coffee (to drink standing up), usually attached to a bakery.

Chocolate and cocoa are popular, with tea and herbal teas much less so.

Apart from the usual soft drinks, one can be sure of splendid quality fruit juices (**Fruchtsaft**). The most popular juices are made from grapes (**Trauben**) and apples (**Äpfel**), but there are many other kinds as well.

BEERS, CIDER, WINES AND SPIRITS

Despite the love for mead (an alcoholic drink made from honey and water) that had dominated Germany for many centuries, beer made its appearance and started to become popular even before the Romans occupied the country. The liking for beer is so deep-seated that every other town has its own brewery, with local characteristics. It is estimated that there are around 1300 such establishments (some say more). The varieties of beer are also staggering, with more than 5000 different kinds.

Germany is a land of festivals and fairs – perhaps more than anywhere else in Europe. The beer festivals are among the best and most popular with **Oktoberfest**, held in Munich, being the most outstanding.

According to statistics, German people drink between 150 and 250 litres of beer each year, depending on the region they live in, with the north having the highest consumption. Beers are of medium to high alcoholic strengths and very characteristically German. In the last few years, brewers have also been producing low-alcohol and non-alcoholic beers (full of flavour, nevertheless) to meet public demand.

German beers vary according to the fermentation methods and formulae of cereals included in each. In Germany beer is actually classified as a food and all the details of its production are closely scrutinised both by the producers and the consumers. Except for the beers made in Bavaria, which are based on wheat (**Weizenbiere**), all the others are made from hops, yeast, water and, of course, malted barley. There are really two

GERMAN FOOD

main types, which are then subdivided. These are bottom-fermented beer, called **untergärig**, and top-fermented, or **obergärig**. Each one of these main streams then has specialities like the **Altbier** (beer from the lower Rhine), and the **Kölsch** (from Cologne), which are top-fermented beers, and **Dunkeles** (dark beer) or **Helles** (light beer), which are bottom-fermented. All the famous beers made especially for the festive seasons (Christmas, Easter or Carnival, and for the beer festivals) are bottom-fermented and quite high in alcohol content, for example **Doppelbockbier** and **Bockbier**. Christmas is a time for specially strong beer, called **Weihnachtsbier**.

Apfelwein (apple wine), a kind of cider which may or may not be sparkling, is produced in substantial quantities, as well as a number of spirits derived from various fruits and cereals. Cereal spirits (made from rye, barley, corn, wheat and oats) are all called **Schnaps** and are served with beer, as a side drink. They can be neutral in taste or flavoured with juniper berries or caraway seeds. **Obstbranntwein** (fruit brandies) are spirits made from cherries (the famous **Kirsch**), from apricots, plums, blackberries, etc. Another common brandy is **Weinbrand**.

The wine industry, however, is relatively small, because of Germany's geography. However, the Rhine and Moselle river valleys do provide the right conditions for productive vineyards, giving mainly white wines (and some rosés) which tend to be light and refreshing, some of them slightly sweet. Some sparkling wines are also produced and there is a selection of low-alcohol and alcohol-free wines as well.

In Germany one can enjoy food, as well as beer or wine, at the **Brauhäuser** or **Weinstuben**. However, if you only want to drink, there are also places where you can do just that (**Kneipen**).

AUSTRIA

Austria is known as a country of good food, where one is certain of eating really well, both in quantity and quality. The Austrian way of life with its old-fashioned dignity is reflected in the elegance of its traditions which scarcely seem to alter with the passing of time.

Austrian cuisine and especially Viennese cuisine are proudly traditional and offer many delightful surprises, flavoured with paprika (a favourite), lots of garlic, ginger, caraway, cumin and poppy seeds, horseradish and various other spices and herbs. Many of these seasonings are not of Austrian origin but were adopted during the seventeenth century, when they became popular in Europe. Historical connections with Hungary brought a strong Hungarian influence on Austrian cuisine, as do those neighbours which share a border with Austria.

Soups are important everywhere and the desserts proverbially out of this world. It is not unusual for an Austrian to eat just soup and dessert as a main meal on many occasions.

During the most important annual festivities (Christmas, Easter, Carnival), many restaurants will serve special dishes. Cake shops will also sell typical Christmas goodies of all types, from meringues to honey cakes and small biscuits to hang on the trees. Carnival is greeted in Vienna with special jam doughnuts made to perfection.

Culinary terms in Austria can be straightforward German but more often than not they consist of colourful local expressions. You will see that many dishes are given extremely long names, generally incorporating either their origin or some of their ingredients. Dividing the words into several sections should help towards understanding what they mean.

Places where you can have a good and reasonably-priced meal are many and varied. The best example is a **Beisel**, also called **Gasthaus**, which has similarities both with a pub and a café and is very popular with the locals. You can stay practically the whole day at a **Gasthaus** if you want to, having endless cups of excellent coffee and sampling the many dishes available, while enjoying the relaxed atmosphere. A **Kaffeehaus** is a café with a difference (though there are many kinds) where you can also stay for long stretches of time, partaking of coffee and food, from breakfast to supper. The tempting cake shops (**Konditoreien**) are also fully licensed.

AUSTRIAN FOOD

Even if you do not go to a restaurant at all in Austria, it is always possible to have something substantial and special, wherever you go. Try one of the colourful street stalls which often specialize in **Wurst** (sausages).

Hotels generally have good restaurants (open to the public as well as to their guests), cafés and brasseries.

Eating places (including restaurants) are normally open all day and even if the main meal is not available at certain times, one can choose something from a **kleine Karte** (snack menu), instead of the **Tageskarte** (full menu). Many establishments close on bank holidays (there are quite a few, counting saints' days) so it is advisable to check beforehand if you want to go to a particular place.

Breakfast can consist of a simple continental coffee and croissant, but Austrians (who love good food) tuck into sausages of various kinds, cakes and cheeses. Bread (**Brot**) is excellent. Try little rolls like **Baunzerl** (with a distinctive cut on top), or **Stangl**, which is a type of croissant covered with cheese or stuffed with crackling bacon (**Grammeln**), or **Bosniakerl**, a wholemeal roll with caraway seeds. **Gebildebroten** (ornamented loaf) is also recommended. Breakfast may include **zwei Eier im Glas** – a couple of soft boiled eggs served in a glass container.

Despite a good breakfast, Austrians also have a mid-morning snack, perhaps a cake or a sandwich but often a proper dish, based either on eggs, ham, lentils, red cabbage or, of course, sausages. Good snacks for this time of day are **Schinkenkipferl** (ham-filled croissants) or **Eierspeispfandl** (a special kind of soft Viennese omelette).

Lunch is often taken from a set menu, called **Mittagsmenü**. Homely places may include **Hausmannskost**, meaning good home cooking.

Mid-afternoon is again snack-time, often taken at a **Konditorei** (cake shop), when a **Sachertorte** (a typical sponge cake filled with apricot and chocolate) would be in order. There are of course many other **Torten** (gateaux). They are generally based on a sponge with various glorious fillings. Try **Linzertorte**, filled with raspberry jam, **Nußtorte** (made with nuts), the obligatory **Mohntorte**, containing poppy seeds, or **Cremeschmitten**, a mille-feuilles (layered cake) filled with egg custard.

Dinner may start with the splendid Austrian **Vorspeisen** (hors d'œuvres), followed by soup, the main dish, cheese, dessert, coffee and a digestif.

AUSTRIAN FOOD

The hors d'œuvres (or starters) can be a **kalte Platte** (cold meats) with various pork delicacies, or perhaps meat in aspic, black pudding (**Blunz'm** or **Blutwurst**), perhaps with **Sauerkraut**, **Gansleber** (foie gras) or dumplings (for example, **Hechtknödel**, pike dumplings).

Good examples of soups are **Frittatensuppe** (beef broth with strips of pancake), **Bröselknödel** (soup with little dumplings prepared with bone marrow and breadcrumbs), **Einmachsuppe** (chicken or veal broth with cream and eggs), **Rahmsuppe** (a garlic soup thickened with potato – as are many soups, as well as with maize), **Kirtagssuppe** (thickened with potato and flavoured with caraway seeds), **Kraftsuppe** (consommé), **Wiener Kartoffelsuppe** (potato soup with mushrooms), and **Burgenländische Krautsuppe** (a thickened vegetable soup). Wine soups such as **grüne Veltlinersuppe** or **Rieslingsuppe**, which consist of a good broth, cream, eggs and wine, are now very popular in Austria. However, there are so many excellent soups that it would be impossible to give a complete list. But look out also for those made with delicate strudel parcels filled with a variety of ingredients, mushroom soups and creamy soups in general.

Sea fish is generally expensive but there are lake and river fish in abundance, including carp, pike, trout, salmon and eels. Fish can be sometimes served in **Sulz** (aspic – Austrians are fond of aspic of all kinds), in quenelles, fried or steamed. As a devout Catholic country, Austria observes Lent and during this time fish is eaten much more widely. Many eating places in the countryside serve a special herring menu during Lent – **Heringsschmaus** (herring feast). Pike tends to be popular, but a large fish that also finds some favour at restaurants is **Wels** (catfish).

Austrians also enjoy eating meat, especially pork, although restaurants like to give more importance to veal and beef. Other meats are poultry (chicken and duck of high quality), wild boar, mutton and lamb. Game is abundant and quails (and their eggs) have become very popular. Every part of the pig and other animals is used, offal being highly esteemed. Lard is the most widely used fat. Smoked meats (**Geselchtes**) are very good, as is the liver pâté.

Specialities from Vienna and other regions are too numerous to list here, but one must not visit Austria without trying some of its famous dishes, such as **Wiener Schnitzel** (a veal or sometimes pork escalope);

AUSTRIAN FOOD

Tafelspitz (which is popular nationally but really a Viennese speciality and consists of perfectly boiled beef of various cuts); **Tafelspitzsulz** (meaning beef in aspic); **gefüllte Kalbsbrust** (stuffed breast of veal); **Fledermaus** (boiled beef in a blanket of horseradish cream, browned in the oven); the indispensable **Gulasch** (a spicy meat stew) which can take many forms; the very popular **Wiener Backhendl** (roast or fried chicken covered in breadcrumbs); **Spanferkel** (suckling pig); **Fleischlaberln** (highly seasoned meat cakes); **gebackene Leber** (calves' liver bread-crumbed and fried); **Gansleber** (goose liver); **Steirisches Lammkarree mit Basilikum** (lamb baked with basil); **Erdäpfelgulasch** (a very spicy sausage and potato stew); or **Zwiebelrostbraten**, which is a large steak made with onions. The Austrians are also very partial to roast pork (**Schweinsrostbraten**). **Gefüllte Kalbsstelze** (knuckle of veal) is another local speciality.

There are endless accompaniments and salads, hot and cold, to go with those dishes or to eat by themselves: dumplings, for example, of which Austrians are extremely fond, producing all kinds of variations. Their generic name is **Knödel** or **Knöderl**, according to size. **Topfenknöderl**, a cheese dumpling, is a must. They are very often used in soups. Larger, stuffed dumplings are served as a main dish, and there are also many sweet dumplings. A nice vegetable dish is **Schwammerlgulasch** (mush-room stew). **Risi lisi** or **Risipisi** is rice with peas. Chanterelles (**Eierschwammerln**) are very plentiful and appear in many dishes or by themselves as starters. The classic accompaniment for the ubiquitous **Tafelspitz** (boiled beef) is **Erdäpfelkren**, a relish made with potato and the much loved horseradish. **Warmer Krautsalat** is a salad made with warm cabbage and crunchy bacon. **Grüner Salat** is a green salad and **Linsenspecksalat** is a lentil salad with **Speck** (bacon). Lentils are used a lot in Austrian cooking. **Sterz**, a sort of polenta, is made in some regions. Gnocchi (**Grießtaler**) made of semolina are delicious. They can be sweet as well as savoury.

Next come the desserts, in a class of their own. Some are splendid chest-nut specialities, such as **Maronitorte** (chestnut tart), **Kastanienreis** (sweet puréed chestnuts) or **Kastanienroulade** (roulade with chestnut fill-ing). The Austrians specialize also in puddings made with pasta. Good examples are **Topfennudeln** (pasta with cheese), **Powidltascherl** (ravioli-like pasta filled with plum jam), or the very popular **Mohnnudeln** (noodles with poppy seeds, cinnamon, sugar and butter). **Apfelstrudel** is perhaps the best-known dessert, with fine strudel pastry and apples. Try also **Marillenknödel** (an apricot dumpling), **Mohr im Hemd** (one of the best chocolate puddings), **Wiener Hofburgtorte** (another chocolate speciality), **Milchrahmstrudel** (a strudel with a filling of egg custard and soft cheese), **B'soffene**, a lovely pudding soaked in mulled wine, or another alcoholic pudding, **Punschpudding**.

Cheeses are not as outstanding in Austria as might be expected, although there are a few good ones, such as **Alpzirler**, a cow's cheese, **Steirischer Selchkäse** (ewe's), **Graf Görz** (a soft cheese), **Zillertaler** (cow's milk), **Ennstaler** (blue cheese from mixed milk), and **Ziegett**, also a mixed milk cheese. Many Austrian cheeses try to imitate French or Italian cheeses, without managing to get it completely right. This seems to be a consequence of the laws governing the making of cheese, which interfere with the ripening process.

COFFEE

Coffee in Austria is a serious business and there are many kinds you can order, the names varying according to the amount of milk they contain. This can be puzzling to foreigners, who would be well advised to write down a list to be consulted at the appropriate moment. Thus:

Espresso is black coffee (normally) but you must state whether you want it really strong and therefore with less, more concentrated liquid (**kurz**) or with more water and therefore weaker (**verlängert**). However, espresso can also be served with milk, as **Brauner** or **eine Schale Braun**.

Schwarzer is also black coffee and again it can be small and strong (**kurz**) or weaker and larger (**verlängert** or **gestreckt**).

Melange is an old name for milky coffee, and you can specify whether you want it with more milk (**mehr licht** – lighter coffee) or less milk (**mehr dunkel** – darker coffee).

Eine Schale Gold and **eine Schale Braun** are similar to **Melange**, with more or less milk.

Kapuziner is meant to be cappuccino, in this case black with just a drop of milk.

Einspänner is coffee with cream, served in a glass (large).

AUSTRIAN FOOD

Kaisermelange is coffee with a beaten egg yolk and no milk. It can be fortified with a little brandy. Some places serve this with whipped cream and no egg.

Türkischer is of course a Turkish coffee.

Eiskaffee is a delicious iced coffee, with lots of cream.

Tea is also drunk in Austria, though not as much as coffee.

BEER

Bier is one of the drinks to have in Austria, but it is less important than in Germany, where beer is much more a part of the local culture. These are the names given to the different measures of beer in Austria: a **Pfiff** is the smallest size (about one eighth of a litre); next comes the **kleines Bier** (small beer), also called **Seidel**; then the **großes Bier** (large) or **Krügel** (measuring half a litre). If asking for bottled beer, a small bottle is **kleine Flasche** (a third of a litre), and the large is **große Flasche** (half a litre).

WINES

The vine has been cultivated in Austria for many centuries and it is known that wine was made well before the Roman occupation. The Romans themselves continued this culture, which has remained ever since, often in ecclesiastical hands. More recently, and after a sad episode that gave Austrian wines a bad name, the industry is flourishing again and, as is the case with anything produced in the country, wines are made with excellence in mind. Geographical conditions favour a great variety of grapes, which in turn make a very good range of wines, mainly whites, some good reds and splendid sweet or dessert wines. Each region has its own good offerings worth trying. You can have house wine (**offene Weine**) or good vintage (**Bouteillenweine**) by the glass. The proper names for the various glass or bottle sizes vary, but **Achtel** (one eighth of a litre), **Viertel** (one quarter of a litre), **Halber** (half a litre) and **Liter** (one litre) are useful to remember.

A good way of tasting various wines more economically is to try **Heuriger** (new wine) in a special restaurant where you have the chance of sampling the season's wines with good food.

There are also fruit wines, like **Birnenmost** (pear wine), some of which are **Sekt** (sparkling), for example **Birnensekt** (sparkling pear wine).

SPIRITS

Austrians produce **Schnaps** with great flair. It may be made from any fruit and is a must after a meal, as a digestif, although many Austrians also drink it at the start. **Schnaps** is a kind of eau-de-vie or dry liqueur, strong but smooth and delicious. **Schnaps** is also given the name of **Geist** or **Brand** with the added name of the particular fruit it is made from, as in **Marillenbrand** (apricot brandy), one of the most popular.

As to the sizes, remember that **klein** goes for small and **groß** for large, but even the large size is quite a small quantity, as it is very strong.

SWITZERLAND

A great part of Switzerland is German-speaking. The most famous Swiss breakfast, one that has become famous the world over, is **Birchermüsli**, a cereal dish created by Dr Bircher-Benner, a renowned doctor from Zurich who believed in the use of uncooked cereals, fruit, vegetables and other foods to promote good health. Muesli is his most famous concoction. The ingredients are oatmeal, lemon juice, apple or other fruit, nuts and honey, with a little cream, yoghurt or condensed milk.

As in Germany, food in Switzerland is prepared with great care. Main meals may start with a soup, which may well be based on bread. Bread is used quite a lot as a main ingredient in various other dishes.

The Swiss lakes provide an abundance of fish used in many recipes.

Cheese is very prominent in the Swiss diet, often served on roasted or fried bread and tarts. The most delicious cheese dish is **Fondue**, with **Gruyère** and **Emmental** (two of the best cheeses) melted with wine and seasonings. Vegetables are often served 'au gratin', as an accompaniment or as a main meal. Veal, kid, tripe, beef, mutton and pork are all popular meats. Many excellent cakes are made with carrots, walnuts, apples and honey.

DRINKS

Alsterwasser lemonade shandy
Altbier top-fermented beer from the lower Rhine
Apfelkorn apple brandy
Apfelsaft apple juice
Apfelwein cider (apple wine)
Barack apricot brandy
Bereich Bernkastel area along the Moselle producing crisp white wines
Berliner Weiße fizzy beer with fruit syrup added
Birnenmost pear wine
Birnensekt sparkling pear wine
Bockbier strong beer (light or dark), drunk especially in Bavaria
Brauner strong black coffee with a little milk
Danziger Goldwasser brandy containing tiny bits of gold leaf
Doppelbockbier like Bock, but still stronger
Dunkeles dark beer
Einspänner coffee with whipped cream served in a glass
Eiskaffee iced coffee served with vanilla ice cream
Eiswein a rich, naturally sweet, white wine made from grapes which are
    harvested only after a period of frost
Erbach area producing scented white wines mainly from Riesling grape
Export Bier premium beer
Früchtetee fruit tea
Fruchtsaft fruit juice
Gespritzer spritzer – white wine and soda water
Glühwein mulled wine
Grog hot rum
Gumpoldkirchen spicy white wine from Austria
halbtrocken medium-dry
Hausbrauerei house beer (own brewery)
Hefe-Weizen wheat beer
Helles light beer
Heuriger new wine
Himbeergeist rasperry brandy
Hochheim strong white wines from the Rheingau region
Kaffee coffee
Kaffee komplett coffee with milk and sugar
Kaffee mit Milch coffee with milk
Kaisermelange black coffee with an egg yolk
Kakao cocoa
Kapuziner Austrian equivalent to cappuccino which is black coffee with
    a drop of milk
Kirschwasser cherry brandy

Kölsch *top-fermented beer from Cologne*
Korn *rye spirit*
Kräutertee *herbal tea*
Kristall-Weizen *a kind of sparkling beer*
Likör *liqueur (generic name)*
Limonade *lemonade*
Malz *dark malt beer (unfermented)*
Märzenbier *beer made for the famous Munich Beer Festival*
Melange *milky coffee*
Milch *milk*
Milchshake *milk shake*
Mineralwasser *mineral water*
Most *fruit juice; (in the south) fruit wine*
Münchener *a kind of dark lager from Munich*
Nierstein *village on the Rhine producing medium to sweet white Rheinwein*
Oppenheim *village on the Rhine producing fine white wines*
Orangensaft *orange juice*
Pils *a strong, slightly bitter lager*
Riesling *Riesling wine*
Roséwein *rosé wine*
Rotwein *red wine*
Saft *juice*
Sahne *cream*
Schnaps *strong spirit*
schwarzer Tee *black tea*
Sekt *sparkling wine like Champagne*
Selters(wasser) *sparkling mineral water*
Slivovitz *plum brandy*
Sprudel *mineral water (sparkling)*
Starkbier *strong beer*
Tee *tea*
Tee mit Milch *tea with milk*
Tee mit Zitrone *tea with lemon*
Tomatensaft *tomato juice*
Traubensaft *grape juice*
Türkischer *Turkish coffee*
Wasser *water*
Weinbrand *brandy*
Weiße *golden wheat beer*
Weißwein *white wine*
Weizenbier *wheat beer (light or dark)*
Zitronentee *lemon tea*

MENU READER

Aal *eel*
Aalsuppe *eel soup*
Allgäuer Emmentaler *whole-milk hard cheese from the Allgäu*
Allgäuer Käsespätzle *cheese noodles from the Allgäu*
Alpzirler *cow's milk cheese from Austria*
Ananas *pineapple*
Apfel *apple*
Apfelsalami *salami with apple*
Apfelstrudel *flaky pastry filled with apples and spices*
Aprikose *apricot*
Art *style or fashion of*
Artischocken *artichokes*
Auflauf *baked pudding or omelette*
Aufschnitt *sliced cold meats*
Austern *oysters*
Bäckerofen *baker's oven (pork and lamb bake) from Saarland*
Backpflaumen *prunes*
Banane *banana*
Barsch *perch*
Bauernfrühstück *scrambled eggs, bacon, cooked diced potatoes, onions, tomatoes*
Baunzerl *little roll with distinctive cut on top*
Bayrisch Kraut *shredded cabbage cooked with sliced apples, wine and sugar*
Bergkäse *cheese from the Alps*
Berliner *doughnut filled with jam*
Berner Erbsensuppe *soup made of dried peas with pig's trotters*
Bierschinken *beer sausage with ham*
Bierwurst *beer sausage*
Birchermüsli *muesli*
Birne *pear*
Blattsalat *green salad*
blau *rare ; poached (fish)*
Blauschimmelkäse *blue cheese*
Blumenkohl *cauliflower*
Blunz'm *black pudding*
Blutwurst *black pudding*
Bockwurst *boiled sausage*
Bohnen *beans*

Bohnensalat *bean salad*
Bohnensuppe *thick bean and bacon soup*
Bosniakerl *wholemeal roll with caraway seeds*
Brathähnchen *roast chicken*
Brathering *fried herring (eaten cold)*
Bratkartoffeln *fried potatoes*
Bratwurst *fried sausage*
Bremer Kükenragout *Bremen chicken fricassée*
Broiler *chicken*
Brombeeren *blackberries*
Bröselknödel *soup with little dumplings prepared with bone marrow and breadcrumbs*
Brot *bread*
Brötchen *bread roll*
Brühwurst *thick frankfurter*
B'soffene *pudding soaked in mulled wine*
Buletten *thick hamburgers*
Buletten mit Kartoffelsalat *meatballs with potato salad*
Bündnerfleisch *raw beef smoked and dried, served thinly sliced*
Burgenländische Krautsuppe *thickened cabbage and vegetable soup*
Butterkäse *high-fat cheese*
Cervelat *fine beef and pork salami*
Chindbettering *ring of bread*
Cremeschnitten *cream slices*
Champignons *button mushrooms*
Damenkäse *mild buttery cheese*
Dampfnudeln *hot yeast dumplings with vanilla sauce*
Deutsches Beefsteak *thick hamburger*
Dorsch *cod*
Dresdner Suppentopf *Dresden vegetable soup with dumplings*
Eier im Glas *soft boiled eggs served in a glass*
Eierkuchen *pancakes*
Eierschwammerln *chanterelles*
Eierspeispfandl *special Viennese omelette*
Einmachsuppe *chicken or veal broth with cream and egg*
Eintopf *stew*
Eis *ice cream*
Eisbecher *knickerbocker glory*
Eisbein *boiled pork knuckle often served with sauerkraut*

MENU READER

Emmentaler *Swiss Emmental, whole-milk hard cheese*
Ennstaler *blue cheese from mixed milk*
Ente *duck*
Erbsen *peas*
Erbsenpüree *green pea purée*
Erbsensuppe *pea soup*
Erdäpfel *potatoes*
Erdäpfelgulasch *spicy sausage and potato stew*
Erdäpfelknödel *potato and semolina dumplings*
Erdäpfelkren *relish with potato and horseradish*
Erdäpfelnudeln *fried, boiled potato balls tossed in fried breadcrumbs*
Erdbeeren *strawberries*
Falscher Hase *baked mince meatloaf*
Fasan *pheasant*
Feigen *figs*
Fenchel *fennel*
Fisch *fish*
Fischfilet *fish fillet*
Fischgerichte *fish and seafood*
Fischklöße *fish dumplings*
Fischsuppe *fish soup*
flambiert *flambé*
Fledermaus *boiled beef in horseradish cream browned in the oven*
Fleischgerichte *meat dishes*
Fleischklößchen *meatballs*
Fleischlaberln *highly seasoned meat cake*
Fleischpflanzerl *meatballs (a Bavarian speciality)*
Fleischsuppe *meat soup served with dumplings*
Flunder *flounder*
Fondue *melted cheese with wine and bread for dipping*
Forelle *trout*
Forelle blau *steamed trout*
Forelle Müllerin *trout fried in batter with almonds*
Forelle Steiermark *trout fillet with bacon in white sauce*
Frikadelle *thick hamburger*
frisch *fresh*
Fritattensuppe *beef broth with strips of pancake*
Froschschenkel *frogs' legs*
Frucht *fresh fruit*

MENU READER

Fünfkernbrot *wholemeal bread made with five different cereals*
Gans *goose*
Gänseleber *foie gras*
Gänseleberpastete *goose liver pâté*
gebackene Leber *calves' liver fried in breadcrumbs*
Gebildebroten *ornamented bread loaf*
gebraten *roasted/fried*
gedämpft *steamed*
Geflügel *poultry*
gefüllt *stuffed/filled*
gefüllte Kalbsbrust *stuffed breast of veal*
gefüllte Kalbsstelze *stuffed knuckle of veal*
gegrillt *grilled*
gegrillter Lachs *grilled salmon*
Gehacktes *mince*
gekochtes Rindfleisch mit grüner Soße *boiled beef with green sauce*
gemischter Salat *mixed salad*
Gemüse und Klöße *vegetables and dumplings*
Gemüseplatte *mixed vegetables*
Gemüsesuppe *vegetable soup*
geräuchert *smoked*
geschmort *braised*
Geschnetzeltes *thinly sliced meat in sauce*
Geselchtes *smoked meats*
Gewürzgurken *gherkins*
Gitziprägel *baked rabbit in batter (Switzerland)*
Graf Görz *Austrian soft cheese*
Grammeln *croissant stuffed with bacon*
Grießklößchensuppe *soup with semolina dumplings*
Grießtaler *gnocchi*
grüne Bohnen *green beans*
grüne Veltlinersuppe *green wine soup*
grüner Salat *green salad*
Gruyère *gruyère cheese*
Güggeli *roast chicken with onions and mushrooms in white wine sauce*
Gulasch *stewed beef with paprika*
Gulaschsuppe *spicy meat soup with paprika*
Gulyas *beef stew with paprika*
Gurke *cucumber*

MENU READER

Gurkensalat *cucumber salad*
Gyros *kebab*
Hackepeter auf Schrippen mit Zwiebeln *spiced minced pork on rolls, with onions*
Hackfleisch *mince*
Hähnchen *chicken*
Hamburger Rundstück *Hamburg meat roll*
Hammel *mutton*
Hartkäse *hard cheese*
hausgemacht *home-made*
Hausmannskost *good traditional home cooking*
Hecht *pike*
Heidschnuckenragout *lamb stew*
heiß *hot*
Hering *herring*
Heringsschmaus *herring in creamy sauce*
Herz *heart*
Himbeeren *raspberries*
Hirsch *venison*
Hühnchen *chicken*
Hühnerfrikasse *chicken fricassée*
Hummer *lobster*
Jägerschnitzel *cutlet served with mushrooms and wine sauce*
Jura Omelette *bacon, potato and onion omelette*
Kabeljau *cod*
Kaiserschmarren *strips of pancake served with raisins, sugar and cinnamon*
Kalb *veal*
Kalbsbraten *roast veal*
Kalbshaxe *knuckle of veal*
Kalbskoteletts *veal cutlets*
Kalbsleber *calf's liver*
Kalbsschnitzel *veal escalope*
kalt *cold*
kalte Platte *cold meat platter*
Kaninchen *rabbit*
Karotten *carrots*
Karpfen blau *poached carp*
Karpfen in Bier *carp poached in beer with herbs*
Kartoffelklöße *potato dumplings*

Kartoffeln *potatoes*
Kartoffelpüree *mashed potatoes*
Kartoffelsalat *potato salad*
Kartoffelsuppe *potato soup*
Käse *cheese*
Käsebrötchen *roll with with small bacon pieces in the dough and melt-ed cheese on top*
Käsefondue *dish made from melted cheese and flavoured with wine and kirsch into which you dip bread*
Käsekuchen *cheesecake*
Käseplatte *cheese platter with various cheeses*
Käsesuppe *cheese soup*
Kasseler *smoked pork*
Kasseler Rippe mit Sauerkraut *saddle of pork with sauerkraut*
Kastanienroulade *roulade with chestnut filling*
Katenspeck *streaky bacon*
Kaviar *caviar*
Kekse *biscuits*
Kirschen *cherries*
Kirtagssuppe *soup with caraway seed thickened with potato*
Klops *rissole*
Klöße *potato dumplings*
Knackwurst *hot spicy sausage*
Knoblauch *garlic*
Knödel *dumpling*
Knöderl *dumplings*
Kohl *cabbage*
Kohlsprossen *Brussels sprouts*
Kompott *stewed fruit*
Königsberger Klopse *meatballs served in thick white sauce with capers*
Kopfsalat *lettuce salad*
Kotelett *pork chop/cutlet dipped in breadcrumbs and deep fried*
Krabben *prawns*
Krabbencocktail *prawn cocktail*
Kraftbrot *wheatgerm bread*
Kraftfleisch *corned beef*
Kraftsuppe *consommé*
Krapfen *doughnut*
Krautwickerl *stuffed cabbage*

MENU READER

Kren *horseradish*
Kroketten *croquettes*
Labskaus *cured pork, herring and potato stew*
Lachs *salmon*
Lachsbrot *smoked salmon with bread*
Lamm *lamb*
Lauche *leeks*
Leber *liver*
Leberkäse *pork liver meatloaf*
Leberknödelsuppe *light soup with chicken liver dumplings*
Leberwurst *liver sausage*
Leinsamenbrot *wholemeal bread with linseed*
Leipziger Allerlei *vegetable dish made from peas, carrots, cauliflower and cabbage*
Limburger *strong cheese flavoured with herbs*
Linsenspecksalat *lentil salad with bacon*
Linsensuppe *lentil and sausage soup*
Linzertorte *latticed tart with jam topping*
Liptauer Quark *cream cheese with paprika and herbs*
Maiskolben *corn on the cob*
Makrele *mackerel*
Mandarine *mandarin*
Marillenknödel *apricot dumplings*
Maronitorte *chestnut tart*
Mastochsenhaxe *knuckle of beef (with sauce) from Sachsen-Anhalt*
Matjes *herring*
Matjeshering *salted herring*
Maultaschen *ravioli-like pasta filled with pork, veal and spinach mixture*
Mehrkornbrötchen *rolls made with several kinds of wholemeal flour*
Melone *melon*
Milchrahmstrudel *strudel filled with egg custard and soft cheese*
Mirabellen *small yellow plums*
Mohnnudeln *noodles with poppy seeds, cinnamon, sugar and butter*
Mohntorte *gâteau with poppy seeds*
Möhren *carrots*
Mohr im Hemd *chocolate pudding*
Muscheln *mussels*
Nachspeisen *desserts*
Nieren *kidneys*

MENU READER

Nockerln small dumplings
Nudeln noodles
Nudelsuppe noodle soup
Nußkuchen nut cake
Nußtorte nut gâteau
Obstkuchen fruit cake
Obstsalat fruit salad
Ochsenschwanzsuppe oxtail soup
Orange orange
Palatschinken pancakes filled with curd mixture or jam or ice cream
Pampelmuse grapefruit
paniert coated with breadcrumbs
Paprika peppers (red or green)
Pellkartoffeln jacket potatoes
Pfannkuchen pancakes
Pfefferkäse mit Schinken ham and pepper cheese log
Pfirsich peach
Pflaumen plums
Pflaumenkuchen plum tart
Pilze mushrooms
Pommes frites chips
Powidltascherl ravioli-like pasta filled with plum jam
Pumpernickel very dark bread made with wholemeal coarse rye flour
Punschpudding pudding containing alcohol
Pute turkey
Putenschnitzel turkey breast in breadcrumbs
Quark curd cheese
Raclette melted cheese and potatoes
Ragout stew
Rahmschnitzel cutlet with a creamy sauce
Rahmsuppe garlic soup thickened with potato
Räucherkäse mit Schinken smoked cheese with bacon pieces in it
Räucherkäse mit Walnüssen smoked cheese with walnuts in it
Räucherlachs smoked salmon
Rehrücken roast saddle of venison
Reibekuchen potato cakes
Reis rice
Rieslingsuppe wine soup made with Riesling
Rind(fleisch) beef

MENU READER

Rinderbraten *roast beef*
Rinderrouladen *rolled beef (beef olives)*
Rippenbraten *roast spare ribs*
Risi lisi, Risipisi *rice with peas*
Rollmops *marinated herring fillets rolled up with small pieces of onion, gherkins and white peppercorns*
Rosenkohl *Brussels sprouts*
Rösti *fried diced potatoes, onions and bacon*
Rotbarsch *rosefish*
rote Bete *beetroot*
rote Grütze *raspberry, red currant and wine jelly served with fresh cream*
rote Rübe *beetroot*
Rotkohl *red cabbage*
Rübe *turnip*
Rührei *scrambled eggs*
Sachertorte *rich chocolate gâteau*
Salat *salad*
Salzkartoffeln *boiled potatoes*
Sardinen *sardines*
Sauerbraten *braised pickled beef*
Sauerkraut *shredded pickled white cabbage*
Scampi *scampi*
Schafskäse *ewe's milk cheese*
Schaschlik *shish kebab*
Schellfisch *haddock*
Schinken *ham*
Schinkenkipferl *ham-filled croissant*
Schinkenwurst *ham sausage*
Schlachtplatte *mixture of cold sausages and meat*
Schmelzkäse *cheese spread*
Schnecke *snail*
Schnitzel *escalope*
Scholle *plaice*
Schwäbischer Apfelkuchen *apple cake*
Schwammerlgulasch *mushroom stew*
Schwarzbrot *wholemeal rye bread*
Schwarzwälder Kirschtorte *Black Forest gâteau*
Schwarzwälder Schinken *Black Forest ham*
Schwarzwäldertorte *fruit compote flan with cream*

MENU READER

Schwein *pork*
Schweinebraten *roast pork*
Schweinefleisch *pork*
Schweinehaxe *knuckle of pork*
Schweinekotelett *pork chop*
Schweinsrostbraten *roast pork*
Schwertfisch *swordfish*
Seezunge *sole*
Semmelknödel *whole roll dumpling*
Sonnenblumenbrot *wholemeal bread with sunflower seeds*
Spanferkel *suckling pig*
Spargel *asparagus*
Spargelcremesuppe *cream of asparagus soup*
Spargelsalat *asparagus (white) salad*
Spätzle *home-made noodles*
Speck *bacon (fat)*
Spiegelei *fried egg*
Spieß *kebab style*
Stachelbeertorte *gooseberry tart*
Stangl *croissant covered with cheese*
Steinbutt *turbot*
Steirischer Selchkäse *ewe's milk cheese*
Steirisches Lammkarree mit Basilikum *lamb baked with basil*
Sterz *Austrian polenta*
Stollen *spiced loaf with candied peel traditionally eaten at Christmas*
Strudel *strudel*
Sulz/Sülze *meat in aspic*
Suppen *soups*
Tafelspitz *boiled beef of various cuts*
Tafelspitzsulz *beef in aspic*
Thunfisch *tuna fish*
Thüringer Rostbratwurst *sausages from Thuringia, grilled or fried*
Tilsiter *savoury cheese with sharpish taste*
Tintenfisch *squid*
Tomaten *tomatoes*
Topf *stew*
Topfen *curd cheese (Austria)*
Topfenknöderl *curd cheese dumplings*
Topfennudeln *pasta with cheese*

MENU READER

Trauben *grapes*
Truthahn *turkey*
Vollkornbrot *wholemeal bread*
Vorspeisen *starters*
warm *warm*
warmer Krautsalat *salad with warm cabbage and crunchy bacon*
Weichkäse *cream cheese*
Weißbrot *wheat bread*
Weißkohl *white cabbage*
Weißwurst *white sausage (veal and pork with herbs)*
Wels *catfish*
Westfälischer Schinken *Westphalian ham*
Wiener *frankfurters*
Wiener Backhendl *roast chicken covered in breadcrumbs*
Wiener Fischfilets *fish fillets baked in sour cream sauce*
Wiener Hofburgtorte *chocolate gâteau*
Wiener Kartoffelsuppe *potato soup with mushrooms*
Wiener Schertorte *chocolate cake*
Wiener Schnitzel *veal escalope fried in breadcrumbs*
Wiener Würstchen *pork sausage*
Wildbraten *roast venison*
Wildgulasch *game stew*
Wildschwein *wild boar*
Wurst *sausage*
Würstchen *frankfurter*
Zander *pike-perch*
Ziegenkäse *goat's milk cheese*
Ziegett *mixed milk cheese*
Zillertaler *cow's cheese from the Zillertal*
Zitrone *lemon*
Zopf *braided bread loaf*
Zuger Köteli *baked dace with herbs and wine*
Zunge *tongue*
Zwetschgendatschi *damson tart*
Zwetschgenknödel *plum dumplings*
Zwiebeln *onions*
Zwiebelrostbraten *large steak with onions*
Zwiebelsalami *salami with onion*
Zwiebelsuppe *onion soup (from Saarland)*

DICTIONARY
english-german
german-english

A

a *(with 'der' words)* ein
  (with 'die' words) eine
  (with 'das' words) ein
abbey die Abtei
abortion die Abtreibung
abortion pill die Abtreibungspille
about *(concerning)* über
  about 4 o'clock ungefähr vier Uhr
above *(overhead)* oben
  (higher than) über
abscess der Abszeß
accelerator das Gaspedal
accent *(pronunciation)* der Akzent
to accept akzeptieren
accident der Unfall
accident and emergency department die Notaufnahme
accommodation die Unterkunft
account *(bill)* die Rechnung
  (in bank) das Konto
acid die Säure
actor der/die Schauspieler(in)
adaptor der Zwischenstecker
address die Adresse
  what is the address? wie ist die Adresse?
adhesive tape das Klebeband
admission fee der Eintrittspreis
adult der/die Erwachsene
  for adults für Erwachsene
advance: *in advance* im voraus
advert *(in newspaper)* die Anzeige
to advise raten
aeroplane das Flugzeug
aerosol die Spraydose
afraid: *to be afraid of* Angst haben vor
after *(afterwards)* danach
  after lunch nach dem Mittagessen
afternoon der Nachmittag
  this afternoon heute nachmittag
  in the afternoon am Nachmittag
aftershave das Rasierwasser

again wieder
against gegen
age das Alter
ago: *a week ago* vor einer Woche
to agree vereinbaren
agreement die Vereinbarung
air conditioning die Klimaanlage
  is there air conditioning? ist es klimatisiert?
airline die Fluggesellschaft
air mail: *by air mail* per Luftpost
air mattress die Luftmatratze
airplane das Flugzeug
airport der Flughafen
air ticket das Flugticket
aisle *(theatre, plane)* der Gang
alarm die Alarmanlage
alarm call der Weckruf
alarm clock der Wecker
alcohol der Alkohol
alcohol-free alkoholfrei
alcoholic alkoholisch
all alle
allergic: *to be allergic to* allergisch sein gegen
  I'm allergic to... ich bin allergisch gegen
allergy die Allergie
to allow erlauben
  to be allowed dürfen
all right *(agreed)* in Ordnung
  are you all right? geht es Ihnen gut?
almond die Mandel
almost fast
alone allein
Alps die Alpen
also auch
altar der Altar
aluminium foil die Alufolie
always immer
am *see* (to be) **GRAMMAR**
amber *(traffic lights)* das Gelb
ambulance der Krankenwagen
America Amerika

American *adj* amerikanisch
m/f der/die Amerikaner(in)
amount: *total amount* die Gesamtsumme
anaesthetic die Narkose
local anaesthetic die örtliche
Betäubung
general anaesthetic die Vollnarkose
anchor der Anker
ancient antik
and und
angina die Angina
angry zornig
animal das Tier
ankle der Knöchel
anniversary der Jahrestag
annual jährlich
another *(additional)* noch ein(e/s)
(different) ein anderer
another beer, please noch ein
Bier, bitte
answer die Antwort
to answer antworten
answerphone der Anrufbeantworter
ant die Ameise
antacid das säurebindende Mittel
antibiotic das Antibiotikum
antifreeze das Frostschutzmittel
antiques die Antiquitäten
antique shop der Antiquitätenladen
antiseptic das Antiseptikum
apartment das Appartement
appendicitis die Blinddarmentzündung
apple der Apfel
appointment der Termin
I have an appointment ich habe
einen Termin
apricot die Aprikose
April der April
apron die Schürze
architect der/die Architekt(in)
architecture die Architektur

are *see* (to be) **GRAMMAR**
arm der Arm
armbands *(to swim)* die Schwimmflügel
armchair der Sessel
to arrange vereinbaren
to arrest verhaften
arrival die Ankunft
to arrive ankommen
art die Kunst
art gallery die Kunsthalle
arthritis die Arthritis
artist der/die Künstler(in)
ashtray der Aschenbecher
asparagus der Spargel
aspirin das Aspirin
asthma das Asthma
I have asthma ich habe Asthma
at: *at the hotel* im Hotel
at home zu Hause
at 8 o'clock um acht Uhr
at once sofort
at night am Abend
Atlantic Ocean der Atlantik
to attack angreifen
attic der Dachboden
attractive attraktiv
auction die Auktion
audience das Publikum
August der August
aunt die Tante
au pair das Au-pair-Mädchen
Australia Australien
Australian *adj* australisch
m/f der/die Australier(in)
Austria Österreich
Austrian *adj* österreichisch
m/f der/die Österreicher(in)
author der/die Autor(in)
automatic automatisch
automatic car das Automatikauto
auto-teller der Geldautomat
autumn der Herbst
available erhältlich
avalanche die Lawine

a

a

a

93

a

avenue die Allee
to avoid *(obstacle)* ausweichen
(person) meiden
awake wach
awful schrecklich
axle *(car)* die Achse

B

baby das Baby
baby food die Babynahrung
baby milk die Babymilch
baby's bottle die Babyflasche
baby seat *(in car)* der Kindersitz
babysitter der/die Babysitter(in)
babysitting service der Babysitter-Service
baby wipes die Babytücher
back *(of body, hand)* der Rücken
backpack der Rucksack
bacon der Speck
bad *(weather, news)* schlecht
(fruit, vegetables) verdorben
bag die Tasche
baggage das Gepäck
baggage allowance das Freigepäck
baggage reclaim die Gepäckausgabe
bait *(for fishing)* der Köder
baked gebacken
baker's die Bäckerei
balcony der Balkon
ball der Ball
ballet das Ballett
balloon der Ballon
banana die Banane
band *(musical)* die Band
bandage der Verband
bank die Bank
(river) das Ufer
bank account das Bankkonto
banknote der Geldschein
bar die Bar
barbecue der Grill

to have a barbecue eine Grillparty geben
barber der (Herren)friseur
to bark bellen
barn die Scheune
barrel *(wine/beer)* das Faß
basement das Souterrain
basil das Basilikum
basket der Korb
Basle Basel
bath das Bad
to have a bath ein Bad nehmen
bathing cap die Badekappe
bathroom das Badezimmer
with bathroom mit Bad
battery die Batterie
bay *(along coast)* die Bucht
bay leaf das Lorbeerblatt
to be sein *see* (to be) **GRAMMAR**
beach der Strand
private beach der Privatstrand
sandy beach der Sandstrand
beach hut der Strandkorb
bean die Bohne
bear *(animal)* der Bär
beard der Bart
beautiful schön
beauty salon der Kosmetiksalon
because weil
bed das Bett
double bed das Doppelbett
single bed das Einzelbett
twin beds zwei Einzelbetten
bed and breakfast Übernachtung mit Frühstück
bedroom das Schlafzimmer
bee die Biene
beef das Rindfleisch
beer das Bier
before vor
before breakfast vor dem Frühstück
to begin beginnen
behind hinter
beige beige

to believe glauben
bell *(church)* die Glocke
(door) die Klingel
to belong to gehören zu
below unterhalb
belt der Gürtel
bend *(in road)* die Kurve
berth *(train, ship)* die Kabine
beside *(next to)* neben
best: *the best* der/die/das beste
to bet on *(auf etwas)* wetten
better besser
better than besser als
between zwischen
bib *(baby's)* das Lätzchen
bicycle das Fahrrad
by bicycle mit dem Fahrrad
bicycle lock das Fahrradschloß
bicycle repair kit das Fahrradflickzeug
big groß
bigger than größer als
bike *(push bike)* das Fahrrad
mountain bike das Mountainbike
bikini der Bikini
bill *(account)* die Rechnung
bin *(dustbin)* der Mülleimer
bin liner der Müllbeutel
binoculars das Fernglas
bird der Vogel
biro der Kugelschreiber
birth die Geburt
birth certificate die Geburtsurkunde
birthday der Geburtstag
happy birthday! alles Gute zum
Geburtstag!
my birthday is on... ich habe
am … Geburtstag
birthday card die Geburtstagskarte
birthday present das Geburtstagsgeschenk
biscuits die Kekse
bit *(piece)* das Stück
a bit (a little) ein bißchen

to bite beißen
(insect) stechen
bitten *(by insect)* gestochen
I've been bitten ich bin
gestochen worden
bitter *(taste)* bitter
black schwarz
blackcurrants die schwarzen
Johannisbeeren
black ice das Glatteis
blanket die Decke
bleach das Bleichmittel
to bleed bluten
blender der Mixer
blind *(person)* blind
blind *(for window)* das Rollo
blister die Blase
blocked *(pipe, road)* verstopft
blond *(person)* blond
blood das Blut
blood group die Blutgruppe
blood pressure der Blutdruck
blood test der Bluttest
blouse die Bluse
to blow-dry fönen
blue blau
dark blue dunkelblau
light blue hellblau
blunt *(knife, blade)* stumpf
boar das Wildschwein
boarding card/pass die
Bordkarte
boarding house die Pension
boat *(large)* das Schiff
(small) das Boot
boat trip die Bootsfahrt
to boil kochen
boiled gekocht
bomb die Bombe
bone der Knochen
fish bone die Gräte
bonnet *(car)* die Motorhaube
book das Buch
to book buchen
booking *(in hotel)* die Reservierung

b

booking office (train) der Fahrkartenschalter
bookshop die Buchhandlung
boot (car) der Kofferraum
boots (long) die Stiefel
(ankle) die Schnürschuhe
border (of country) die Grenze
boring langweilig
born: I was born in 1960 ich bin
neunzehnhundertsechzig
geboren
to borrow borgen
boss der/die Chef(in)
both beide
bottle die Flasche
a bottle of wine eine Flasche
Wein
a half-bottle eine kleine Flasche
bottle bank der Altglascontainer
bottle opener der Flaschenöffner
bowl (for soup, etc) die Schüssel
bow tie die Fliege

b

box (of wood) die Kiste
(of cardboard) der Karton
box office (theatre) die Kasse
boy der Junge
boyfriend der Freund
bra der BH
bracelet das Armband
to brake bremsen
brake fluid die Bremsflüssigkeit
brake light das Bremslicht
brakes die Bremsen
branch (of tree) der Ast
(of bank, etc) die Filiale
brand (make) die Marke
brandy der Kognak
brass das Messing
brave mutig
bread das Brot
brown bread das Schwarzbrot
French bread das Baguette
sliced bread geschnittenes Brot
white bread das Weißbrot
bread roll das Brötchen
to break (object) kaputtmachen

breakable zerbrechlich
breakdown (car) die Panne
(nervous) der Nervenzusammenbruch
breakdown van der Abschleppwagen
breakfast das Frühstück
when is breakfast? wann gibt
es Frühstück?
breast (chicken) die Brust
to breathe atmen
brick der Ziegel
bride die Braut
bridegroom der Bräutigam
bridge die Brücke
briefcase die Aktentasche
to bring bringen
Britain Großbritannien
British britisch
brochure die Broschüre
broken gebrochen
broken down (car, etc) kaputt
bronchitis die Bronchitis
bronze die Bronze
brooch die Brosche
brother der Bruder
brother-in-law der Schwager
brown braun
bruise der Bluterguß
brush die Bürste
(for sweeping floor) der Besen
bucket der Eimer
buffet car der Speisewagen
to build bauen
building das Gebäude
bulb (electric) die Glühbirne
bumbag die Gürteltasche
bumper (on car) die Stoßstange
bunch (flowers) der Blumenstrauß
(grapes) die Weintraube
bungee jumping das Bungee-
Springen
bureau de change die Wechselstube
burger der Hamburger

burglar der/die Einbrecher(in)
burn (on skin) die Brandwunde
to burn verbrennen
bus der Bus
bus station der Busbahnhof
bus stop die Bushaltestelle
bus ticket der Busfahrschein
bus tour die Busfahrt
bush der Busch
business das Geschäft
  on business geschäftlich
business address die Geschäftsadresse
business card die Visitenkarte
business class die Business-Class
businessman/woman der/die
  Geschäftsmann/Geschäftsfrau
business trip die Dienstreise
busy beschäftigt
but aber
butcher's die Fleischerei
butter die Butter
butterfly der Schmetterling
button der Knopf
to buy kaufen
by (beside) bei
  (via) über
  by bus mit dem Bus
  by car mit dem Auto
  by train mit dem Zug
bypass die Umgehungsstraße

C

cab (taxi) das Taxi
cabaret das Varieté
cabbage der Kohl
cabin (on ship) die Kabine
cable car die Seilbahn
cable TV das Kabelfernsehen
café das Café
  internet café das Internet-Café
cake der Kuchen
  (big) die Torte
  (small) das Törtchen

cake shop die Konditorei
calculator der Taschenrechner
calf (young cow) das Kalb
call (on phone) der Anruf
  long-distance call das Ferngespräch
to call (on phone) anrufen
calm (person) ruhig
  (weather) windstill
camcorder der Camcorder
camera die Kamera
camera case die Kameratasche
camera shop das Fotogeschäft
to camp campen
camping gas das Campinggas
camping stove der Campingkocher
campsite der Campingplatz
can die Dose
can opener der Dosenöffner
can (to be able) können
  I can/we can ich kann/wir können
  can I...? kann ich...?
  I cannot... ich kann nicht...
  can we...? können wir...?
  we cannot... wir können nicht...
Canada Kanada
Canadian adj kanadisch
  m/f der/die Kanadier(in)
canal der Kanal
to cancel (ticket etc) stornieren
cancellation die Stornierung
cancer der Krebs
candle die Kerze
canoe das Kanu
cap (hat) die Mütze
  (diaphragm) das Pessar
capital (city) die Hauptstadt
car das Auto
car alarm die Autoalarmanlage
car ferry die Autofähre
car hire die Autovermietung
car insurance die Kfz-Versicherung
car keys die Autoschlüssel
car park der Parkplatz
car parts die Ersatzteile

C

car seat *(children's)* der Kindersitz
caravan der Wohnwagen
carburettor der Vergaser
card *(greetings)* die (Glückwunsch)karte
  (playing) die Spielkarte
cardboard die Pappe
cardigan die Strickjacke
careful vorsichtig
  be careful! passen Sie auf!
carpenter der/die Tischler(in)
carpet *(fitted)* der Teppichboden
  (rug) der Teppich
carriage *(railway)* der Wagen
carrot die Karotte
to carry tragen
carton der Karton
case *(suitcase)* der Koffer
cash das Bargeld
to cash *(cheque)* einlösen
cash desk die Kasse
cash dispenser *(autoteller)* der Geldautomat
cashier der/die Kassierer(in)
casino das Kasino
casserole die Kasserolle
cassette die Kassette
cassette player der Kassettenrecorder
castle das Schloß
  (medieval fortress) die Burg
casualty department die Unfallstation
cat die Katze
catalogue der Katalog
to catch *(bus, train)* nehmen
cathedral der Dom
Catholic katholisch
cave die Höhle
CD die CD
CD player der CD-Spieler
ceiling die Decke
cellar der Keller
cemetery der Friedhof
centimetre der Zentimeter

central zentral
central heating die Zentralheizung
central locking *(car)* die Zentralverriegelung
centre das Zentrum
century das Jahrhundert
ceramic die Keramik
certain *(sure)* sicher
certificate die Bescheinigung
chain die Kette
chair der Stuhl
chairlift der Sessellift
chalet das Appartment
chambermaid das Zimmermädchen
champagne der Champagner
change *(money)* das Wechselgeld
to change *(to alter)* ändern
  to change money Geld wechseln
  to change clothes sich umziehen
  to change bus/train umsteigen
changing room die Umkleidekabine
Channel *(English)* der Kanal
chapel die Kapelle
charcoal die Holzkohle
charter flight der Charterflug
cheap billig
cheaper billiger
cheap rate *(phone)* der Billigtarif
check *(to examine)* überprüfen
  (passports, tickets) kontrollieren
to check in *(at airport)* einchecken
  (at hotel) sich an der Rezeption anmelden
check-in der Check-in
cheers! *(toast)* Prost!
cheese der Käse
chef der/die Koch/Köchin
chemical toilet die chemische Toilette
chemist's die Drogerie
  (for medicines) die Apotheke
cheque der Scheck
cheque book das Scheckheft
cheque card die Scheckkarte**

cherries die Kirschen
chest *(body)* die Brust
chest of drawers die Kommode
chestnut die Kastanie
chewing gum der Kaugummi
chicken das Hühnchen
chickenpox die Windpocken
child das Kind
child car seat der Kindersitz
children die Kinder
  for children für Kinder
chimney der Schornstein
chin das Kinn
chips *(french fries)* die Pommes
  frites
chives der Schnittlauch
chocolate die Schokolade
chocolates die Pralinen
choir der Chor
to choose auswählen
chopping board das Küchenbrett
Christmas Weihnachten
  merry Christmas! frohe
  Weihnachten!
Christmas card die Weihnachtskarte
Christmas Eve Heiligabend
Christmas present das Weihnachtsgeschenk
church die Kirche
cider der Apfelwein
cigar die Zigarre
cigarette die Zigarette
cigarette lighter das Feuerzeug
cigarette papers das Zigarettenpapier
cinema das Kino
circle *(theatre)* der Rang
circuit breaker der Unterbrecher
circus der Zirkus
cistern *(of toilet)* der Spülkasten
citizen der/die Bürger(in)
city die Stadt
city centre das Stadtzentrum
class: *first class* erste Klasse

  second class zweite Klasse
clean sauber
to clean säubern
cleanser *(facial)* das Gesichtswasser
clear klar
client der/die Kunde/Kundin
cliff *(along coast)* die Klippe
  (in mountains) der Felsen
to climb *(mountains)* klettern
climbing boots die Bergschuhe
clingfilm® die Frischhaltefolie
clinic die Klinik
cloakroom die Garderobe
clock die Uhr
to close schließen
closed *(shop, etc)* geschlossen
cloth *(rag)* der Lappen
  (fabric) der Stoff
clothes die Kleider
clothes line die Wäscheleine
clothes peg die Wäscheklammer
clothes shop das Bekleidungsgeschäft
cloudy bewölkt
club der Club
clutch *(car)* die Kupplung
coach *(bus)* der Bus
coach station der Busbahnhof
coach trip die Busreise
coal die Kohle
coast die Küste
coastguard die Küstenwache
coat der Mantel
coat hanger der Kleiderbügel
Coca cola® die Cola
cockroach die Kakerlake
cocoa der Kakao
coconut die Kokosnuß
cod der Kabeljau
code der Kode
coffee der Kaffee
  black coffee schwarzer Kaffee
  white coffee Kaffee mit Milch
  decaffeinated coffee koffeinfreier Kaffee

C

coil (IUD) die Spirale
coin die Münze
Coke® die Cola
colander das Sieb
cold kalt
  I'm cold mir ist kalt
  it's cold es ist kalt
cold (illness) die Erkältung
  I have a cold ich habe mich
  erkältet
cold sore der Ausschlag
collar der Kragen
collar bone das Schlüsselbein
colleague der/die
  Kollege/Kollegin
to collect (someone) (jemanden)
  abholen
  (something) (etwas) sammeln
Cologne Köln
colour die Farbe
colour-blind farbenblind
colour film der Farbfilm
comb der Kamm
to come kommen
  (to arrive) ankommen
to come back zurückkommen
to come in hereinkommen
  come in! herein!
comedy die Komödie
comfortable bequem
company (firm) die Firma
compartment (in train) das Abteil
compass der Kompaß
to complain sich beschweren
complaint die Klage
composer der/die Komponist(in)
compulsory obligatorisch
computer der Computer
computer disk (floppy) die
  Diskette
computer program das Computerprogramm
computer programmer der/die
  Programmierer(in)
computer software die Software

concert das Konzert
concert hall die Konzerthalle
concession die Ermäßigung
concussion die Gehirnerschütterung
conditioner (hair) der Conditioner
condoms die Kondome
conference die Konferenz
to confirm bestätigen
  please confirm bitte bestätigen
  Sie
confirmation (flight, etc) die
  Bestätigung
confused verwirrt
congratulations! herzlichen
  Glückwünsch!
connection (train, etc) die Verbindung
constipated verstopft
consulate das Konsulat
to contact sich in Verbindung
  setzen mit
contact lens cleaner der Kontaktlinsenreiniger
contact lenses die Kontaktlinsen
to continue weitermachen
contraceptive das Verhütungsmittel
contract der Vertrag
convenient: is it convenient?
  paßt es so?
to cook kochen
cooked gekocht
cooker der Herd
cool kühl
cool-box (for picnic) die Kühlbox
copy (duplicate) die Kopie
to copy kopieren
cork der Korken
corkscrew der Korkenzieher
corner die Ecke
cornflakes die Cornflakes
corridor der Flur
cost (price) die Kosten (pl)
to cost kosten

how much does it cost? wieviel kostet es?
costume *(swimming)* der Badeanzug
cot das Kinderbett
cotton die Baumwolle
cotton bud der Wattebausch
cotton wool die Watte
couchette der Liegewagen
cough der Husten
to cough husten
cough mixture der Hustensaft
cough sweets die Hustenbonbons
counter *(in shop, bar)* die Theke
country das Land
countryside die Landschaft
couple *(two people)* das Paar
courier service der Kurierdienst
course *(of study)* der Kurs
(of meal) der Gang
cousin der/die Cousin(e)
cover charge *(in restaurant)* die Gedeckkosten
cow die Kuh
crab die Krabbe
crafts die Kunstgewerbearbeiten
craftsperson der/die Handwerker(in)
cramps die Krämpfe
crash *(collision)* der Zusammenstoß
to crash einen Unfall haben
crash helmet der Sturzhelm
cream *(lotion)* die Creme
(on milk) die Sahne
soured cream saure Sahne
whipped cream Schlagsahne
credit card die Kreditkarte
crime das Verbrechen
crisps die Chips
to cross *(road)* überqueren
cross-country skiing der Skilanglauf
crossing *(sea)* die Überfahrt
crossroads die Kreuzung
crossword das Kreuzworträtsel
crowd die Menge

crowded *(train, shop)* überfüllt
crown die Krone
cruise die Kreuzfahrt
crutches die Krücken
to cry *(weep)* weinen
crystal das Kristall
cucumber die Gurke
cufflinks die Manschettenknöpfe
cup die Tasse
cupboard der Schrank
currency die Währung
current *(electric)* der Strom
(water) die Strömung
curtain der Vorhang
cushion das Kissen
custard die Vanillesoße
custom *(tradition)* der Brauch
customer der/die Kunde/Kundin
customs *(duty)* der Zoll
cut die Schnittwunde
to cut schneiden
cutlery das Besteck
cycle *(bicycle)* das Fahrrad
to cycle radfahren
cycle track der Radweg
cyst die Zyste
cystitis die Blasenentzündung

D

daily *(each day)* täglich
dairy products die Milchprodukte
damage der Schaden
damp feucht
dance der Tanz
to dance tanzen
danger die Gefahr
dangerous gefährlich
dark dunkel
after dark nach Einbruch der Dunkelheit
date das Datum
date of birth das Geburtsdatum
daughter die Tochter

101

d

daughter-in-law die Schwiegertochter
dawn die Morgendämmerung
day der Tag
dead tot
deaf taub
dear *(in letter)* liebe(r/s) *(expensive)* teuer
debts die Schulden
decaffeinated coffee der koffeinfreie Kaffee
December der Dezember
deck chair der Liegestuhl
to declare: *nothing to declare* nichts zu verzollen
deep tief
deep freeze die Tiefkühltruhe
to defrost entfrosten
to de-ice enteisen
delay die Verspätung
how long is the delay? wieviel beträgt die Verspätung?

d

delayed verspätet
delicates das Feinkostgeschäft
delicious köstlich
dental floss die Zahnseide
dentist der/die Zahnarzt/Zahnärztin
dentures das Gebiß
deodorant das Deo
to depart abfahren
department die Abteilung
department store das Kaufhaus
departure *(train, bus)* die Abfahrt *(plane)* der Abflug
departure lounge die Abflughalle
deposit die Anzahlung
to describe beschreiben
desk der Schreibtisch
dessert der Nachtisch

d

details die Details
detergent das Waschmittel
detour der Umweg
to develop *(photos)* entwickeln
diabetes der Diabetes

diabetic person der/die Diabetiker(in)
to dial wählen
dialling code die Vorwahl
dialling tone der Wählton
diamond der Diamant
diapers die Windeln
diarrhoea der Durchfall
diary der Terminkalender
dice der Würfel
dictionary das Wörterbuch
to die sterben
diesel der Diesel
diet die Diät
I'm on a diet ich muß eine Diät einhalten
different verschieden
difficult schwierig
dinghy *(rubber)* das Schlauchboot
dining room das Eßzimmer
dinner *(evening meal)* das Abendessen
to have dinner zu Abend essen
diplomat der/die Diplomat(in)
direct *(route)* direkt *(train, bus, etc)* durchgehend
directions: *to ask for directions* nach dem Weg fragen
directory *(phone)* das Telefon-buch
directory enquiries die Auskunft
dirty schmutzig
disabled *(person)* behindert
to disappear verschwinden
disco die Disko
discount der Rabatt
to discover entdecken
disease die Krankheit
dish die Schale *(food)* das Gericht *side dish* die Beilage
dishtowel das Geschirrtuch
dishwasher die Geschirrspülmaschine
disinfectant das Desinfektionsmittel

disk *(computer)* die Diskette
to dislocate *(joint)* auskugeln
disposable nappies die Wegwerfwindeln
distance die Entfernung
distilled water das destillierte
Wasser
district der Bezirk
to disturb stören
to dive tauchen
diversion die Umleitung
divorced geschieden
DIY shop der Baumarkt
dizzy schwindelig
to do machen
doctor der/die Arzt/Ärztin
documents die Dokumente
dog der Hund
dog lead die Hundeleine
doll die Puppe
dollar der Dollar
domestic *(flight, etc)* Inland-
donor card der Organspenderausweis
door die Tür
doorbell die Klingel
double Doppel-
double bed das Doppelbett
double room das Doppelzimmer
doughnut der Berliner
down: to go down nach unten
gehen
downstairs unten
drain der Abfluß
draught *(of air)* der Durchzug
there's a draught hier zieht es
draught lager das Faßbier
drawer die Schublade
drawing die Zeichnung
dress das Kleid
to dress *(get dressed)* sich anziehen
dressing *(for food)* die Soße
dressing gown der Morgenmantel
drill *(tool)* der Bohrer
drink das Getränk

to drink trinken
drinking chocolate die heiße
Schokolade
drinking water das Trinkwasser
to drive fahren
driver *(of car)* der/die Fahrer(in)
driving licence der Führerschein
to drown ertrinken
drug *(medicine)* das Medikament
(narcotic) die Droge
drunk betrunken
dry trocken
to dry trocknen
dry cleaner's die Reinigung
dryer der Wäschetrockner
duck die Ente
due: when's it due? *(train, bus)*
wann soll er ankommen?
dummy *(for baby)* der Schnuller
during während
dust der Staub
duster das Staubtuch
dustpan and brush Schaufel und
Handfeger
duty-free zollfrei
duvet die Bettdecke
duvet cover der Bettbezug
dye färben
dynamo die Lichtmaschine

E

each jede(r/s)
eagle der Adler
ear das Ohr
earache die Ohrenschmerzen *(pl)*
I have earache ich habe Ohrenschmerzen
earlier früher
early früh
earphones die Kopfhörer
earrings die Ohrringe
earth die Erde
earthquake das Erdbeben
east der Osten

e

Easter Ostern
  Happy Easter! fröhliche Ostern!
Easter egg das Osterei
easy leicht
to eat essen
to eat out auswärts essen
economic ökonomisch
economy die Wirtschaft
economy class die Touristenklasse
edge der Rand
eel der Aal
egg das Ei
  fried egg das Spiegelei
  hard-boiled egg das hart-
  gekochte Ei
  scrambled egg das Rührei
  soft-boiled egg das weich-
  gekochte Ei
either ... or entweder ... oder
elastic elastisch
elastic band das Gummiband
Elastoplast® das Pflaster
elbow der Ellbogen
electric elektrisch
electric razor der Elektrorasierer
electric shock der elektrische
  Schlag
electrician der/die Elektriker(in)
electricity die Elektrizität
electricity meter der Stromzähler
elevator der Fahrstuhl
e-mail die E-Mail
e-mail address die E-Mail-Adresse
embassy die Botschaft
emergency der Notfall
emergency exit der Notausgang
emery board die Nagelfeile
empty leer
end das Ende
engaged *(to be married)* verlobt
  (toilet, telephone) besetzt
engine der Motor
engineer der/die Ingenieur(in)
England England
English *adj* englisch

Englishman/-woman der/die
  Engländer(in)
to enjoy *(to like)* mögen
  I enjoy dancing ich tanze gern
enough genug
  that's enough das reicht
enquiry desk die Auskunft
to enter eintreten
entrance der Eingang
entrance fee der Eintrittpreis
envelope der Umschlag
epileptic der/die Epileptiker(in)
epileptic fit der epileptische Anfall
equipment die Ausrüstung
eraser der Radiergummi
escalator die Rolltreppe
to escape entkommen
essential wesentlich
estate agent's der Grundstücksmakler
EU die EU
Eurocheque der Euroscheck
Europe Europa
European Union die Europäische
  Union
eve: *Christmas Eve* Heiligabend
  New Year's Eve Silvester
even *(number)* gerade
evening der Abend
  this evening heute abend
  tomorrow evening morgen abend
  in the evening am Abend
evening dress das Abendkleid
evening meal das Abendessen
every *(each)* jede(r/s)
everyone jeder
everything alles
everywhere überall
examination *(medical)* die Untersuchung
  (school) die Prüfung
example: *for example* zum Beispiel
excellent ausgezeichnet
excess luggage das Übergewicht
exchange der Austausch

to exchange tauschen
(money) wechseln
exchange rate der Wechselkurs
exciting aufregend
excursion der Ausflug
excuse me! *(sorry)* Entschuldigung
(when passing) entschuldigen Sie bitte
exhaust pipe das Auspuffrohr
exhibition die Ausstellung
exit der Ausgang
expenses die Spesen
expensive teuer
expert der Experte/die Expertin
to expire *(ticket, etc)* ungültig werden
to explain erklären
explosion die Explosion
export der Export
to export exportieren
exposure *(film)* die Belichtung
express *(train)* der Schnellzug
express *(parcel, etc)* per Expreß
extension lead das Verlängerungskabel
extra *(spare)* übrig
(more) noch ein(e)
an extra towel ein zusätzliches Handtuch
eye das Auge
eye drops die Augentropfen
eye liner der Eyeliner
eye shadow der Lidschatten

F

fabric der Stoff
face das Gesicht
facial die Gesichtspflege
factory die Fabrik
to faint ohnmächtig werden
fainted ohnmächtig
fair *(hair)* blond
fair *(trade fair)* die Messe
(funfair) die Kirmes

fall *(autumn)* der Herbst
to fall fallen
he/she has fallen er/sie ist hingefallen
false teeth das Gebiß
family die Familie
famous berühmt
fan *(electric)* der Ventilator
(football) der Fan
fan belt der Keilriemen
far weit
how far is it? wie weit ist es?
fare *(train, bus, etc)* der Fahrpreis
farm der Bauernhof
farmer der/die Bauer/Bäuerin
farmhouse das Bauernhaus
fashionable modern
fast schnell
too fast zu schnell
to fasten *(seatbelt, etc)* sich anschnallen
fat dick
father der Vater
father-in-law der Schwiegervater
fault *(defect)* der Fehler
it wasn't my fault das war nicht meine Schuld
favourite Lieblings-
fax das Fax
by fax per Fax
to fax faxen
fax number die Faxnummer
February der Februar
to feed füttern
feeding bottle die Babyflasche
to feel fühlen
I don't feel well ich fühle mich nicht wohl
I feel sick mir ist schlecht
feet die Füße *(pl)*
female weiblich
ferry die Fähre
festival das Fest
to fetch *(bring)* holen
fever das Fieber

f

few: *a few* ein paar
fiancé(e) der/die Verlobte
field das Feld
to fight kämpfen
file *(nail)* die Feile
  (computer) die Datei
  (for papers) der Ordner
to fill füllen
to fill in *(form)* ausfüllen
to fill up *(tank)* volltanken
fillet das Filet
filling *(in tooth)* die Plombe
film der Film
  colour film der Farbfilm
  black and white film der
  Schwarzweißfilm
Filofax® der Terminkalender
filter der Filter
to find finden
fine *(to be paid)* die Geldstrafe
finger der Finger
to finish beenden
fire das Feuer
fire alarm der Feuermelder
fire brigade die Feuerwehr
fire engine das Feuerwehrauto
fire escape die Feuertreppe
fire exit der Notausgang
fire extinguisher der Feuerlöscher
fireplace der Kamin
fireworks das Feuerwerk
first erste(r/s)
first aid die Erste Hilfe
first aid kit der Verbandskasten
first class *(travel)* erster Klasse
first name der Vorname
fish der Fisch
to fish angeln
fishing permit der Angelschein
fishing rod die Angelrute
fishmonger's die Fischhandlung
fit *(seizure)* der Anfall
to fit passen
  it doesn't fit me es paßt mir nicht

to fix reparieren
  can you fix it? können Sie es
  reparieren?
fizzy sprudelnd
flag die Fahne
flannel *(face cloth)* der Wasch-
  lappen
flash *(for camera)* das Blitzlicht
flashlight die Taschenlampe
flask *(thermos)* die Thermosflasche
flat *(level)* flach
flat *(apartment)* die Wohnung
flat battery die leere Batterie
flat tyre die Reifenpanne
flavour der Geschmack
  what flavour? welchen
  Geschmack?
flaw der Mangel
fleas die Flöhe
flight der Flug
flip flops die Badelatschen
flippers die Schwimmflossen
flood die Flut
  flash flood die Überschwemmung
floor *(of building)* die Etage
  (of room) der Boden
  which floor? auf welcher Etage?
floorcloth der Scheuerlappen
floppy disk die Diskette
florist's shop der Blumenladen
flour das Mehl
flowers die Blumen
flu die Grippe
fly die Fliege
to fly fliegen
fly sheet das Überzelt
foggy neblig
to follow folgen
food das Essen
food poisoning die Lebensmittelvergiftung
foot der Fuß
  on foot zu Fuß
football der Fußball
football match das Fußballspiel

football pitch der Fußballplatz
football player der/die Fuß-
baller(in)
footpath der Fußweg
for für
  for me für mich
  for him/her für ihn/sie
  for us für uns
  for you für Sie/dich
forbidden verboten
forehead die Stirn
foreign ausländisch
foreigner der/die Ausländer(in)
forest der Wald
forever für immer
to forget vergessen
to forgive vergeben
fork *(for eating)* die Gabel
  (in road) die Gabelung
form *(document)* das Formular
formal dress die Abendgarderobe
fortnight zwei Wochen
fountain der Brunnen
four wheel drive der Allradantrieb
fox der Fuchs
fracture der Bruch
fragile zerbrechlich
frame *(picture)* der Rahmen
France Frankreich
free *(not occupied)* frei
  (costing nothing) umsonst
freelance freiberuflich
freezer die Tiefkühltruhe
French *adj* französisch
French beans die grünen Bohnen
French fries die Pommes frites
Frenchman/-woman der/die
Franzose/Französin
frequent häufig
fresh frisch
fresh water das frische Wasser
Friday der Freitag
fridge der Kühlschrank

fried gebraten
friend der/die Freund(in)
friendly freundlich
frog der Frosch
from von
  from Scotland aus Schottland
  from England aus England
front die Vorderseite
  in front of vor
front door die Eingangstür
frost der Frost
frozen gefroren
fruit das Obst
  dried fruit das Trockenobst
fruit juice der Fruchtsaft
fruit tea der Früchtetee
to fry braten
frying pan die Bratpfanne
fuel *(petrol)* das Benzin
fuel gauge die Tankanzeige
fuel tank der Tank
full voll
  (occupied) besetzt
full board die Vollpension
fun der Spaß
funeral die Beerdigung
funfair die Kirmes
funny *(amusing)* komisch
fur der Pelz
fur coat der Pelzmantel
furnished möbliert
furniture die Möbel *(pl)*
further on weiter
fuse die Sicherung
fuse box der Sicherungskasten
future die Zukunft

G

gallery die Galerie
gallon = approx. 4.5 litres
game das Spiel
  (meat) das Wild
garage *(private)* die Garage
  (for repairs) die Werkstatt

g

garden der Garten
gardener der/die Gärtner(in)
garlic der Knoblauch
gas das Gas
gas cooker der Gasherd
gas cylinder die Gasflasche
gastritis die Gastritis
gate *(airport)* das Gate
gay *(person)* der/die Homosexuelle
gears das Getriebe
  first gear der erste Gang
  second gear der zweite Gang
  third gear der dritte Gang
  fourth gear der vierte Gang
  neutral der Leerlauf
  reverse der Rückwärtsgang
generous großzügig
gents *(toilet)* die Herrentoilette
genuine echt
German *adj* deutsch
  m/f der/die Deutsche
German measles die Röteln
Germany Deutschland

g

to get *(to obtain)* bekommen
  (to fetch) holen
to get in(to) *(bus, etc)* einsteigen
to get off *(bus, etc)* aussteigen
gift das Geschenk
gift shop der Geschenkeladen
girl das Mädchen
girlfriend die Freundin
to give geben
to give back zurückgeben
glacier der Gletscher
glass das Glas
  a glass of water ein Glas Wasser
glasses *(spectacles)* die Brille
glasses case das Brillenetui
gloves die Handschuhe
glue der Klebstoff
to go *(on foot)* gehen
  (in car) fahren
  I'm going to... ich fahre nach...
  we're going to... wir fahren nach...
  to go home nach Hause fahren

g

to go on foot zu Fuß gehen
to go back zurückgehen
to go down heruntergehen
to go in hineingehen
to go out ausgehen
goat die Ziege
God Gott
goggles *(swimming)* die Taucherbrille
  (skiing) die Schneebrille
gold das Gold
golf das Golf
golf ball der Golfball
golf clubs die Golfschläger
golf course der Golfplatz
good gut
  (pleasant) schön
good afternoon guten Tag
goodbye auf Wiedersehen
good day guten Tag
good evening guten Abend
good morning guten Morgen
good night gute Nacht
goose die Gans
Gothic gotisch
gram das Gramm
granddaughter die Enkelin
grandfather der Großvater
grandmother die Großmutter
grandparents die Großeltern
grandson der Enkel
grapefruit die Grapefruit
grapes die Trauben
grass das Gras
grated *(cheese)* gerieben
greasy fettig
great *(big)* groß
Great Britain Großbritannien
green grün
green card *(car insurance)* die
  grüne Versicherungskarte
greengrocer's der Gemüseladen
greetings card die Grußkarte
grey grau
grill der Grill

to grill grillen
grilled gegrillt
grocer's der Lebensmittelladen
ground der Boden
ground floor das Erdgeschoß
  on the ground floor im Erdgeschoß
groundsheet der Zeltboden
group die Gruppe
guarantee die Garantie
guard *m/f (on train)* der/die Schaffner(in)
guest der Gast
guesthouse die Pension
guide *m/f (tour guide)* der/die Fremdenführer(in)
guidebook der Reiseführer
guided tour die Führung
guitar die Gitarre
gun die Waffe
gym shoes die Turnschuhe

H

haberdasher's das Kurzwarengeschäft
haemorrhoids die Hämorrhoiden
hail der Hagel
hair die Haare *(pl)*
hairbrush die Haarbürste
haircut der Haarschnitt
hairdresser der Friseur
hairdryer der Fön
hair dye die Tönung
hair gel das Haargel
hairgrip die Haarklemme
hair mousse der Schaumfestiger
hair spray das Haarspray
half halb
  a half bottle eine kleine Flasche
  half an hour eine halbe Stunde
half board die Halbpension
half fare der halbe Fahrpreis
half price der halbe Preis
halibut der Heilbutt

ham der Schinken
  (cooked) Kochschinken
  (cured) geräucherter Schinken
hamburger der Hamburger
hammer der Hammer
hand die Hand
handbag die Handtasche
hand luggage das Handgepäck
hand-made handgearbeitet
handicapped behindert
handkerchief das Taschentuch
handle der Griff
handlebars der Lenker
handsome gutaussehend
hanger *(coat hanger)* der Bügel
hang gliding das Drachenfliegen
hangover der Kater
to hang up *(phone)* auflegen
to happen geschehen ; passieren
  what happened? was ist passiert?
happy glücklich
  happy birthday! alles Gute zum Geburtstag!
harbour der Hafen
hard *(difficult)* schwierig
  (not soft) hart
hard disk die Festplatte
hardware shop die Eisenwarenhandlung
hare der Hase
harvest die Ernte
hat der Hut
to have haben *see* **GRAMMAR**
  I have... ich habe...
  we have... wir haben...
  do you have...? haben Sie...?
to have to müssen
hay fever der Heuschnupfen
hazelnuts die Haselnüsse
he er *see* **GRAMMAR**
head der Kopf
headache die Kopfschmerzen *(pl)*
headlights die Scheinwerfer
headphones die Kopfhörer
health food shop das Reformhaus

h

healthy gesund
to hear hören
hearing aid das Hörgerät
heart das Herz
heart attack der Herzanfall
heartburn das Sodbrennen
to heat up *(food, milk)* aufwärmen
heater das Heizgerät
heating die Heizung
heavy schwer
heel der Absatz
height die Höhe
helicopter der Helikopter
hello hallo
helmet *(for bike)* der Schutzhelm
help! Hilfe!
to help helfen
  can you help me? können Sie
  mir helfen?
hem der Saum
hepatitis die Hepatitis

h

her ihr
  (with der-words) ihr
  (with das-words) ihr
  (with die-words) ihre
herbs die Kräuter
herb tea der Kräutertee
here hier
  here is... hier ist...
hernia der Eingeweidebruch
hi! hallo!
to hide verstecken
high hoch
  (number, speed) groß
high blood pressure der hohe
  Blutdruck
high chair der Kinderstuhl
high tide die Flut
hill der Hügel
hill-walking das Bergwandern

h

him ihm
hip die Hüfte
hip replacement die künstliche
  Hüfte
hire die Vermietung

car hire die Autovermietung
bike hire die Fahrradvermietung
boat hire der Bootsverleih
ski hire der Skiverleih
to hire mieten
hire car das Mietauto
his sein
  (with der-words) sein
  (with das-words) sein
  (with die-words) seine
historic historisch
history die Geschichte
to hit schlagen
to hitchhike trampen
hobby das Hobby
to hold halten
  (to contain) enthalten
hold-up *(traffic jam)* der Stau
hole das Loch
holiday der Feiertag
  holidays der Urlaub
  on holiday in den Ferien
  public holiday der gesetzliche
  Feiertag
holy heilig
home das Zuhause
  at home zu Hause
homesick *(to be)* Heimweh haben
  I'm homesick ich habe Heimweh
homosexual homosexuell
honest ehrlich
honey der Honig
honeymoon die Flitterwochen *(pl)*
hood *(of jacket)* die Kapuze
to hope hoffen
  I hope so/not hoffentlich/hof-
  fentlich nicht
horn *(car)* die Hupe
hors d'œuvre die Vorspeise
horse das Pferd
horse racing das Pferderennen
to horse ride reiten
hosepipe der Schlauch
hospital das Krankenhaus
hostel das Wohnheim
hot heiß

I'm hot mir ist heiß
it's hot (weather) es ist heiß
hot water das Warmwasser
hot chocolate die heiße
Schokolade
hot-water bottle die
Wärmflasche
hotel das Hotel
hour die Stunde
1 hour eine Stunde
2 hours zwei Stunden
half an hour eine halbe Stunde
house das Haus
housewife/husband die/der
Hausfrau/Hausmann
house wine der Hauswein
housework die Hausarbeit
hovercraft das Luftkissenboot
how wie
how much? wieviel
how many? wie viele
how are you? wie geht es
Ihnen?
hundred hundert
five hundred fünfhundert
hungry *(to be)* Hunger haben
to hunt jagen
hunting permit die Jagderlaubnis
hurry: *I'm in a hurry* ich habe es
eilig
to hurt *(be painful)* weh tun
my back hurts mir tut der
Rücken weh
that hurts das tut weh
husband der Mann
hut *(beach)* der Strandkorb
(mountain) die Hütte
hydrofoil das Tragflügelboot
hypodermic needle die Spritze

I

I ich see **GRAMMAR**
ice das Eis
with ice mit Eis
ice box die Kühlbox

ice cream das Eis
ice cube der Eiswürfel
ice rink die Schlittschuhbahn
ice skates die Schlittschuhe
iced: *iced coffee* der Eiskaffee
iced tea der Eistee
identity card der Personalausweis
if wenn
ignition die Zündung
ignition key der Zündschlüssel
ill krank
I'm ill ich bin krank
immediately sofort
immersion heater der Boiler
immunisation die Immunisierung
important wichtig
impossible unmöglich
it's impossible das ist unmöglich
in in
in 2 hours in zwei Stunden
in London in London
in front of vor
inch = approx. 2.5 cm
included inbegriffen
indicator *(in car)* der Blinker
indigestion die
Magenverstimmung
indigestion tablets die
Magentabletten
indoors drinnen
(at home) zu Hause
infection die Infektion
infectious ansteckend
information die Auskunft
information office das
Informationsbüro
ingredients die Zutaten
inhaler *(for medication)* der
Inhalationsapparat
injection die Spritze
to injure verletzen
injured *(person)* verletzt
injury die Verletzung
ink die Tinte
inn das Gasthaus

i

inner tube der Schlauch
insect das Insekt
insect bite der (Insekten)stich
insect repellent das Insekten-schutzmittel
inside in
instant coffee der Pulverkaffee
instructor der/die Lehrer(in)
(ski) der/die Skilehrer(in)
insulin das Insulin
insurance die Versicherung
insurance certificate die Ver-sicherungsbescheinigung
insured *(to be)* versichert sein
intelligent intelligent
interesting interessant
international international
(arrivals, departures) Ausland
internet das Internet
internet café das Internet-Café
interpreter der/die Dolmetscher(in)
interval die Pause
into in
  into town in die Stadt
  into the centre ins Zentrum
to introduce vorstellen
invitation die Einladung
to invite einladen
invoice die Rechnung
Ireland Irland
Irish *adj* irisch
Irishman/-woman der/die Ire/Irin
iron *(for clothes)* das Bügeleisen
  (metal) das Eisen
to iron bügeln
ironing board das Bügelbrett
ironmonger's die Eisenwaren-handlung
is see (to be) GRAMMAR
island die Insel
it er/sie/es see GRAMMAR
Italian *adj* italienisch
  m/f der/die Italiener(in)
Italy Italien
to itch jucken

J

jack *(for car)* der Wagenheber
jacket die Jacke
jacuzzi der Whirlpool
jam *(food)* die Marmelade
jammed *(camera, lock)* blockiert
January der Januar
jar *(honey, jam, etc)* das Glas
jaundice die Gelbsucht
jaw der Kiefer
jazz der Jazz
J cloth® der Abwaschlappen
jealous eifersüchtig
jeans die Jeans
jellyfish die Qualle
jet ski das Wassermotorrad
jetty die Mole
Jew der/die Jude/Jüdin
jeweller's der Juwelier
jewellery der Schmuck
jiffy bag® der gefütterte Briefumschlag
job *(employment)* die Stelle
to jog joggen
to join *(club)* beitreten
joint *(of body)* das Gelenk
to joke scherzen
joke der Witz
journalist der/die Journalist(in)
journey die Reise
joy die Freude
judge der/die Richter(in)
jug der Krug
juice der Saft
  apple juice der Apfelsaft
  orange juice der Orangensaft
  tomato juice der Tomatensaft
  carton of juice der Saftkarton
July der Juli
to jump springen
jumper der Pullover
jump leads *(for car)* das Starthilfe-kabel

junction *(road)* die Kreuzung

June der Juni

just: *just two* nur zwei
I've just arrived ich bin gerade angekommen

K

to keep *(retain)* behalten
keep the change! stimmt so!

kettle der Wasserkocher

key der Schlüssel
cardkey die Schlüsselkarte

keyring der Schlüsselring

to kick *(ball)* schießen
(person) treten

kidneys die Nieren

to kill töten

kilo das Kilo

kilogram das Kilogramm

kilometre der Kilometer

kind *(person)* nett

king der König

kiosk der Kiosk

kiss der Kuß

to kiss küssen

kitchen die Küche

kitchen paper das Küchenpapier

kiwi fruit die Kiwi

knee das Knie

knickers der Slip

knife das Messer

to knit stricken

knitting needle die Stricknadel

to knock stoßen

to knock over *(object)* umstoßen

knot der Knoten

to know *(facts)* wissen
(to be acquainted with) kennen
I don't know ich weiß nicht
(to be acquainted with) kennen

to know how to können
to know how to swim schwimmen können

L

label das Schild

lace *(of shoe)* der Schnürsenkel
(fabric) die Spitze

ladder die Leiter

ladies *(toilet)* die Damentoilette

lady die Dame

lager das helle Bier
bottled lager das Flaschenbier
draught lager das Faßbier

lake der See

lamb das Lammfleisch

lamp *(for table)* die Lampe

lamppost die Straßenlampe

to land landen

landlady die Vermieterin

landlord der Vermieter

landslide der Erdrutsch

lane die Gasse
(of motorway/main road) die Spur

language die Sprache

laptop der Laptop

large groß

last *(final)* letzte(r/s)
the last bus der letzte Bus
last night gestern abend
last week letzte Woche
last year letztes Jahr

late spät
the train is late der Zug hat Verspätung
sorry we're late es tut uns leid, daß wir zu spät sind

later später

to laugh lachen

launderette der Waschsalon

laundry room der Wäscheraum

laundry service der Wäscherei-service

lavatory die Toilette

law das Gesetz

lawyer der/die Rechtsanwalt/Rechtsanwältin

laxative das Abführmittel

layby die Haltebucht
lazy faul
lead *(metal)* das Blei
to lead führen
lead-free bleifrei
leaf das Blatt
leak *(of gas, liquid)* das Leck
to learn lernen
lease *(rental)* der Mietvertrag
leather das Leder
to leave *(a place)* weggehen/weg-fahren
 when does the train leave? wann fährt der Zug ab?
 to leave behind zurücklassen
leek der Porree
left: *on/to the left* links/nach links
left-handed *(person)* der/die Links-händer(in)
left-luggage locker das Schließ-fach
left-luggage office die Gepäck-aufbewahrung
leg das Bein
leisure centre das Freizeitzentrum
lemon die Zitrone
lemon tea der Zitronentee
lemonade die Limonade
to lend leihen
length *(size)* die Länge
 (duration) die Dauer
lens die Linse
lenses *(contact)* die Kontaktlinsen
lentils die Linsen
lesbian lesbisch
less weniger
lesson die Unterrichtsstunde
to let *(to allow)* erlauben
 (room, house) vermieten
letter *(written)* der Brief
 (of alphabet) der Buchstabe
letterbox der Briefkasten
lettuce der Kopfsalat
level crossing der Bahnübergang
library die Bibliothek

licence *(driving)* der Führerschein
lid der Deckel
lie *(untruth)* die Lüge
lifebelt der Rettungsring
lifeboat das Rettungsboot
lifeguard der/die Rettungs-schwimmer(in)
life insurance die Lebens-versicherung
life jacket die Schwimmweste
life raft die Rettungsinsel
lift *(elevator)* der Aufzug
 can you give me a lift? können Sie mich mitnehmen?
lift pass *(on ski slopes)* der Liftpaß
light *(not heavy)* leicht
light das Licht
 have you a light? haben Sie Feuer?
light bulb die Glühbirne
lighter das Feuerzeug
lighthouse der Leuchtturm
lightning der Blitz
to like mögen
 I like coffee ich trinke gern Kaffee
 I don't like... ich mag... nicht
 we'd like... wir möchten...
lilo® die Luftmatratze
lime *(fruit)* die Limone
line *(row, of railway)* die Linie
 (telephone) die Leitung
linen das Leinen
lingerie die Unterwäsche
lion der Löwe
lips die Lippen
lip salve der Lippenpflegestift
lipstick der Lippenstift
liqueur der Likör
list die Liste
to listen to zuhören
litre der Liter
 a litre of milk ein Liter Milch
litter *(rubbish)* der Abfall
little *(small)* klein
 a little milk ein bißchen Milch

to live (exist) leben
  (reside) wohnen
  I live in London ich wohne in
  London
liver die Leber
living room das Wohnzimmer
loaf of bread das Brot
local (wine, speciality) hiesig
lock (on door, box) das Schloß
  the lock is broken das Schloß
  ist geöffnet worden
to lock zuschließen
locker (luggage) das Schließfach
log book (car) die Zulassung
London London
  in London in London
  to London nach London
long lang
  for a long time lange Zeit
long-sighted weitsichtig
to look after sich kümmern um
to look at anschauen
to look for suchen
loose (screw, tooth) locker
lorry der Lastwagen
to lose verlieren
lost (object) verloren
  I've lost my wallet ich habe
  meine Brieftasche verloren
  I'm lost (on foot) ich habe mich
  verlaufen
  I'm lost (in car) ich habe mich
  verfahren
lost property office das Fundbüro
lot: *a lot* viel
lotion die Lotion
loud laut
lounge (hotel/airport) die Lounge
  (in house) das Wohnzimmer
love die Liebe
to love lieben
  I love you ich liebe dich
lovely schön
low niedrig
  (standard, quality) minderwertig
low-fat fettarm

low tide die Ebbe
lucky glücklich
luggage das Gepäck
luggage allowance das Freigepäck
luggage rack die Gepäckablage
luggage tag der Kofferanhänger
luggage trolley der Gepäckwagen
lump (swelling) die Beule
lunch das Mittagessen
lung die Lunge

M

machine die Maschine
magazine die Zeitschrift
maggot die Made
magnet der Magnet
magnifying glass die Lupe
maid (in hotel) das Zimmermädchen
maiden name der Mädchenname
mail die Post
  by mail per Post
main (principal) Haupt-
main course (of meal) das Hauptgericht
major road die Hauptstraße
make (brand) die Marke
to make machen
  (meal) zubereiten
make-up das Make-up
male männlich
man der Mann
  men die Männer
to manage (be in charge) managen
manager der/die Geschäfts-
  führer(in)
managing director der/die
  Direktor(in)
man-made fibre die Kunstfaser
manual (gear change) das
  Schaltgetriebe
many viele
map die Karte
  (of region, country) die Landkarte
  (of town) der Stadtplan

m

marble der Marmor
March der März
margarine die Margarine
marina der Jachthafen
marinated mariniert
mark *(stain)* der Fleck
market der Markt
marmalade die Orangen-
marmelade
married verheiratet
I'm married ich bin verheiratet
are you married? sind Sie verheiratet?
to marry *(get married)* heiraten
marsh der Sumpf
mascara die Wimperntusche
mashed potato das Kartoffelpüree
mass *(in church)* die Messe
mast der Mast
masterpiece das Meisterwerk
match *(sport)* der Wettkampf
matches die Streichhölzer
material das Material
matter: *no matter!* macht nichts!
it doesn't matter das macht
nichts
what's the matter? was ist los?
mattress die Matratze
May der Mai
mayonnaise die Mayonnaise
me *(direct object)* mich
(indirect object) mir
meal das Essen
to mean bedeuten
what does this mean? was
bedeutet das?
measles die Masern *(pl)*
to measure messen
meat das Fleisch
I don't eat meat ich esse kein
Fleisch
mechanic der/die Mechaniker(in)
medical insurance die Krankenkasse
medicine die Medizin
medieval mittelalterlich

Mediterranean das Mittelmeer
medium rare *(meat)* halb durch
to meet *(by chance)* treffen
(by arrangement) sich treffen mit
pleased to meet you! sehr
erfreut
meeting das Treffen
melon die Melone
to melt schmelzen
member *(of club, etc)* das Mitglied
men die Männer
to mend reparieren
meningitis die Hirnhautentzündung
menu die Speisekarte
set menu die Tageskarte
meringue das Baiser
message die Nachricht
metal das Metall
meter der Zähler
metre der Meter
metro *(underground)* die U-Bahn
microwave oven die Mikrowelle
midday der Mittag
at midday am Mittag
middle die Mitte
middle-aged in den mittleren
Jahren
midge die Mücke
midnight die Mitternacht
at midnight um Mitternacht
migraine die Migräne
I have a migraine ich habe
Migräne
mile die Meile
milk die Milch
fresh milk frische Milch
hot milk heiße Milch
long-life milk H-Milch
powdered milk das Milchpulver
semi-skimmed milk Halb-
fettmilch
skimmed milk Magermilch
soya milk die Sojamilch
with milk mit Milch
millimetre der Millimeter
million die Million

mince *(meat)* das Hackfleisch
mind: *do you mind if...?* haben Sie etwas dagegen, wenn...?
I don't mind es ist mir egal
mineral water das Mineralwasser
minimum das Minimum
minister *(church)* der/die Pfarrer(in)
(political) der/die Minister(in)
minor road die Nebenstraße
mint *(herb)* die Minze
(sweet) das Pfefferminzbonbon
minute die Minute
mirror der Spiegel
miscarriage die Fehlgeburt
to miss *(plane, train)* verpassen
Miss Fräulein
missing *(object)* verschwunden
my son's missing mein Sohn ist weg
mistake der Fehler
misty dunstig
misunderstanding das Mißverständnis
to mix mischen
mixer der Mixer
mobile phone das Mobiltelefon
modem das Modem
modern modern
moisturizer die Feuchtigkeitscreme
moment: *just a moment* einen Moment, bitte
monastery das Kloster
Monday der Montag
money das Geld
I have no money ich habe kein Geld
moneybelt die Gürteltasche
money order die Postanweisung
monkey der Affe
month der Monat
this month diesen Monat
last month letzten Monat
next month nächsten Monat
monthly monatlich
monument das Denkmal

moon der Mond
mooring der Anlegeplatz
moped das Moped
more mehr
more than 3 mehr als drei
more wine noch etwas Wein
morning der Morgen
in the morning am Morgen
this morning heute morgen
tomorrow morning morgen früh
mosque die Moschee
mosquito die Stechmücke
mosquito net das Moskitonetz
most: *most of* das meiste von
moth *(clothes)* die Motte
mother die Mutter
mother-in-law die Schwiegermutter
motor der Motor
motorbike das Motorrad
motorboat das Motorboot
motorway die Autobahn
mountain der Berg
mountain bike das Mountainbike
mountain rescue die Bergwacht
mountaineering das Bergsteigen
mouse *(animal, computer)* die Maus
moustache der Schnurrbart
mouth der Mund
mouthwash das Mundwasser
to move bewegen
Mr Herr
Mrs Frau
Ms Frau
much viel
too much zuviel
mugging der Überfall
mumps der Mumps
Munich München
muscle der Muskel
museum das Museum
mushrooms die Pilze
music die Musik
musical das Musical
mussel die Muschel

m

must müssen
mustard der Senf
mutton das Hammelfleisch
my mein
  (with der-words) mein
  (with das-words) mein
  (with die-words) meine

N

n

nail *(fingernail)* der Fingernagel
  (metal) der Nagel
nailbrush die Nagelbürste
nail file die Nagelfeile
nail polish/varnish der Nagellack
nail polish remover der Nagellackentferner
nail scissors die Nagelschere
name der Name
  my name is... mein Name ist...
  what is your name? wie ist Ihr
  Name?
nanny das Kindermädchen
napkin die Serviette
nappy die Windel
narrow eng
national national
national park der Nationalpark
nationality die Nationalität
nature die Natur
nature reserve das Naturschutzgebiet
nature trail der Naturlehrpfad
navy blue marineblau
near *(place, time)* nahe
  near the bank in der Nähe der
  Bank
necessary notwendig
neck der Hals
necklace die Halskette
nectarine die Nektarine
to need brauchen
  I need an aspirin ich brauche
  ein Aspirin
  I need to go ich muß gehen
  we need... wir brauchen...

needle die Nadel
  needle and thread Nadel und
  Faden
negative *(photo)* das Negativ
neighbour der/die Nachbar(in)
nephew der Neffe
nest das Nest
net das Netz
never nie
  I never drink wine Wein trinke
  ich nie
new neu
news die Nachrichten
newspaper die Zeitung
newsstand der Zeitungskiosk
New Year (1 Jan) Neujahr
  happy New Year! ein gutes
  neues Jahr
New Year's Eve Silvester
New Zealand Neuseeland
next nächste(r/s)
  next to neben
  next week nächste Woche
  the next bus der nächste Bus
  the next train der nächste Zug
nice *(person)* nett
  (place, holiday) schön
niece die Nichte
night die Nacht
  at night am Abend
  last night gestern abend
  per night pro Nacht
  tomorrow night (evening) morgen abend
  tonight heute abend
night club der Nachtklub
nightdress das Nachthemd
no nein
  no thanks nein danke
  (without) ohne
  no sugar ohne Zucker
  no ice ohne Eis
nobody niemand
noise der Lärm
noisy laut
  it's very noisy es ist sehr laut

non-alcoholic alkoholfrei
none keine(r/s)
non-smoking Nichtraucher-
north der Norden
Northern Ireland Nordirland
North Sea die Nordsee
nose die Nase
not nicht
  I do not know ich weiß nicht
note *(banknote)* der Geldschein
  (written) die Notiz
note pad der Notizblock
nothing nichts
  nothing else nichts weiter
notice *(sign)* das Schild
notice board das Anschlagbrett
novel der Roman
November der November
now jetzt
nuclear nuklear
nudist beach der FKK-Strand
number die Zahl
number plate das Nummernschild
nurse die/der Krankenschwester/
  Krankenpfleger
nursery school die Vorschule
nut *(to eat)* die Nuß
  (for bolt) die Schraubenmutter

O

oak die Eiche
oar das Ruder
oats der Hafer
to obtain erhalten
occasionally gelegentlich
occupation *(work)* der Beruf
ocean der Ozean
October der Oktober
odd *(number)* ungerade
of von
  a glass of water ein Glas Wasser
  made of... aus...
off *(light, radio, etc)* aus
  (rotten) schlecht

office das Büro
office block das Bürogebäude
often oft
  how often? wie oft?
oil das Öl
oil filter der Ölfilter
oil gauge der Ölstandsanzeiger
ointment die Salbe
OK okay
old alt
  how old are you? wie alt sind
  Sie?
  I'm... years old ich bin... Jahre
  alt
old age pensioner der/die
  Rentner(in)
olive die Olive
olive oil das Olivenöl
omelette das Omelett
on *(light, radio, etc)* an
on auf
  on the table auf dem Tisch
  on time pünktlich
once einmal
  at once sofort
one ein
  (as number) eins
one-way street die Einbahnstraße
onion die Zwiebel
only nur
open geöffnet
to open öffnen
opera die Oper
operation *(surgical)* die Operation
operator *(phone)* die Vermittlung
opposite gegenüber
optician's der Optiker
or oder
  tea or coffee Tee oder Kaffee
orange *(colour)* orange
orange *(fruit)* die Orange
orange juice der Orangensaft
orchestra das Orchester
order *(in restaurant)* die Bestellung
  out of order kaputt

o to order (in restaurant) bestellen
organic organisch
to organize organisieren
other: the other one der/die/das andere
ounce = approx. 30 g
our unser
  (with der-words) unser
  (with das-words) unser
  (with die-words) unsere
out (light, etc) aus
  she's out sie ist nicht da
out of order kaputt
outdoor (pool, etc) im Freien
outside draußen
oven der Herd
ovenproof dish die feuerfeste Form
over (on top of, above) über
to overbook überbuchen
to overcharge zuviel berechnen
overcoat der Überzieher
overdone (food) verkocht
to overheat überhitzen
to overtake (in car) überholen
to owe schulden
  I owe you... ich schulde Ihnen...
  you owe me... Sie schulden mir...
owl die Eule
owner der/die Besitzer(in)
oxygen der Sauerstoff

P

pacemaker der Herzschrittmacher
to pack (luggage) packen
package das Paket
package tour die Pauschalreise
packet das Paket
paddling pool das Planschbecken
padlock das Vorhängeschloß
page die Seite
paid bezahlt
  I've paid ich habe bezahlt
pain der Schmerz

painful schmerzhaft
painkiller das Schmerzmittel
to paint malen
painting (picture) das Bild
pair das Paar
palace der Palast
pale blaß
pan (saucepan) der Kochtopf
  (frying pan) die Bratpfanne
pancake der Pfannkuchen
panniers (for bike) die Satteltaschen
pants (underwear) der Slip
panty liner die Slipeinlage
paper das Papier
paper napkins die Papierserviette
paracetamol® die Schmerztablette
parcel das Paket
pardon? wie bitte?
  I beg your pardon! Entschuldigung!
parents die Eltern
park der Park
to park parken
parking disk die Parkscheibe
parking meter die Parkuhr
parking ticket (fine) der Strafzettel
  (to display) der Parkschein
parsley die Petersilie
partner (business) der/die Geschäftspartner(in)
  (boy/girlfriend) der/die Partner(in)
party (of tourists) die Reisegruppe
  (celebration) die Party
  (political) die Partei
pass der Paß
passenger der Fahrgast
passport der Reisepaß
passport control die Paßkontrolle
pasta die Nudeln (pl)
pastry der Teig
  (cake) das Gebäck
path der Weg
patient (in hospital) der/die Patient(in)
pavement der Bürgersteig

to pay zahlen
payment die Bezahlung
payphone das Münztelefon
peach der Pfirsich
peak rate der Höchsttarif
peanut die Erdnuß
pear die Birne
pearls die Perlen
peas die Erbsen
pedal das Pedal
pedalo der Wassertreter
pedestrian der/die Fußgänger(in)
pedestrian crossing der Fußgängerübergang
to peel *(fruit)* schälen
peg *(clothes)* die Wäscheklammer
(tent) der Hering
pen der Füller
pencil der Bleistift
penicillin das Penizillin
peninsula die Halbinsel
penis der Penis
penknife das Taschenmesser
pensioner der/die Rentner(in)
people die Leute
pepper *(spice)* der Pfeffer
(vegetable) die Paprikaschote
per pro
per day pro Tag
per hour pro Stunde
per person pro Person
100 km per hour einhundert Kilometer pro Stunde
perfect perfekt
performance: *the next performance* die nächste Vorstellung
perfume das Parfüm
perhaps vielleicht
period *(menstruation)* die Periode
perm die Dauerwelle
permit die Genehmigung
person die Person
per person pro Person
personal organizer der Terminplaner

personal stereo der Walkman®
pet das Haustier
petrol das Benzin
4-star petrol Superbenzin
unleaded petrol bleifreies Benzin
petrol cap der Tankdeckel
petrol pump die Tanksäule
petrol station die Tankstelle
pharmacy die Apotheke
to phone telefonieren
phone das Telefon
by phone per Telefon
phonebook das Telefonbuch
phone call der Anruf
phonebox die Telefonzelle
phonecard die Telefonkarte
photocopy die Fotokopie
I need a photocopy ich brauche eine Fotokopie
to photocopy fotokopieren
photograph das Foto
to take a photograph fotografieren
phrase book der Sprachführer
piano das Klavier
pickpocket der Taschendieb
picnic das Picknick
to have a picnic ein Picknick machen
picnic rug die Picknickdecke
picnic table der Campingtisch
picture *(painting)* das Bild
(photo) das Foto
picture frame der Bilderrahmen
pie *(sweet)* der Obstkuchen
(savoury) die Pastete
piece das Stück
pier die Pier
pig das Schwein
pill die Pille
to be on the Pill die Pille nehmen
pillow das (Kopf)kissen
pillowcase der (Kopf)kissenbezug
pilot der/die Pilot(in)
pin die Stecknadel

p

pineapple die Ananas
pink rosa
pint = approx. 0.5 litre
  a pint of beer eine Halbe
pipe *(smoker's)* die Pfeife
  (drain, etc) das Rohr
pizza die Pizza
place der Platz
plain *(unflavoured)* einfach
plait der Zopf
plane *(airplane)* das Flugzeug
plant die Pflanze
plaster *(sticking)* das Pflaster
  (for broken limb) der Gips
plastic *(made of)* Plastik-
plastic bag der Plastikbeutel
plate der Teller
platform *(at station)* der Bahnsteig
  which platform? welcher
  Bahnsteig?
play *(theatre)* das Stück
to play spielen

p

playground der Spielplatz
playroom das Spielzimmer
please bitte
pleased erfreut
  pleased to meet you sehr erfreut
pliers die Zange *(sgl)*
plug *(electrical)* der Stecker
  (in sink) der Stöpsel
plum die Pflaume
plumber der/die Klempner(in)
poached *(egg, fish)* pochiert
pocket die Tasche
points *(in car)* die Unterbrecherkontakte
poison das Gift
poisonous giftig
police *(force)* die Polizei
policeman/woman der/die
  Polizist(in)

p

police station das Polizeirevier
polish *(for shoes)* die Schuhcreme
  (for furniture) die Möbelpolitur
polite höflich

polluted verschmutzt
pony das Pony
pony trekking das Ponyreiten
poor arm
poppy der Mohn
pop socks die Kniestrümpfe
popular beliebt
pork das Schweinefleisch
port *(seaport)* der Hafen
porter *(for door)* der Portier
  (in station) der Gepäckträger
portion die Portion
portrait das Portrait
Portugal Portugal
Portuguese *adj* portugiesisch
  m/f der/die Portugiese/
  Portugiesin
possible möglich
post: *by post* per Post
to post aufgeben
postbox der Briefkasten
postcard die Ansichtskarte
postcode die Postleitzahl
postman/woman der/die
  Briefträger(in)
post office das Postamt
poster das Poster
to postpone verschieben
potato die Kartoffel
  boiled potatoes die Salzkartoffeln
  fried potatoes die Bratkartoffeln
  mashed potatoes das Kartoffelpüree
  sautéed potatoes die Röstkartoffeln
potato salad der Kartoffelsalat
pothole das Schlagloch
pottery die Töpferwaren *(pl)*
pound das Pfund
to pour eingießen
powder: *in powder form* pulverförmig
powdered milk die Trockenmilch
pram der Kinderwagen

prawn die Garnele
to pray beten
to prefer vorziehen
pregnant schwanger
  I'm pregnant ich bin schwanger
to prepare vorbereiten
to prescribe verschreiben
prescription das Rezept
present *(gift)* das Geschenk
pressure: *tyre pressure* der
  Reifendruck
  blood pressure der Blutdruck
pretty hübsch
price der Preis
price list die Preisliste
priest der Priester
prince der Prinz
princess die Prinzessin
print *(photo)* der Abzug
prison das Gefängnis
private privat
prize der Preis
probably wahrscheinlich
problem das Problem
programme das Programm
prohibited verboten
to promise versprechen
to pronounce aussprechen
  how's it pronounced? wie
  spricht man das aus?
Protestant protestantisch
public öffentlich
public holiday der gesetzliche
  Feiertag
pudding die Nachspeise
to pull ziehen
  to pull a muscle sich einen
  Muskel verziehen
pullover der Pullover
pump *(bike, etc)* die Luftpumpe
  (petrol) die Tanksäule
puncture die Reifenpanne
puppet die Puppe
puppet show das Puppenspiel
purple violett

purse der Geldbeutel
to push stoßen
pushchair die Kinderkarre
to put *(place)* stellen
to put back verschieben
pyjamas der Pyjama

Q

quality die Qualität
quantity die Quantität
quarantine die Quarantäne
to quarrel streiten
quarter das Viertel
quay der Kai
queen die Königin
question die Frage
queue die Schlange
to queue anstehen
quick(ly) schnell
quiet ruhig
quilt die Bettdecke
quite *(rather)* ziemlich
  it's quite good es ist ganz gut
  it's quite expensive es ist ziemlich teuer
quiz show das Quiz

R

rabbit das Kaninchen
rabies die Tollwut
race *(sport)* das Rennen
race course die Rennbahn
racket *(tennis, etc)* der Schläger
radiator *(car)* der Kühler
  (heater) der Heizkörper
radio das Radio
radishes die Radieschen
rag der Lappen
railway die Eisenbahn
railway station der Bahnhof
rain der Regen
to rain regnen
  it's raining es regnet

r

raincoat der Regenmantel
raisins die Rosinen
rake die Harke
rape die Vergewaltigung
to rape vergewaltigen
rare *(unique)* selten
(steak) blutig
rash *(skin)* der Ausschlag
raspberries die Himbeeren
rate *(price)* der Preis
rate of exchange der Wechselkurs
raw roh
razor der Rasierapparat
(electric) der Elektrorasierer
razor blades die Rasierklingen
to read lesen
ready fertig
to get ready sich fertig machen
real echt
to realize erkennen
rearview mirror der Rückspiegel
receipt die Quittung

r

receiver *(of phone)* der Hörer
reception *(desk)* der Empfang
receptionist der/die Empfangs-
che/Empfangsdame
to recharge *(battery)* wieder
aufladen
recipe das Rezept
to recognize erkennen
to recommend empfehlen
record *(music)* die Schallplatte
to recover *(from illness)* genesen
red rot
redcurrants die roten Johannisbeeren
to reduce reduzieren
reduction die Ermäßigung
refill *(for pen)* die Ersatzmine
(for lighter) die Nachfüllpatrone
refund die Rückerstattung
to refund rückerstatten
to refuse ablehnen
region das Gebiet
to register *(at hotel)* sich anmelden

registered letter das Einschreiben
registration form das Anmeldeformular
to reimburse entschädigen
relation *(family)* der/die Ver-
wandte
to remain *(to stay)* bleiben
to remember sich erinnern
I don't remember ich kann mich
nicht erinnern
remote control die Fernbedienung
rent die Miete
to rent mieten
repair die Reparatur
to repair reparieren
to repeat wiederholen
to reply antworten
report der Bericht
to request bitten um
to require benötigen
to rescue retten
reservation die Reservierung ;
die Buchung
to reserve reservieren ; buchen
reserved reserviert
resident der/die Bewohner(in)
resort *(holiday)* das Urlaubsgebiet
rest *(repose)* die Ruhe
the rest of the wine der Rest
des Weins
to rest ruhen
restaurant das Restaurant
restaurant car der Speisewagen
to retire in den Ruhestand treten
retired pensioniert
to return *(in car)* zurückfahren
(on foot) zurückgehen
(return something) zurückgeben
return ticket *(train)* die Rückfahrkarte
(plane) das Rückflugticket
to reverse *(car)* rückwärts fahren
reverse charge call das R-
Gespräch
reverse gear der Rückwärtsgang

rheumatism der Rheumatismus
ribbon das Band
rice der Reis
rich *(person)* reich
  (food) reichhaltig
to ride *(horse)* reiten
right *(correct)* richtig
right: on the right rechts
  to the right nach rechts
ring der Ring
to ring *(bell, phone)* klingeln
ring road die Umgehungsstraße
ripe reif
river der Fluß
road die Straße
road map die Straßenkarte
roadworks die Straßenarbeiten
roast Rost-
roll *(bread)* das Brötchen
Romanesque romanisch
roof das Dach
roof-rack der Dachgepäckträger
room *(in house, hotel)* das Zimmer
  (space) der Platz
  double room das Doppelzimmer
  family room das Familienzimmer
  single room das Einzelzimmer
room number die Zimmernummer
room service der Zimmerservice
rope das Seil
rose *(flower)* die Rose
rotten *(fruit, etc)* verfault
rough rauh
round rund
roundabout *(traffic)* der Kreisverkehr
to row *(boat)* rudern
rowing *(sport)* das Rudern
rowing boat das Ruderboot
royal königlich
rubber *(eraser)* der Radiergummi
  (material) das Gummi
rubber band das Gummiband
rubber gloves die Gummihandschuhe

rubbish der Abfall
rubella die Röteln *(pl)*
rucksack der Rucksack
rudder das Ruder
rug der Teppich
ruin *(eg castle)* die Ruine
ruler *(for measuring)* das Lineal
to run rennen
rush hour die Rush-hour
rusty rostig
rye bread das Roggenbrot

S

saccharin der Süßstoff
sad traurig
saddle der Sattel
safe *(for valuables)* der Safe
safe *(not dangerous)* ungefährlich
  is it safe? ist das ungefährlich?
safety belt der Sicherheitsgurt
safety pin die Sicherheitsnadel
sail das Segel
sailboard das Segelbrett
sailing *(sport)* das Segeln
sailing boat das Segelboot
salad der Salat
  green salad grüner Salat
  mixed salad gemischter Salat
salad dressing die Salatsoße
sale *(in general)* der Verkauf
  (seasonal bargains) der Schlußverkauf
salesperson der/die Verkäufer(in)
sales rep der/die Vertreter(in)
salmon der Lachs
salt das Salz
salt water das Salzwasser
salty salzig
same gleich
sand der Sand
sandals die Sandalen
sandwich das Sandwich
  toasted sandwich das
  getoastete Sandwich

S

sanitary pads die Damenbinden
satellite TV das Satellitenfernsehen
Saturday der Samstag
sauce die Soße
tomato sauce die Tomatensoße
saucepan der Kochtopf
saucer die Untertasse
sauerkraut das Sauerkraut
sauna die Sauna
sausage die Wurst
to save *(person)* retten
(money) sparen
savoury pikant
to say sagen
scales *(weighing)* die Waage
scampi die Scampi *(pl)*
scarf *(headscarf)* das Kopftuch
(round neck) das Halstuch
scenery die Landschaft
school die Schule
scissors die Schere
to score a goal ein Tor schießen
score *(of match)* der Endstand
Scot der/die Schotte/Schottin
Scotland Schottland
Scottish schottisch
scouring pad der Topfschrubber
screen *(TV, etc)* der Bildschirm
screenwash das Scheibenputzmittel
screw die Schraube
screwdriver der Schraubenzieher
(phillips) der Kreuzschraubenzieher
scuba diving das Sporttauchen
sculpture die Skulptur
sea das Meer
seafood die Meeresfrüchte *(pl)*
seasickness die Seekrankheit
seaside die Küste
at the seaside an der Küste
seaweed die Alge
season *(of year)* die Jahreszeit
in season Saison haben
season ticket die Zeitkarte

seasonal saisonal
seasoning das Gewürz
seat *(chair)* der Sitz
(in bus, train, theatre) der Platz
seat belt der Sicherheitsgurt
second *(time)* die Sekunde
second zweite(r/s)
second class zweiter Klasse
second-hand gebraucht
secretary der/die Sekretär(in)
security guard die Wache
to see sehen
self-catering für Selbstversorger
self-employed freiberuflich
self-service die Selbstbedienung
to sell verkaufen
do you sell...? verkaufen Sie...?
sell-by date das Haltbarkeitsdatum
Sellotape® der Tesafilm®
semi-skimmed milk die Halbfettmilch
to send schicken
senior citizen der/die Rentner(in)
sentence der Satz
separated *(couple)* getrennt
separately: *to pay separately*
getrennt bezahlen
September der September
septic tank die Klärgrube
serious schlimm
service *(church)* der Gottesdienst
(in shop, etc) die Bedienung
is service included? ist die
Bedienung inbegriffen?
service charge die Bedienung
service station die Raststätte
serviette die Serviette
set menu die Tageskarte
several verschiedene
to sew nähen
sex *(gender)* das Geschlecht
(intercourse) der Sex
shade der Schatten
in the shade im Schatten
shallow *(water)* seicht

126

shampoo das Shampoo
to share teilen
sharp scharf
to shave rasieren
shaving cream die Rasiercreme
she sie *see* GRAMMAR
sheep das Schaf
sheet *(on bed)* das Bettuch
shelf das Regal
shell *(seashell)* die Muschel
(egg, nut) die Schale
sheltered geschützt
to shine scheinen
shingles die Gürtelrose
ship das Schiff
shirt das Hemd
shock absorber der Stoßdämpfer
shoe der Schuh
shoelaces die Schnürsenkel
shoe mender's der Schuster
shoe polish die Schuhcreme
shoe shop der Schuhladen
shop der Laden
shop assistant der/die Verkäufer(in)
shop window das Schaufenster
shopping das Einkaufen
to go shopping einkaufen gehen
shopping centre das Einkaufszentrum
shore das Ufer
short kurz
short cut die Abkürzung
shorts die Shorts
short-sighted kurzsichtig
shoulder die Schulter
to shout rufen
show *(theatrical)* die Aufführung
to show zeigen
shower *(bath)* die Dusche
(of rain) der Schauer
shower cap die Duschhaube
shower curtain der Duschvorhang
shrimp die Garnele
to shrink einlaufen

shut *(closed)* geschlossen
to shut schließen
shutter *(on window)* der Fensterladen
sick *(ill)* krank
(nauseous) übel
I feel sick mir ist schlecht
side dish die Beilage
sidelight das Standlicht
sidewalk der Bürgersteig
sieve das Sieb
sight die Sehenswürdigkeit
to sightsee Sehenswürdigkeiten besichtigen
sign *(notice)* das Schild
to sign unterschreiben
signature die Unterschrift
signpost der Wegweiser
silk die Seide
silver das Silber
similar ähnlich
since seit
to sing singen
single *(unmarried)* ledig
(not double) Einzel-
(ticket) einfach
single bed das Einzelbett
single room das Einzelzimmer
sink *(kitchen)* das Spülbecken
sister die Schwester
sister-in-law die Schwägerin
to sit sitzen
size *(of clothes, shoes)* die Größe
to skate *(on ice)* Schlittschuh laufen
skates *(ice)* die Schlittschuhe
(roller) die Rollschuhe
skating rink die Eisbahn
ski der Ski
to ski Ski fahren
ski boot der Skistiefel
skiing das Skilaufen
ski instructor der/die Skilehrer(in)
ski jacket die Skijacke
ski jump die Sprungschanze
ski lift der Skilift

S

ski pants die Skihose
ski pass der Skipaß
ski run/piste die Abfahrt
ski stick/pole der Skistock
ski suit der Skianzug
skimmed milk die Magermilch
skin die Haut
skin diving das Tauchen
skirt der Rock
sky der Himmel
sledge der Schlitten
to sleep schlafen
sleeper (on train) der Schlafwagen
sleeping bag der Schlafsack
sleeping car der Schlafwagen
sleeping pills die Schlaftabletten
slice die Scheibe
sliced bread geschnittenes Brot
slide (photograph) das Dia
to slip rutschen
slippers die Hausschuhe
slow(ly) langsam

S

to slow down langsamer werden
small klein
smaller kleiner
smell der Geruch
  (unpleasant) der Gestank
  a nice smell ein angenehmer
  Duft
to smell riechen
smile das Lächeln
to smile lächeln
smoke der Rauch
to smoke rauchen
  I don't smoke ich bin
  Nichtraucher(in)
smoke alarm der Feuermelder
smoked (food) geräuchert
smoked salmon geräucherter
  Lachs
smokers (sign) Raucher

S

snack der Snack
  to have a snack einen Imbiß
  essen
snack bar die Snackbar

snake die Schlange
snake bite der Schlangenbiß
to sneeze niesen
to snore schnarchen
snorkel der Schnorchel
snow der Schnee
to snow: *it's snowing* es schneit
snow board das Snowboard
snow chains die Schneeketten
snowed up eingeschneit
snowplough der Schneepflug
snow tyres die Winterreifen
soap die Seife
sober nüchtern
socket (for plug) die Steckdose
socks die Socken
soda water das Soda
sofa das Sofa
sofa bed das Sofabett
soft weich
soft drink das alkoholfreie Getränk
sole (of shoe) die Sohle
  (fish) die Seezunge
soluble löslich
some einige
someone irgend jemand
something etwas
sometimes manchmal
son der Sohn
son-in-law der Schwiegersohn
song das Lied
soon bald
  as soon as possible so bald wie
  möglich
sore throat die Halsschmerzen (pl)
sorry: *I'm sorry!* tut mir leid!
soup die Suppe
sour sauer
soured cream die saure Sahne
south der Süden
souvenir das Souvenir
spa das Bad
spade der Spaten
Spain Spanien
Spaniard m/f der/die Spanier(in)

Spanish *adj* spanisch
spanner der Schraubenschlüssel
spare parts die Ersatzteile
spare wheel das Ersatzrad
sparkling perlend
  sparkling wine der Schaumwein
spark plugs die Zündkerzen
to speak sprechen
  do you speak English?
  sprechen Sie Englisch?
speciality die Spezialität
speed die Geschwindigkeit
speedboat das Schnellboot
speed limit die Geschwindigkeitsbegrenzung
  to exceed the speed limit die
  Geschwindigkeitsbegrenzung
  überschreiten
speedometer der Tachometer
to spell: *how is it spelt?* wie
  buchstabiert man das?
to spend ausgeben
spice das Gewürz
spicy würzig
to spill verschütten
spinach der Spinat
spine das Rückgrat
spirits *(alcohol)* die Spirituosen
splinter der Splitter
to spoil verderben
sponge der Schwamm
spoon der Löffel
sport der Sport
sports shop das Sportgeschäft
sprain die Verstauchung
spring *(season)* der Frühling
spring onion die Frühlingszwiebel
square *(in town)* der Platz
stadium das Stadion
stain der Fleck
stainless steel der rostfreie Stahl
stairs die Treppe
stale *(bread)* trocken
stalls *(in theatre)* das Parkett
stamp die Briefmarke

stapler der Klammeraffe
staples die Heftklammern
star der Stern
  (film) der Star
to start *(begin)* anfangen
starter *(in meal)* die Vorspeise
  (in car) der Anlasser
station der Bahnhof
stationer's die Schreibwarenhandlung
statue die Statue
to stay *(to remain)* bleiben
  I'm staying at a hotel ich wohne
  in einem Hotel
steak das Steak
  medium steak Steak medium
  well-done steak durch-
  gebratenes Steak
  rare steak blutiges Steak
to steal stehlen
steamed gedünstet
steel der Stahl
steep: *is it steep?* ist es steil?
steering wheel das Lenkrad
stepfather der Stiefvater
stepmother die Stiefmutter
stereo die Stereoanlage
sterling das Pfund Sterling
stew das Eintopfgericht
steward/stewardess der/die
  Steward(eß)
to stick *(with glue)* kleben
sticking plaster das Heftpflaster
still *(yet)* noch
  (motionless) still
  still water stilles Wasser
sting der Stachel
to sting stechen
to stitch *(wound)* eine Wunde
  nähen
stock cubes die Brühwürfel
stockings die Strümpfe
stolen gestohlen
stomach der Magen
stomachache die Magenschmerzen *(pl)*

S

stone der Stein
stop (sign) das Stoppschild
to stop halten
store (shop) das Geschäft
storey das Geschoß
storm der Sturm
straight away sofort
straight on geradeaus
strange (odd) seltsam
straw (for drinking) der Strohhalm
strawberries die Erdbeeren
stream der Bach
street die Straße
street map der Stadtplan
stress der Streß
strike (of workers) der Streik
string die Schnur
striped gestreift
stroke (medical) der Schlaganfall
strong stark
  strong coffee starker Kaffee
  strong tea starker Tee

S

stuck: it's stuck es klemmt
student m/f der/die Student(in)
student discount die Studentenermäßigung
stuffed gefüllt
stung gestochen
stupid dumm
subtitles die Untertitel
suddenly plötzlich
suede das Wildleder
sugar der Zucker
  icing sugar Puderzucker
sugar-free zuckerfrei
suit (man's) der Anzug
  (woman's) das Kostüm
suitcase der Koffer
summer der Sommer
summer holidays die Sommerferien

S

summit der Gipfel
sun die Sonne
to sunbathe sonnenbaden
sunblock die Sonnencreme

sunburn der Sonnenbrand
Sunday der Sonntag
sunglasses die Sonnenbrille
sunny sonnig
sunrise der Sonnenaufgang
sunroof (car) das Sonnendach
sunset der Sonnenuntergang
sunshade der Sonnenschirm
sunstroke der Sonnenstich
suntan die Sonnenbräune
suntan lotion das Sonnenöl
supermarket der Supermarkt
supper das Abendessen
supplement (to pay) der Zuschlag
to surf surfen
surfboard das Surfbrett
surgery (treatment) die Operation
surname der Nachname
suspension (in car) die Federung
surrounded by umgeben von
to swallow verschlucken
to sweat schwitzen
sweater der Pullover
sweet (not savoury) süß
sweetener der Süßstoff
sweets die Süßigkeiten
to swell anschwellen
to swim schwimmen
swimming costume der Badeanzug
swimming pool das Schwimmbad
swimsuit der Badeanzug
swing (for children) die Schaukel
Swiss adj schweizerisch
  m/f der/die Schweizer(in)
switch der Schalter
to switch off (light) ausschalten
  (machine) abschalten
  (gas, water) abstellen
to switch on (light, machine) einschalten
  (gas, water) anstellen
Switzerland die Schweiz
swollen geschwollen
synagogue die Synagoge

T

table der Tisch
tablecloth die Tischdecke
tablespoon der Eßlöffel
tablet *(pill)* die Tablette
table tennis das Tischtennis
table wine der Tafelwein
to take *(medicine)* einnehmen
  how long does it take? wie lange dauert es?
take-away food das Essen zum Mitnehmen
to take off abfliegen
talc der Körperpuder
to talk to sprechen mit
tall groß
tampons die Tampons
tangerine die Mandarine
tank *(petrol)* der Tank
  (fish) das Aquarium
tap der Wasserhahn
tape die Kassette
tape measure das Maßband
tape recorder der Kassettenrecorder
tart der Obstkuchen
to taste probieren
  can I taste it? darf ich es probieren?
tax die Steuer
taxi das Taxi
taxi driver der/die Taxifahrer(in)
taxi rank der Taxistand
tea der Tee
  herbal tea Kräutertee
  tea with milk Tee mit Milch
  strong tea starker Tee
tea bag der Teebeutel
teapot die Teekanne
teaspoon der Teelöffel
tea towel das Geschirrtuch
to teach unterrichten
teacher *(school)* der/die Lehrer(in)
  (university) der/die Dozent(in)

tear *(in material)* der Riß
teat *(on bottle)* der Sauger
teeshirt das T-shirt
teeth die Zähne
telegram das Telegramm
telephone das Telefon
  mobile phone das Mobiltelefon
to telephone telefonieren
telephone box die Telefonzelle
telephone call der Anruf
telephone card die Telefonkarte
telephone directory das Telefonbuch
telephone number die Telefonnummer
television das Fernsehen
telex das Telex
to tell erzählen
temperature die Temperatur
  to have a temperature Fieber haben
temple der Tempel
temporary provisorisch
tendon die Sehne
tennis das Tennis
tennis ball der Tennisball
tennis court der Tennisplatz
tennis racket der Tennisschläger
tent das Zelt
tent peg der Hering
terminal das Terminal
terrace die Terrasse
terrorist der/die Terrorist(in)
testicles die Hoden
to thank danken
  thank you danke
  thanks very much vielen Dank
that das
  that one das dort
the der, die, das
theatre das Theater
theft der Diebstahl
their *m/nt* ihr
  f ihre
them ihnen

t

there *(over there)* dort
there is/there are es gibt
thermometer das Thermometer
these diese
  these ones diese hier
they sie *see* **GRAMMAR**
thief der/die Dieb(in)
thigh der Oberschenkel
thin dünn
thing das Ding
  my things meine Sachen
to think denken
  (to be of opinion) glauben
thirsty durstig
  to be thirsty Durst haben
this dies
  this one das hier
thorn der Dorn
those jene
  those ones jene dort
thousand tausend
thread der Faden
throat die Kehle
throat lozenges die Halspastillen
through durch
thrush *(candida)* die Pilzkrankheit
thumb der Daumen
thunder der Donner
thunderstorm das Gewitter
Thursday der Donnerstag
thyme der Thymian
ticket die Karte
  (train, bus, etc) die Fahrkarte
  a single ticket eine einfache
  Fahrkarte
  a return ticket eine Rückfahrkarte
  tourist ticket ein Touristenticket
  book of tickets ein Fahrscheinheft
  (entrance fee) die Eintrittskarte
ticket collector der/die Schaff-
ner(in)
ticket office der Fahrkartenschalter
tide die Gezeiten *(pl)*
  high tide die Flut
  low tide die Ebbe

tie die Krawatte
tights die Strumpfhose
till *(cash desk)* die Kasse
till *(until)* bis
  till 2 o'clock bis zwei Uhr
time *(of day)* die Zeit
  what time is it? wie spät ist es?
  do you have time? haben Sie
  Zeit?
timer die Schaltuhr
timetable der Fahrplan
tin *(can)* die Dose
tin-opener der Dosenöffner
to tip Trinkgeld geben
tip *(to waiter, etc)* das Trinkgeld
tipped *(cigarettes)* Filter-
tired müde
tissues die Papiertaschentücher
to zu (zum/zur)
  (with names of places) nach
  to London nach London
  to the airport zum Flughafen
toast der Toast
tobacco der Tabak
tobacconist's die Tabakwarenhandlung
today heute
toe die Zehe
together zusammen
toilet die Toilette
  toilet for disabled die Behindertentoilette
toilet brush die Toilettenbürste
toilet paper das Toilettenpapier
toiletries die Toilettenartikel
token *(for bus)* der Fahrschein
  (for phone) die Marke
toll *(motorway)* die Maut
tomato die Tomate
  tinned tomatoes Tomaten in
  Dosen
tomato juice der Tomatensaft
tomato purée das Tomatenpüree
tomato sauce die Tomatensoße
tomorrow morgen
  tomorrow morning morgen früh

tomorrow afternoon morgen nachmittag

tomorrow evening morgen abend

tongue die Zunge

tonic water das Tonic

tonight heute abend

tonsillitis die Mandelentzündung

too *(also)* auch
too big zu groß
too small zu klein

tool das Werkzeug

toolkit der Werkzeugkasten

tooth der Zahn

toothache die Zahnschmerzen *(pl)*
I have toothache ich habe Zahnschmerzen

toothbrush die Zahnbürste

toothpaste die Zahnpasta

toothpick der Zahnstocher

top: *the top floor* das oberste Stockwerk

top *(of mountain)* der Gipfel
(lid) der Deckel
on top of... oben auf...

torch *(flashlight)* die Taschenlampe

torn zerrissen

total *(amount)* die Endsumme

tough *(meat)* zäh

tour die Fahrt
guided tour die Besichtigungstour

tour guide der/die Reiseführer(in)

tour operator der Reiseveranstalter

tourist der/die Tourist(in)

tourist information die Touristen-Information

tourist office das Fremdenverkehrsbüro

tourist route die Touristenroute

tourist ticket die Touristenkarte

to tow *(car)* abschleppen

towel das Handtuch

tower der Turm

town die Stadt

town centre das Stadtzentrum

town hall das Rathaus

town plan der Stadtplan

tow rope das Abschleppseil

toy das Spielzeug

toy shop der Spielzeugladen

tracksuit der Jogginganzug

traditional traditionell

traffic der Verkehr

traffic jam der Stau

traffic lights die Ampel

trailer der Anhänger

train der Zug
by train mit dem Zug

trainers die Trainingsschuhe

tram die Straßenbahn

tranquillizer das Beruhigungsmittel

to translate übersetzen

translation die Übersetzung

to travel reisen

travel agent's das Reisebüro

travel documents die Reisepapiere

travel guide der Reiseführer

travel sickness die Reisekrankheit

traveller's cheques die Reisechecks

tray das Tablett

tree der Baum

trip der Ausflug

trolley *(luggage)* der Gepäckwagen
(shopping) der Einkaufswagen

trousers die Hose

trout die Forelle

truck der Laster

trunk *(for luggage)* der Koffer

trunks *(swimming)* die Badehose

to try versuchen

to try on *(clothes, etc)* anprobieren

T-shirt das T-shirt

tuna der Thunfisch

tunnel der Tunnel

turkey der Truthahn

to turn *(right/left)* abbiegen

to turn around umdrehen

t

t

t

t

to turn off (light) ausmachen
(TV, radio, etc) ausschalten
(tap) zudrehen
to turn on (light) anmachen
(TV, radio, etc) anschalten
(tap) aufdrehen
turquoise (colour) türkis
tweezers die Pinzette
twice zweimal
twin-bedded room das Zwei-
bettzimmer
twins die Zwillinge
to type maschineschreiben
typical typisch
tyre der Reifen
tyre pressure der Reifendruck

U

u

ugly häßlich
ulcer das Geschwür
umbrella der Regenschirm
(sunshade) der Sonnenschirm
uncle der Onkel
uncomfortable unbequem
unconscious bewußtlos
under unter
underground (metro) die U-Bahn
underpants die Unterhose
underpass die Unterführung
understand verstehen
I don't understand ich verstehe
nicht
do you understand? verstehen
Sie?
underwater unter Wasser
underwear die Unterwäsche
unemployed arbeitslos
to unfasten aufmachen
United States die Vereinigten
Staaten
university die Universität
unleaded petrol das bleifreie
Benzin
to unlock aufschließen

to unpack auspacken
to unscrew aufschrauben
unusual ungewöhnlich
up: *to get up* aufstehen
upside down verkehrt herum
upstairs oben
urgent dringend
urine der Urin
us uns
USA die USA (pl)
to use benutzen
useful nützlich
usual gewöhnlich
usually gewöhnlich
U-turn die Wende

V

vacancy (in hotel) Zimmer frei
vaccination die Impfung
vacuum cleaner der Staubsauger
vagina die Vagina
valid (ticket, licence, etc) gültig
valley das Tal
valuable wertvoll
valuables die Wertsachen
value der Wert
valve das Ventil
van der Lieferwagen
vanilla die Vanille
vase die Vase
VAT die Mehrwertsteuer (MWST)
veal das Kalbsfleisch
vegetables das Gemüse
vegetarian vegetarisch
I'm vegetarian ich bin Vegetarier
vehicle das Fahrzeug
vein die Ader
Velcro® das Klettband
vending machine der Automat
venereal disease die Geschlechtskrankheit
ventilator der Ventilator
very sehr

vest das Unterhemd
vet der/die Tierarzt/Tierärztin
via über
to video (from TV) auf Video
 aufnehmen
 (to film) filmen
video das Video
video camera die Videokamera
video cassette/tape die Videokassette
video recorder der Videorecorder
view die Aussicht
villa die Villa
village das Dorf
vinegar der Essig
vineyard der Weinberg
violet (flower) das Veilchen
virus der Virus
visa das Visum
to visit (person) besuchen
 (place) besichtigen
visiting hours (hospital) die
 Besuchszeit
visitor der Besucher
vitamin das Vitamin
vodka der Wodka
voice die Stimme
volcano der Vulkan
volleyball der Volleyball
voltage die Spannung
to vomit erbrechen
voucher der Gutschein

W

wage der Lohn
waist die Taille
waistcoat die Weste
to wait for warten auf
waiter/waitress der/die Kellner(in)
waiting room der Warteraum
to wake up aufwachen
Wales Wales
walk wandern
 to go for a walk einen

 Spaziergang machen
to walk zu Fuß gehen
walking boots die Wanderschuhe
walking stick der Wanderstock
Walkman® der Walkman®
wall die Mauer
wallet die Brieftasche
walnut die Walnuß
to want wollen
 I want... ich möchte...
 we want... wir möchten...
war der Krieg
ward (hospital) die Station
wardrobe der Kleiderschrank
warehouse die Lagerhalle
warm warm
 it's warm (weather) es ist warm
warning triangle das Warndreieck
to wash waschen
 (to wash oneself) sich waschen
to wash and blow dry waschen
 und fönen
washbasin das Waschbecken
washing machine die Waschmaschine
washing powder das Waschpulver
washing-up liquid das Spülmittel
wasp die Wespe
waste bin der Abfalleimer
to watch zuschauen
watch die Armbanduhr
watch strap das Uhrarmband
water das Wasser
 hot/cold water warmes/kaltes
  Wasser
 drinking water Trinkwasser
 mineral water Mineralwasser
 sparkling/still water
  Sprudelwasser/stilles Wasser
waterfall der Wasserfall
water heater das Heißwassergerät
water melon die Wassermelone
waterproof wasserdicht
waterproof material das
 wasserundurchlässige Material
to water ski Wasserski fahren

135

W

water wings die Schwimmflügel
waves *(on sea)* die Wellen
waxing *(hair removal)* die Wachsbehandlung
way: *which is the way to...?* wie kommt man zu/nach...?
way in *(entrance)* der Eingang
way out *(exit)* der Ausgang
we wir *see* **GRAMMAR**
weak schwach
  (tea, coffee) dünn
to wear tragen
weather das Wetter
weather forecast die Wettervorhersage
wedding die Hochzeit
wedding anniversary der Hochzeitstag
wedding cake die Hochzeitstorte
wedding dress das Hochzeitskleid
wedding present das Hochzeitsgeschenk
Wednesday der Mittwoch
week die Woche
  last week letzte Woche
  next week nächste Woche
  per week pro Woche
  this week diese Woche
weekday der Werktag
weekend das Wochenende
  next weekend nächstes Wochenende
  this weekend dieses Wochenende
weekly wöchentlich
to weigh wiegen
weight das Gewicht
welcome willkommen
well gut
  he's not well ihm geht's nicht gut
well-done *(steak)* durch
wellington boots die Gummistiefel
Welsh *adj* walisisch
  m/f der/die Waliser(in)
west der Westen
wet naß

wetsuit der Taucheranzug
what? was?
wheel das Rad
wheelchair der Rollstuhl
wheel clamp die Parkkralle
when? wann?
where? wo?
which: *which man?* welcher Mann?
  which woman? welche Frau?
  which book? welches Buch?
while während
whipped cream die Schlagsahne
white weiß
who wer?
whole vollständig
wholemeal bread das Vollkornbrot
whose? wessen?
why? warum?
wide breit
widow die Witwe
widower der Witwer
wife die Frau
wig die Perücke
to win gewinnen
windbreak *(camping)* der Windschutz
wind der Wind
windmill die Windmühle
window das Fenster
  (of shop) das Schaufenster
windscreen die Windschutzscheibe
windscreen wipers die Scheibenwischer
to windsurf surfen
windy: *it's windy* es ist windig
wine der Wein
  red wine Rotwein
  white wine Weißwein
  dry wine trockener Wein
  sweet wine süßer Wein
  rosé wine Roséwein
  sparkling wine Schaumwein
  house wine Hauswein
wine list die Weinkarte
wing mirror der Seitenspiegel

winter der Winter
with mit
  with ice mit Eis
  with milk mit Milch
  with sugar mit Zucker
without ohne
  without ice ohne Eis
  without milk ohne Milch
  without sugar ohne Zucker
wolf der Wolf
woman die Frau
wood *(material)* das Holz
woods der Wald
wool die Wolle
word das Wort
work die Arbeit
to work *(person)* arbeiten
  (machine) funktionieren
  it doesn't work es funktioniert
  nicht
world die Welt
worldwide website die Internet-
  Seite
worried besorgt
worse schlechter
worth: *it's worth £50* es ist
  fünfzig Pfund wert
to wrap up *(parcel)* einwickeln
wrapping paper das Geschenkpapier
wrinkles die Falten
wrist das Handgelenk
to write schreiben
  please write it down bitte
  schreiben Sie das auf
writing paper das Briefpapier
wrong falsch
  what's wrong? was stimmt nicht?

X

X-ray die Röntgenaufnahme

Y

yacht die Jacht

year das Jahr
  this year dieses Jahr
  next year nächstes Jahr
  last year letztes Jahr
yearly jährlich
yellow gelb
Yellow Pages die Gelben Seiten
yes ja
yesterday gestern
yet: *not yet* noch nicht
yoghurt der Joghurt
  plain yoghurt Naturjoghurt
yolk das Eigelb
you *(polite sing. and pl.)* Sie *see*
  GRAMMAR
  (familiar sing.) du ; ihr *(pl.)*
young jung
your dein/Ihr
  (with der-words) dein/Ihr
  (with das-words) dein/Ihr
  (with die words) deine /Ihre
youth hostel die Jugendherberge

Z

zero null
zip der Reißverschluß
zone die Zone
zoo der Zoo

y

z

A

Aal *m* eel
ab off ; from
  ab 8 Uhr from 8 o'clock
  ab Mai from May onward
abbestellen to cancel
abbiegen to turn *(right/left)*
Abbildung *f* illustration
abblenden to dip *(headlights)*
Abblendlicht *nt* dipped headlights
Abend *m* evening
Abendessen *nt* dinner ; supper
Abendgarderobe *f* formal dress
Abendkleid *nt* evening dress
abends in the evening(s)
aber but
abfahren to depart ; to leave

ABFAHRT departures *(train, bus)*

Abfahrtszeit *f* departure time
Abfall *m* rubbish
Abfertigungsschalter *m* check-in desk
abfliegen to take off *(plane)*

ABFLUG departures *(plane)*

  Abflug Inland domestic departures
  Abflug Ausland international departures
Abflughalle *f* departure lounge
Abflugzeit *f* departure time
Abfluß *m* drain
Abführmittel *nt* laxative
abheben to withdraw *(money)*
abholen to fetch ; to claim *(baggage, etc)*
  abholen lassen to send for
Abkürzung *f* short cut
abladen to dump ; to offload
ablaufen to expire
ablehnen to refuse
Abonnement *nt* subscription
Abreise *f* departure

absagen to cancel
Absatz *m* heel
abschalten to switch off *(machine)*
abschicken to dispatch
Abschleppdienst *m* breakdown service
abschleppen to tow *(car)*
Abschleppseil *nt* towrope
Abschleppstange *f* towbar
Abschleppwagen *m* breakdown van
Absender *m* sender
abstellen to turn off ; to park car
Abszeß *m* abscess
Abtei *f* abbey
Abteil *nt* compartment *(on train)*
Abteilung *f* department
Abtreibung *f* abortion
Abtreibungspille *f* abortion pill
Abwaschlappen *m* J cloth®
Abzug *m* print *(photo)*
Achse *f* axle
achten auf to pay attention to

ACHTUNG caution

Ader *f* vein
Adler *m* eagle
Adreßbuch *nt* address book
Adresse *f* address
adressieren to address *(letter)*
Affe *m* monkey
ähnlich similar
Aktentasche *f* briefcase
Akzent *m* accent *(pronunciation)*
akzeptieren to accept
Alarmanlage *f* alarm
Alge *f* seaweed
Alkohol *m* liquor ; alcohol
alkoholfrei non-alcoholic
alkoholisch alcoholic *(drink)*
alle all ; everybody ; everyone
  alle zwei Tage every other day
Allee *f* avenue
allein alone

139

a **Allergie** f allergy
allergisch gegen allergic to
Allerheiligen nt All Saints' Day
alles everything ; all *(singular)*
allgemein general ; universal
Allradantrieb m four wheel drive
Alpen pl Alps
als than ; when *(with past tense)*
alt old
Altar m altar
Altbier nt top-fermented dark beer
Alter nt age *(of person)*
ältere(r/s) older ; elder
Altglascontainer m bottle bank
Alufolie f aluminium foil
am at ; in ; on
  am Bahnhof at the station
  am Abend in the evening
  am Freitag on Friday
Ameise f ant
Amerika nt America
a **Amerikaner(in)** m/f American
amerikanisch American *adj*
Ampel f traffic light
Amtszeichen nt dialling tone
Amüsierviertel nt nightclub
  district
an at ; on *(light, radio, etc)* ; near
  Frankfurt an 1300 arriving
  Frankfurt 1300
  an/aus on/off
Ananas f pineapple
anbauen to grow *(cultivate)*
anbieten to offer
andere(r/s) other
ändern to change *(to alter)*
Änderung f change
Anfall m fit *(seizure)*
Anfang m start *(beginning)*
anfangen to begin ; to start
a **Anfänger(in)** m/f beginner
Anfängerhügel m nursery slope
Anfrage f enquiry
Angaben pl details ; directions *(to
  a place)*

angeben to give
Angebot nt offer
  im Angebot on offer
Angehörige(r) m/f relative
angeln to fish
Angeln nt fishing ; angling
  Angeln verboten no fishing
Angelrute f fishing rod
Angelschein m fishing permit
angenehm pleasant
Angestellte(r) m/f employee
Angina f angina
angreifen to attack
Angst haben vor to be afraid of
Anhänger m trailer ; fan *(supporter)*
Anker m anchor
ankommen to arrive
ankündigen to announce

ANKUNFT arrivals

Anlage f park ; grounds ; facilities
  öffentliche Anlage public park
Anlasser m starter *(in car)*
Anlegeplatz m mooring
Anlegestelle f landing stage ;
  jetty
anmachen to turn on *(light, radio)*
Anmeldeformular nt registration
  form
Anmeldung f registration ; reception *(place)*
Annahme f acceptance ; reception
annehmen to assume ; to accept
anprobieren to try on *(clothes, etc)*
Anruf m phone call
Anrufbeantworter m answerphone
anrufen to phone
anschalten to turn on *(TV, etc)*
anschauen to look at
Anschlagbrett nt notice board
Anschluß m connection *(train, etc)*
Anschlußflug m connecting flight
anschnallen to fasten *(seatbelt)*
Anschrift f address

140

anschwellen to swell
Ansicht f view
Ansichtskarte f picture postcard
anstatt instead of
ansteckend infectious
anstehen to queue
anstellen to switch on *(gas, water)*
Anteil m share *(part)*
Antenne f aerial
Antibiotikum nt antibiotic
antik ancient
Antiquitäten pl antiques
Antiquitätenladen m antique shop
Antiseptikum nt antiseptic
Antwort f answer ; reply
antworten to answer ; to reply
Anweisungen pl instructions
Anzahl f number
Anzahlung f deposit
Anzeige f advertisement ; report *(to police)*
Anzug(-züge) m suit(s) *(man's)*
anzünden to light ; to set fire to
Apfel (Äpfel) m apple(s)
Apfelkuchen m apple cake
Apfelsaft m apple juice
Apfelsine(n) f orange(s)
Apfelwein m cider
Apotheke f pharmacy
Apparat m appliance ; camera ; extension
Aprikose(n) f apricot(s)

APRIL April

Aquarium nt fish tank
Arbeit f employment ; work
arbeiten to work *(person)*
arbeitslos unemployed
Architekt(in) m/f architect
Architektur f architecture
arm poor
Arm m arm
Armband nt bracelet

Armbanduhr f watch
Ärmelkanal m English Channel
Art f type ; sort ; manner
Arthritis f arthritis
Artikel m article ; item
Arznei f medicine
Arzt/Ärztin m/f doctor
Aschenbecher m ashtray
Aspirin nt aspirin
Ast m branch *(of tree)*
Asthma nt asthma
Atlantik m Atlantic Ocean
atmen to breathe
attraktiv attractive
auch also ; too ; as well
auf onto ; on ; upon ; on top of
  auf deutsch in German
  auf Wiedersehen goodbye
aufdrehen to turn on *(tap)*
Aufenthalt m stay ; visit
Aufenthaltsraum m lounge
Auffahrt f slip-road
Aufführung f performance ; show
aufgeben to quit ; to check in *(baggage)* ; to post
aufhalten to delay ; to hold up
  sich aufhalten to stay
auflegen to hang up *(phone)*
aufmachen to open *(shop, bank)* ; to unfasten
  sich aufmachen to set off
aufregend exciting
aufschließen to unlock
aufschrauben to unscrew
aufschreiben to write down
aufstehen to get up
Aufstieg m ascent
aufwachen to wake up
aufwärmen to heat up *(food, milk)*

AUFZUG lift/elevator

Auge(n) nt eye(s)
Augenblick m moment ; instant
Augentropfen pl eye drops

AUGUST August

Auktion f auction
Au-pair-Mädchen nt au pair
aus off (light, radio, etc) ; made of… ; from ; out of
Ausdruck m expression ; print-out ; term (word)

AUSFAHRT exit (motorway)

Ausfall m failure (mechanical)
Ausflug(-flüge) m trip(s) ; excursion(s)
Ausfuhr f export(s)
ausführen to export ; to carry out (job)
ausfüllen to fill in (form)
  bitte nicht ausfüllen please leave blank (on form)
Ausgabe f issue (of magazine) ; issuing counter

AUSGANG exit/gate (at airport)

ausgeben to spend (money)
ausgehen to go out (for amusement)
ausgeschaltet off (radio)
ausgestellt issued at (passport)
ausgezeichnet excellent
auskugeln to dislocate (joint)

AUSKUNFT information

Ausland nt foreign countries ; abroad ; international
  aus dem Ausland from overseas
Ausländer(in) m/f foreigner
ausländisch foreign
Auslandsgespräch nt international call
auslassen to leave out ; to omit
auslaufen to sail (ship)
ausmachen to turn off (light) ; to put out (fire, cigarette)
Ausnahme(n) f exception(s)
auspacken to unpack

Auspuffrohr nt exhaust pipe
Ausrüstung f kit ; equipment
ausschalten to switch off (light, TV, radio)
Ausschank m bar ; drinks
Ausschlag m cold sore ; skin rash
ausschließlich excluding ; exclusive(ly)
Außenseite f outside
Außenspiegel m outside mirror

AUSSER BETRIEB out of order

äußerlich exterior
Aussicht f view ; prospect
aussprechen to pronounce
Ausstattung f equipment (of car)
aussteigen to get out of (vehicle)
Ausstellung f show ; exhibition
Ausstellungsdatum nt date of issue
Austausch m exchange
Australien nt Australia
Australier(in) m/f Australian
australisch Australian adj

AUSVERKAUF sale

ausverkauft sold out
Auswahl f choice
auswählen to choose
auswärts essen to eat out
ausweichen to avoid (obstacle)
Ausweis m identity card ; pass (permit)
auszahlen to pay
Auto(s) nt car(s)

AUTOBAHN motorway

Autobahngebühr f toll
Autofähre f car-ferry
Autokarte f road map
Automat m vending machine
  Automat wechselt change given
Automatikauto nt automatic car
automatisch automatic
Automobilklub m automobile

association
Autor(in) *m/f* author
Autoreisezug *m* motorail service
Autoschlüssel *pl* car keys
Autovermietung *f* car hire

B

Baby *nt* baby
Babyflasche *f* baby's bottle
Babymilch *f* baby milk
Babynahrung *f* baby food
Babyraum *m* mother and baby room
Babysitter(in) *m/f* babysitter
Babytücher *pl* baby wipes
Bach *m* stream
Bäckerei *f* baker's
Backofen *m* oven
Bad *nt* bath ; spa
Badeanzug *m* swimsuit
Badehose *f* swimming trunks
Badekappe *f* bathing cap
Badelatschen *pl* flip flops
baden to bathe ; to swim

BADEN VERBOTEN no swimming

Badezimmer *nt* bathroom
Baguette *nt* French bread
Bahn *f* railway ; rink
  per Bahn by rail
Bahnhof *m* station ; depot
Bahnlinie *f* line *(railway)*

BAHNSTEIG platform

Bahnübergang *m* level crossing
bald soon
Balkon *m* balcony
Ball *m* ball
Ballett *nt* ballet
Ballon *m* balloon
Banane(n) *f* banana(s)
Band (Bänder) *nt* ribbon(s) ; tape(s) *(audio, video)*
Band *f* band *(musical)*

Bank *f* bank *(financial)* ; bench
Bankkonto *nt* bank account
Bar *f* nightclub ; bar
Bär *m* bear *(animal)*
Bargeld *nt* cash
Bart *m* beard
Basel Basle
Batterie *f* battery
Bauarbeiten *pl* roadworks ; construction work
bauen to build
Bauer(Bäuerin) *m/f* farmer
Bauernhaus *nt* farmhouse
Bauernhof *m* farm(yard)
Baum *m* tree
Baumarkt *m* DIY shop
Baumwolle *f* cotton *(fabric)*
Baustelle *f* roadworks ; construction site
beachten to observe ; to obey
beantworten to answer
Bedarfshaltestelle *f* request stop
bedeckt cloudy *(weather)*
Bedeutung *f* meaning
bedienen to serve ; to operate
  sich bedienen to help oneself
Bedienung *f* service *(charge)*
Bedingung *f* condition *(proviso)*
Beefsteak *nt* steak
  deutsches Beefsteak hamburger; beefburger
beenden to end ; to finish
Beerdigung *f* funeral
Beere *f* berry
beginnen to begin
begrüßen to greet ; to welcome
behalten to keep *(retain)*
Behandlung *f* treatment
beheizt heated
behindert disabled *(person)*

BEHINDERTENTOILETTE toilet for disabled

Behinderung *f* obstruction ; handicap

b

bei near ; by *(beside)* ; at ; on ; during
beide both
Beilage *f* side-dish ; vegetables ; side-salad
Bein *nt* leg
Beisel *nt* pub *(Austria)*
Beispiel(e) *nt* example(s)
  zum Beispiel for example
beißen to bite
Beitrag *m* contribution ; subscription *(to club)*
beitreten to join *(club)*
Bekleidungsgeschäft *nt* clothes shop
bekommen to get *(receive, obtain)*
beladen to load *(truck, ship)*
Belastung *f* load

BELEGT no vacancies

Beleuchtung *f* lighting
Belichtung *f* exposure *(film)*
beliebt popular
Belohnung *f* reward
benachrichtigen to inform
Benachrichtigung *f* advice note
benötigen to require
benutzen to use
Benzin *nt* petrol
Benzinpumpe *f* fuel pump *(in car)*
bequem comfortable
Beratungsstelle *f* advice centre
berechtigt zu entitled to
Berechtigte(r) *m/f* authorized person
bereit ready
Bereitschaftsdienst *m* emergency service
Berg(e) *m* mountain(s)
bergab downhill
bergauf uphill
Bergführer(in) *m/f* mountain guide
Bergschuhe *pl* climbing boots
Bergsteigen *nt* mountaineering
Bergtour *f* hillwalk ; climb

Bergwacht *f* mountain rescue
Bergwanderung *f* hill-walking
Bericht(e) *m* report(s) ; bulletin(s)
berichten to report
Berliner *m* doughnut
Beruf *m* profession ; occupation
beruflich professional
Beruhigungsmittel *nt* tranquillizer
berühmt famous
berühren to handle ; to touch
beschädigen to damage
beschäftigt busy
Beschäftigung *f* employment ; occupation
Bescheinigung *f* certificate
beschreiben to describe
Beschreibung *f* description
Besen *m* brush *(for sweeping floor)*

BESETZT engaged/occupied

besichtigen to visit *(place)*
Besichtigungen *pl* sightseeing
Besichtigungstour *f* guided tour
Besitzer(in) *m/f* owner
besondere(r/s) particular ; special
besorgt worried
besser better
Besserung(en) *f* improvement(s)
  gute Besserung get well soon
bestätigen to confirm
Bestätigung *f* confirmation *(flight, etc)*
beste(r/s) best
Besteck *nt* cutlery
bestellen to book ; to order
Bestellung *f* order *(in restaurant)*
Bestimmungen *pl* regulations
Bestimmungsort *m* destination
besuchen to visit *(person)*
Besucher(in) *m/f* visitor
Besuchszeit *f* visiting hours
beten to pray
Betrag *m* amount
  Betrag erhalten payment received

betreffs concerning
betreten to enter
  Betreten verboten keep off
Betrieb m business
betrunken drunk
Bett(en) nt bed(s)
Bettbezug m duvet cover
Bettdecke f duvet ; quilt
Bettuch nt sheet (on bed)
Bettzeug nt bedclothes
Beule f lump (swelling)
bewacht guarded
bewegen to move
Bewohner(in) m/f resident
bewölkt cloudy
bewußtlos unconscious
bezahlen to pay ; to settle (bill)
bezahlt paid
Bezahlung f payment
Bezirk m district
BH m bra
Bibliothek f library
Biene f bee
Bienenstich m bee sting ; type of
  cream cake
Bier nt beer
  Bier vom Faß draught beer
Biergarten m beer garden
Bierkeller m beer cellar
Bierstube f pub that specializes
  in beer
bieten to offer
Bikini m bikini
Bild(er) nt picture(s)
Bilderrahmen m picture frame
Bildschirm m screen (TV, computer)
billig cheap ; inexpensive
billiger cheaper
Billigtarif m cheap rate (phone)
Birne(n) f pear(s) ; lightbulb(s)
bis until ; till
  bis jetzt up till now
  bis zu 6 up to 6
  bis bald see you soon
bißchen: ein bißchen a little ; a
  bit of

bitte please
bitte? pardon?
bitten um to request
bitter bitter (taste)
blaß pale
Blase f blister
Blasenentzündung f cystitis
Blatt (Blätter) nt sheet(s) (of
  paper) ; leaf (leaves)
blau blue
Blaue Zone f limited parking
  zone (parking disk required)
Blei nt lead (metal)
bleiben to stay (to remain)
Bleichmittel nt bleach
Bleiersatz-Additiv nt lead additive
bleifreies Benzin nt unleaded
  petrol
Bleistift m pencil
blind blind (person)
Blinddarmentzündung f appen-
  dicitis
Blinker m indicator (in car)
Blitz m lightning
Blitzlicht nt flash (for camera)
blockiert jammed (camera, lock)
Blockschrift f block letters
blond fair (hair) ; blond
Blumen pl flowers
Blumenladen m florist's shop
Bluse f blouse
Blut nt blood
Blutdruck m blood pressure
bluten to bleed
Bluterguß m bruise
Blutgruppe f blood group
blutig rare (steak)
Bluttest m blood test
Blutvergiftung f blood poisoning
Bockbier nt bock (strong beer)
Boden m floor (of room) ; ground
Bohnen pl beans
  grüne Bohnen french beans
Bohrer m drill (tool)

b

Boiler m immersion heater
Bombe f bomb
Bonbon nt sweet
Boot nt boat (small)
Bootsfahrt f cruise
Bootsrundfahrt f round boat trip
Bootsverleih m boat hire
Bordkarte f boarding pass
borgen to borrow
Böschung f embankment
botanischer Garten m botanical gardens
Botschaft f embassy
Bowle f punch (drink)
Brandwunde f burn (on skin)
Brat- fried ; roast
braten to fry ; to roast
Bratkartoffeln pl fried potatoes
Bratpfanne f frying pan
Bratwurst f sausage
Brauch m custom (tradition)
brauchen to need
Brauerei f brewery
braun brown
Bräune f suntan
Braut f bride
Bräutigam nt bridegroom
Brechreiz m nausea
breit wide
Bremse(n) f brake(s)
bremsen to brake
Bremsflüssigkeit f brake fluid
Bremslicht nt brake light
brennen to burn
Brief m letter (message)
Briefkasten m letterbox ; postbox
Briefmarke(n) f stamp(s)
Briefpapier nt writing paper
Brieftasche f wallet
Briefträger(in) postman/woman
Brille f glasses (spectacles)
Brillenetui nt glasses case
bringen to bring
britisch British

Brombeeren pl blackberries
Bronchitis f bronchitis
Bronze f bronze
Brosche f brooch
Broschüre f brochure
Brot nt bread ; loaf
Brötchen nt bread roll
Bruch m fracture
Brücke f bridge
Bruder (Brüder) m brother(s)
Brühe f stock (for soup, etc)
Brühwürfel pl stock cubes
Brunnen m well (for water) ; fountain
Brust f breast ; chest
Buch nt book
buchen to book
Buchhandlung f bookshop
Büchsen- canned
Büchsenöffner m can-opener
Buchstabe m letter (of alphabet)
Bucht f bay (along coast)
Buchung f booking
Bügel m coat hanger
 Bügel drücken! press down!
Bügelbrett nt ironing board
Bügeleisen nt iron (for clothes)
bügeln to iron
Bundes- federal
Bundesrepublik Deutschland f Federal Republic of Germany
Bungee-Springen nt bungee jumping
bunt coloured
Burg f castle (medieval) ; fortress
Bürger(in) m/f citizen
bürgerlich middle-class
Bürgermeister(in) m/f mayor(-ess)
Bürgersteig m pavement ; side-walk
Büro nt agency ; office
Bürogebäude nt office block
Bürste f brush
Bus(se) m bus(es) ; coach(es)
Busbahnhof m bus/coach station

Busfahrschein m bus ticket
Busfahrt f bus tour
Bushaltestelle f bus stop
Buslinie f bus route
Busreise f coach trip
Busverbindung f bus service
Büstenhalter m bra
Butangas nt Calor gas®
Butter f butter

C

campen to camp
Campingführer m camping guide(book)
Campingkocher m camping stove
Campingplatz m campsite
Campingtisch m picnic table
CD-Spieler m CD player
Champignon(s) m mushroom(s)
Charterflug m charter flight
Check-in m check-in
Chef(in) m/f boss
chemische Toilette f chemical loo
Chinarestaurant nt Chinese restaurant
Chips pl crisps ; chips (gambling)
Chor m choir
Cola f Coke®
Computer m computer
Computerprogramm nt computer program
Computerspiel nt computer game
Conditioner m conditioner (hair)
Cousin(e) m/f cousin
Creme f cream (lotion)
Creme(speise) f mousse

D

da there
  nicht da out (not at home)
Dach nt roof
Dachboden m attic

Dachgepäckträger m roof-rack
daheim at home

DAMEN ladies

Damenbinde(n) f sanitary towel(s)
Dampfer m steamer (boat)
danach after (afterwards)
danke thank you
danken to thank
Darmgrippe f gastric flu
das the ; that ; this ; which
Datei f file (computer)
Datum nt date (day)
Dauer f length ; duration
Dauerwelle f perm
Daumen m thumb
Decke f blanket ; ceiling
Deckel m top ; lid
dein your (singular familiar)
denken to think
Denkmal(-mäler) nt monument(s)
Deo nt deodorant
der the ; who(m)
Desinfektionsmittel nt disinfectant
desinfizieren to disinfect
destilliertes Wasser nt distilled water
Details pl details
deutsch adj German
Deutsch nt German (language)
Deutsche(r) m/f German
Deutschland nt Germany
Devisen pl foreign currency

DEZEMBER December

Dia(s) nt slide(s)
Diabetes m diabetes
Diabetiker(in) m/f diabetic person
Diamant m diamond
Diät f diet (special)
dick fat
die the ; who(m)
Dieb(in) m/f thief
Diebstahl m theft

d

Dienst *m* service
im Dienst on duty

DIENSTAG Tuesday

dienstbereit open *(pharmacy)* ; on duty *(doctor)*
Dienstreise *f* business trip
Dienstzeit *f* office hours
dies this
diese these
diese(r/s) this (one)
Diesel *m* diesel
Dieselöl *nt* diesel oil
Ding(e) *nt* thing(s)
Diplomat(in) *m/f* diplomat
direkt direct *(route, train)*
Direktflug *m* direct flight
Direktor(in) *m/f* managing director
Diskette *f* computer disk *(floppy)*
Disko *f* disco
Dokumente *pl* documents
Dollar *m* dollar
Dolmetscher(in) *m/f* interpreter
Dom *m* cathedral
Donner *m* thunder

DONNERSTAG Thursday

Doppel- double
Doppelbett *nt* double bed
doppelt double
Doppelzimmer *nt* double room
Dorf (Dörfer) *nt* village(s)
Dorn *m* thorn
dort there *(over there)* ; that one
Dose *f* box ; tin ; can
Dosenöffner *m* tin-opener
Dozent(in) *m/f* teacher *(university)*
Drachenfliegen *nt* hang gliding
Draht *m* wire
Drahtseilbahn *f* cable railway
draußen outdoors ; outside
drehen to turn ; to twist
Dreibettabteil *nt* three-berth compartment

Dreieck *nt* triangle
Dreikönigstag *m* Epiphany
dringend urgent
drinnen indoors
Droge *f* drug
Drogerie *f* chemist's *(not for prescriptions)*

DRÜCKEN push

Druckschrift *f* block letters
du you *(familiar form)*
dumm stupid
dunkel dark
dunkelblau dark blue
dünn thin ; weak *(tea)*
dunstig misty
durch through ; well-done *(steak)*
Durchfahrt verboten no through traffic
Durchfall *m* diarrhoea
Durchgang *m* way ; passage
Durchgangsverkehr *m* through traffic
durchgehend direct *(train, bus)* ; 24 hour
Durchsage *f* announcement
durchwählen to dial direct
Durchzug *m* draught *(of air)*
dürfen to be allowed
Dürre *f* drought
Durst haben to be thirsty
durstig thirsty
Dusche *f* shower
Duschhaube *f* shower cap
Duschvorhang *m* shower curtain
Dutzend *nt* dozen

E

Ebbe *f* low tide
echt real ; genuine
Ecke *f* corner
Edelstein *m* jewel ; gem
ehemalig ex-
ehrlich honest

Ei(er) nt egg(s)
Eiche f oak
eifersüchtig jealous
Eigelb nt egg yolk
Eigentum nt property
Eigentümer(in) m/f owner
Eil- urgent
Eilbrief m express letter
Eilzustellung f special delivery
Eimer m bucket
ein a (with 'das'/'der' words) ; one
ein(geschaltet) on (machine)
Einbahnstraße f one-way street
Einbrecher(in) m/f burglar
einchecken to check in
eine a (with 'die' words)
einfach simple ; single ticket ; plain (unflavoured)
Einfuhr f import
einführen to insert ; to import

Eingangstür f front door
eingeschlossen included (in price)
eingeschneit snowed up
Eingeweidebruch m hernia
eingießen to pour
einige(r/s) some ; a few
einkaufen to shop
Einkaufswagen m shopping trolley
Einkaufszentrum nt shopping centre
einladen to invite
Einladung f invitation
Einlaß ab 18 no entry for under 18s
einlaufen to shrink
einlösen to cash (cheque)
einmal once
einnehmen to take (medicine)
einordnen to get in lane
Einrichtungen pl facilities
eins one
einschalten to switch on (light, TV)

einschieben to insert
einschließlich including
Einschreiben nt registered letter
per Einschreiben by recorded delivery
einsteigen to get in(to) (bus, etc)
einstellen to adjust ; to appoint ; to stop
Eintopfgericht nt stew
eintreten to enter
Eintritt m entry ; admission (fee)

EINTRITT FREI free entry

Eintrittskarte(n) f ticket(s)
Eintrittspreis m admission charge/fee
einwerfen to post ; to insert
einwickeln to wrap up (parcel)
Einwurf m slot ; slit
Einwurf 2 Mark insert 2 marks
Einzahlung f deposit
Einzel- (not double)
Einzelbett nt single bed
Einzelfahrschein m single ticket
einzeln single ; individual
Einzelzimmer nt single room
Eis nt ice cream ; ice
Eisbahn f skating rink
Eisbecher m knickerbocker glory
Eisdiele f ice-cream parlour
Eisen nt iron (metal)
Eisenbahn f railway
Eisenwarenhandlung f hardware shop
Eiskaffee m iced coffee
Eistee m iced tea
Eiswürfel pl ice cubes
Eiweiß nt egg white
Elastikbinde f elastic bandage
elastisch elastic
Elektriker(in) m/f electrician
elektrisch electric(al)
elektrischer Schlag m electric shock
Elektrizität f electricity

e

e

Elektrorasierer m electric razor
Ellbogen m elbow
Eltern pl parents
E-Mail f e-mail
E-Mail-Adresse f e-mail address
Empfang m reception
empfangen to receive (guest) ; to greet
Empfangschef m receptionist
Empfangsdame f receptionist
Empfangsschein m receipt
empfehlen to recommend
Ende nt end ; bottom (of page, etc)
Endstand m final score (of match)
Endstation f terminal
Endsumme f total (amount)
eng narrow ; tight (clothes)
England nt England
Engländer(in) m/f Englishman/woman
Englisch nt English (language)
Enkel m grandson

e

Enkelin f granddaughter
entdecken to discover
Ente f duck
enteisen to de-ice
entfernt distant
   2 Kilometer entfernt 2 km away
Entfernung f distance
entfrosten to defrost
Enthaarungscreme f depilatory cream
enthalten to hold (to contain)
entkoffeinierter Kaffee m decaffeinated coffee
entkommen to escape
entrahmte Milch f skimmed milk
entschädigen to reimburse
Entschuldigung f pardon ; excuse me
entweder ... oder either ... or

e

entwickeln to develop (photos)
Entzündung f inflammation
Epileptiker(in) m/f epileptic
epileptischer Anfall m epileptic fit

er he ; it
erbrechen to vomit
Erbsen pl peas
Erdbeben nt earthquake
Erdbeeren pl strawberries
Erde f earth
Erdgeschoß nt ground floor
Erdnuß(-nüsse) f peanut(s)
Erdrutsch m landslide
erfreut pleased
Erfrischungen pl refreshments
erhalten to obtain ; to receive
erhältlich available
Erkältung f cold (illness)
erkennen to realize ; to recognize
erklären to explain
Erklärung f explanation
erlauben to permit (something) ; to allow
Ermäßigung f reduction
Ernte f harvest
Ersatz m substitute ; replacement
Ersatzrad nt spare wheel
Ersatzteile pl car parts
erste(r/s) first
   Erste Hilfe f first aid
   erste Klasse f first class
ertrinken to drown
Erwachsene(r) m/f adult
erzählen to tell
es it
eßbar edible
essen to eat
Essen nt food ; meal
Essen zum Mitnehmen take away food
Essig m vinegar
Eßlöffel m tablespoon
Eßzimmer nt dining room
Etage f floor ; storey
Etagenbetten pl bunk beds
etwas something
Eule f owl
Euro m Euro (currency)
Europa nt Europe

europäisch European
Europäische Union (EU) f
  European Union (EU)
Eurocheck m Eurocheque
Exemplar nt copy (of book, etc)
Experte/Expertin m/f expert
exportieren to export

F

Fabrik f works ; factory
Facharzt/Fachärztin m/f specialist
  (medical)
Fächer m fan (hand-held)
Faden m thread
Fahne f flag
Fahrbahn f carriageway
Fähre f ferry
fahren to drive ; to go
Fahrer(in) m/f driver (of car)
Fahrgast m passenger
Fahrkarte f ticket (train, bus, etc)
Fahrkartenschalter m ticket office
Fahrplan m timetable (trains, etc)
Fahrplanhinweise pl travel infor-
  mation
Fahrpreis(e) m fare(s)
Fahrrad(-räder) nt bicycle(s)
Fahrradflickzeug nt bicycle repair
  kit
Fahrradschloß nt bicycle lock
Fahrradvermietung f bike hire
Fahrschein(e) m ticket(s)
Fahrscheinentwerter m ticket
  stamping machine
Fahrscheinheft nt book of tickets
Fahrspur(en) f lane(s)
Fahrstuhl m lift ; elevator
Fahrt f journey ; drive ; ride (in
  vehicle)
  gute Fahrt! safe journey!
Fahrzeug nt vehicle
Fall m instance
  im Falle von in case of
fallen to fall

fällig due (owing)
falsch false (name, etc) ; wrong
Falten pl wrinkles
Familie f family
Familienname m surname
Familienstand m marital status
Familienzimmer nt family room
Fan m fan (football)
Farbe f colour ; paint ; suit (cards)
färben dye
farbenblind colour-blind
Farbfilm m colour film
farbig coloured
Farbstoff m dye
Fasching m carnival
Faß nt barrel
  vom Faß on tap ; on draught
Faßbier nt draught beer
Fastnachtsdienstag m Shrove
  Tuesday
faul lazy
Fax nt fax
faxen to fax
Faxnummer f fax number

FEBRUAR February

Feder f spring (coil) ; feather
Federball m badminton
Federung f suspension (in car)
fehlen to be missing
Fehler m fault ; mistake
Fehlgeburt f miscarriage
feiern to celebrate
Feiertag m holiday
Feile f file (nail)
Feinkostgeschäft nt delicatessen
Feld nt field
Felsen m cliff (in mountains)
Fenster nt window
Fensterladen m shutter (on window)
Fensterplatz m window seat
Ferien pl holiday(s)
Ferienhaus nt chalet (holiday)
Ferienwohnung f holiday flat

f

Fern- long-distance
Fernbedienung f remote control
Ferngespräch nt long-distance call
Fernglas nt binoculars
Fernlicht nt full beam *(headlights)*
Fernsehen nt television
Fernseher m TV set
Fernsprecher m public phone
fertig ready ; finished
Fest nt celebration ; party ; festival
Festplatte f hard disk
Fett nt fat ; grease
fettarm low-fat
fettarme Milch f low-fat milk
fettig greasy
feucht damp
Feuchtigkeitscreme f moisturizer
Feuer nt fire
feuerfeste Form f ovenproof dish
feuergefährlich inflammable
Feuerlöscher m fire extinguisher
Feuermelder m fire/smoke alarm
Feuertreppe f fire escape

FEUERWEHR fire brigade

Feuerwehrauto nt fire engine
Feuerwerk nt fireworks
Feuerzeug nt cigarette lighter
Fieber nt fever
  Fieber haben to have temperature
Filet nt sirloin ; fillet *(of meat, fish)*
Filiale f branch *(of store, bank, etc)*
Film m film *(at cinema, for camera)*
filmen to film
Filter m filter
Filzstift m felt-tip pen
finden to find
Finger m finger
Fingernagel m fingernail
Firma f company *(firm)*
Fisch m fish
Fischladen m fishmonger's
FKK-Strand m nudist beach

flach flat *(level)*
Flamme f flame
Flasche f bottle
Flaschenbier nt bottled beer
Flaschenöffner m bottle opener
Fleck m mark *(stain)*
Fleckenmittel nt stain-remover
Fleisch nt meat ; flesh
Fleischerei f butcher's
Flickzeug nt puncture repair kit
Fliege f bow tie ; fly
fliegen to fly
Flitterwochen pl honeymoon
Flöhe pl fleas
Flohmarkt m flea market
Flug (Flüge) m flight(s)
Fluggast m passenger
Fluggesellschaft f airline
Flughafen m airport
Flughafenbus m airport bus
Flugplan m flight schedule
Flugauskunft f flight information
Flugschein(e) m plane ticket(s)
Flugsteig m gate
Flugstrecke f route ; flying distance
Flugticket(s) nt plane ticket(s)
Flugzeug nt plane, aircraft
Flur m corridor
Fluß (Flüsse) m river(s)
Flußfahrt f river trip
Flüssigkeit f liquid
Flut f flood ; high tide
folgen to follow
Fön® m hairdryer
fönen to blow-dry
Forelle f trout
Form f shape ; form
Formular nt form *(document)*
Fortsetzung f sequel *(book, film)*
Foto nt photo
Fotoapparat m camera
Fotogeschäft nt photo shop
Fotografie f photography

fotografieren to take a photo
Fotokopie f photocopy
fotokopieren to photocopy
Fracht f cargo ; freight
Frage f question
fragen to ask
frankieren to stamp *(letter)*
Frankreich nt France
Franzose/Französin m/f
  Frenchman/woman
französisch adj French
Frau f wife ; Mrs ; Ms ; woman
Fräulein nt Miss

FREI free / vacant

im Freien outdoor ; open-air
Freibad nt open-air pool
freiberuflich freelance ; self-
  employed
Freigepäck nt baggage allowance
freimachen to stamp

FREITAG Friday

Freizeichen nt ringing tone
Freizeit f spare time ; leisure
Freizeitzentrum nt leisure centre
fremd foreign ; strange *(unknown)*
Fremde(r) m/f stranger
Fremdenführer(in) m/f tourist
  guide
Fremdenverkehrsbüro nt tourist
  office
Freude f joy
Freund m friend ; boyfriend
Freundin f friend ; girlfriend
freundlich friendly
Frieden m peace
Friedhof m cemetery
frisch fresh ; wet *(paint)*
Frischhaltefolie f cling film
Frischkäse m cream cheese
Friseur(Friseuse) m/f hairdresser
Frosch m frog
Frost m frost
Frostschutzmittel nt antifreeze

Früchte pl fruit
Früchtetee m fruit tea
Fruchtsaft m fruit juice
früh early
früher earlier
Frühling m spring *(season)*
Frühstück nt breakfast
Fuchs m fox
fühlen to feel
führen to lead
Führer(in) m/f guide
Führerschein m driving licence
Führung(en) f guided tour(s)
füllen to fill
Füller m pen

FUNDBÜRO lost property office

Fundsachen pl lost property
funktionieren to work *(machine)*
für for
  Benzin für DM 50 DM50 worth
  of petrol
für immer forever
Fuß (Füße) m foot (feet)
  zu Fuß gehen to walk
Fußball m football ; soccer
Fußballer(in) m/f football player
Fußballplatz m football pitch
Fußballspiel nt football match
Fußgänger(in) m/f pedestrian
Fußgängerüberweg m pedestrian
  crossing
Fußgängerzone f pedestrian
  precinct
Fußweg m footpath
füttern to feed

G

Gabel f fork *(for eating)*
Gabelung f fork *(in road)*
Galerie f gallery
Gang m course *(of meal)* ; aisle
  (theatre, plane)
Gangschaltung f gears

Gans f goose
ganz whole ; quite
ganztägig full-time
Garage f garage (private)
Garantie f guarantee ; warrant(y)

GARDEROBE cloakroom

Garten m garden
Gartenlokal nt garden café
Gärtner(in) m/f gardener
Gas nt gas
Gasflasche f gas cylinder
Gasherd m gas cooker
Gaspedal nt accelerator
Gasse f alley ; lane (in town)
Gast m guest
  nur für Gäste patrons only
Gästezimmer nt guest-room
Gasthaus nt inn
Gasthof m inn ; guesthouse
Gastritis f gastritis
Gaststätte f restaurant
Gaststube f lounge
Gate nt gate (airport)
Gebäck nt pastry (cake)
gebacken baked
Gebäude nt building
gebeizt cured ; marinated
geben to give
Gebiet nt region ; area
Gebiß nt dentures
geboren born
  geborene Schnorr née Schnorr
gebraten fried
gebrauchen to use
Gebraucht- used (car, etc)
gebrochen broken
Gebühr f fee
gebührenpflichtig subject to fee
Geburt f birth
Geburtsdatum nt date of birth
Geburtsort m place of birth
Geburtstag m birthday
Geburtstagsgeschenk nt birthday

present
Geburtstagskarte f birthday card
Geburtsurkunde f birth certificate
Gedeckkosten pl cover charge (in restaurant)
gedünstet steamed

GEFAHR danger

gefährlich dangerous
Gefälle nt gradient
Gefängnis nt prison
Geflügel nt poultry ; fowl
gefroren frozen (food)
gefüllt stuffed
gegen versus ; against ; toward(s)
Gegend f district ; region
gegenüber opposite ; facing
Gegenverkehr m two-way traffic
gegrillt grilled
gehen to go ; to walk
  wie geht es Ihnen? how are you?
Gehirnerschütterung f concussion
gehören to belong to
gekocht boiled ; cooked
gelb nt yellow ; amber (traffic lights)
Gelbe Seiten pl Yellow Pages
Gelbsucht f jaundice
Geld nt money
  Geld einwerfen insert money
Geldautomat m cash dispenser
Geldbeutel m purse
Geldrückgabe f coin return
Geldschein m banknote
Geldstrafe f fine (to be paid)
Geldstück nt coin
gelegentlich occasionally
Gelenk nt joint (of body)
Geltungsdauer f period of validity
gemischt mixed ; assorted
Gemüse nt vegetables
Gemüseladen m greengrocer's
genau accurate ; precise ; exact
Genehmigung f approval ; permit

genug enough
Genuß m enjoyment

GEÖFFNET open

Gepäck nt luggage
Gepäckablage f luggage rack
Gepäckaufbewahrung f left-luggage office

GEPÄCKAUSGABE baggage reclaim

Gepäckermittlung f luggage desk *(for queries)*
Gepäcknetz nt luggage rack *(in train)*
Gepäckschließfach nt left-luggage locker
Gepäckträger m luggage rack *(on car)* ; porter
Gepäckversicherung f luggage insurance
Gepäckwagen m luggage trolley
gerade even *(number)*
geradeaus straight ahead
Gerät nt appliance ; gadget
geräuchert smoked *(food)*
Gericht nt court *(law)* ; dish *(food)*
gerieben grated *(cheese)*
geröstet sauté ; fried ; toasted
Geruch m smell
Gesamtsumme f total amount
Geschäft(e) nt business ; shop(s)
Geschäftsadresse f business address
Geschäftsführer(in) m/f manager
Geschäftspartner(in) m/f partner *(business)*
Geschäftsstunden pl business hours
geschehen to happen
Geschenk(e) nt gift(s)
Geschenkeladen m gift shop
Geschenkpapier nt wrapping paper
Geschichte f history
geschieden divorced

Geschirrspülmaschine f dishwasher
Geschirrspülmittel nt washing-up liquid
Geschirrtuch nt tea/dish towel
Geschlecht nt gender ; sex
Geschlechtskrankheit f venereal disease

GESCHLOSSEN closed/shut

Geschmack m taste ; flavour
geschmort braised
geschnittenes Brot nt sliced bread
Geschoß nt storey
geschützt sheltered
Geschwindigkeit f speed
geschwollen swollen
Geschwür nt ulcer
Gesellschaft f company
Gesetz nt law
gesetzlicher Feiertag m public holiday
Gesicht nt face
Gesichtswasser f cleanser *(for face)*
Gesichtspflege f facial *(beauty treatment)*
gesperrt closed
Gespräch nt talk ; phone call
Gestank m smell *(unpleasant)*
gestattet permitted
gestern yesterday
gestochen stung ; bitten *(by insect)*
gestreift striped
gesund healthy
Gesundheit f health ; bless you!
Getränk(e) nt drink(s)
Getränkekarte f list of beverages
getrennt separated *(couple)*
  getrennt bezahlen to pay separately
Getriebe nt gearbox ; gears
Gewehr nt gun
Gewicht nt weight

gewinnen to win
Gewitter nt thunderstorm
gewöhnlich usual(ly)
Gewürz nt spice ; seasoning
Gezeiten pl tide
gibt es...? is/are there...?

GIFT poison

giftig poisonous
Gipfel m summit ; mountain top
Gips m plaster (for broken limb)
Gitarre f guitar
Glas nt glass ; lens (of glasses) ; jar
Glatteis nt black ice
Glatteisgefahr f danger-black ice
glatzköpfig bald (person)
glauben to believe ; to think (be of opinion)
gleich same
Gleise pl platforms ; tracks
Gletscher m glacier
Glocke f bell

Glück nt happiness ; luck
glücklich happy ; lucky
Glühbirne f light bulb
Gold nt gold
Golf nt golf
Golfplatz m golf course
Golfschläger m golf club
gotisch Gothic
Gott m God
Gottesdienst m church service
Grad m degree (of heat, cold)
Gramm nt gram(me)
Grapefruit f grapefruit
Gras nt grass
Gräte f fish bone
grau grey
Grenze f frontier ; border (of country)

Grenzpolizei f border police
Griff m handle ; knob
Grill m barbecue ; grill
grillen to grill

Grillstube f steak house ; grillroom
Grillteller m mixed grill
Grippe f flu
groß tall ; great ; big ; high (number, speed)
Großbritannien nt Great Britain
Großbuchstabe m capital letter
Größe f size (of clothes, shoes) ; height
Großeltern pl grandparents
Großmutter f grandmother
Großvater m grandfather
großzügig generous
grün green ; fresh (fish)
Grünanlage f park
Grundstücksmakler m estate agent's
grüne Versicherungskarte f green card (car insurance)
grüner Salat m green salad
Gruppe f group
Gruß m greeting
Grußkarte f greetings card
Gulasch nt goulash
gültig valid
Gummi m rubber ; elastic
Gummiband nt rubber band
Gummihandschuhe pl rubber gloves
Gummistiefel pl wellington boots
günstig convenient
Gurke(n) f cucumber(s) ; gherkin(s)
Gürtel m belt
Gürtelrose f shingles
Gürteltasche f bumbag ; money-belt
gut good ; well ; all right (yes)
alles Gute all the best ; with best wishes
guten Abend good evening
guten Appetit enjoy your meal
guten Morgen good morning
gute Nacht good night
guten Tag hello ; good day/after-noon

Güter *pl* goods
Gutschein *m* voucher ; coupon

H

H-Milch *f* long-life milk
Haar *nt* hair
Haarbürste *f* hairbrush
Haare *pl* hair
Haargel *nt* hair gel
Haarklemme *f* hairgrip
Haarschnitt *m* haircut
Haarspray *nt* hair spray
haben to have *see* GRAMMAR
Hackfleisch *nt* mince meat
Hacksteak *nt* hamburger
Hafen *m* harbour ; port
Hafer *m* oats
Haftung *f* liability
Hagel *m* hail
Hahn *m* tap *(for water)* ; cockerel
Hähnchen *nt* chicken
halb half
  zum halben Preis half-price
halb durch medium rare *(meat)*
halber Fahrpreis *m* half fare
Halbfettmilch *f* semi-skimmed milk
Halbinsel *f* peninsula
Halbpension *f* half board
Hälfte *f* half
hallo hello
Hals *m* neck ; throat
Halskette *f* necklace
Halspastillen *pl* throat lozenges
Halsschmerzen *pl* sore throat
Halstuch *nt* scarf *(round neck)*
Halt *m* stop
Haltbarkeitsdatum *nt* sell-by date
Haltebucht *f* layby
halten to hold ; to stop
Halten verboten no stopping
Haltestelle *f* bus stop
Hammer *m* hammer

Hämorrhoiden *pl* haemorrhoids
Hand *f* hand
Handel *m* trade ; commerce
Handgelenk *nt* wrist
handgemacht handmade
Handgepäck *nt* hand-luggage
Handschuhe *pl* gloves
Handtasche *f* handbag
Handtuch *nt* towel
Handwerker(in) *m/f* craftsperson
Harke *f* rake
hart hard *(not soft)*
hartgekochtes Ei *nt* hard-boiled egg
Hase *m* hare
Haselnuß(-nüsse) *f* hazelnut(s)
häßlich ugly
häufig frequent ; common
Haupt- major ; main
Hauptbahnhof *m* main station
Hauptgericht *nt* main course
Hauptstadt *f* capital *(city)*
Hauptstraße *f* major road
Hauptverkehrszeit *f* peak hours
Haus *nt* house ; home
  zu Hause at home
Hausarbeit *f* housework
Hausfrau(Hausmann) *f/m* housewife/househusband
Haushaltswaren *pl* household goods
Hausschuhe *pl* slippers
Haustier *nt* pet
Hauswein *m* house wine
Haut *f* hide *(leather)* ; skin
Hecht *m* pike
Hefe *f* yeast
Heft *nt* exercise book
Hefter *m* stapler
Heftklammern *pl* staples
Heftpflaster *nt* sticking plaster
Heidelbeeren *pl* bilberries
heilig holy

Heiligabend m Christmas Eve
Heim nt home (institution) ; hostel
Heimweh haben to be homesick
heiraten to marry (get married)

HEIß hot

heißen to be called
  wie heißen Sie? what's your name?
heiße Schokolade f hot chocolate
Heißwassergerät nt water heater
Heizgerät nt heater
Heizkörper m radiator
Heizung f heating
helfen to help
Helikopter m helicopter
hell light (pale) ; bright
hellblau light blue
helles Bier nt lager
helles Fleisch nt white meat
Helm m helmet
Hemd(en) nt shirt(s)
Hepatitis f hepatitis
Herbst m autumn
Herd m cooker ; oven
herein in ; come in
hereinkommen to come in
Hering m herring ; tent peg
Herr m gentleman ; Mr

HERREN gents

heruntergehen to go down
Herz nt heart
Herzanfall m heart attack
herzliche Glückwünsche! congratulations!
Herzschrittmacher m pacemaker
Heuschnupfen m hay fever
heute today
heute abend tonight
hier here
hiesig local (wine, speciality)
Hilfe f help
Himbeeren pl raspberries

Himmel m heaven ; sky
hin there
Hin- und Rückfahrt f round trip
hineingehen to go in
hinten behind

HINTEN EINSTEIGEN enter at rear

hinter behind
Hinweis m notice ; information
Hirnhautentzündung f meningitis
historisch historic
hoch high
Hochsaison f high season
Höchstgeschwindigkeit f maximum speed
Höchsttarif m peak rate
Hochzeit f wedding
Hochzeitsgeschenk nt wedding present
Hochzeitskleid nt wedding dress
Hochzeitstag m wedding anniversary
Hochzeitstorte f wedding cake
Hoden pl testicles
Hof m court
hoffen to hope
höflich polite
Höhe f altitude ; height
hoher Blutdruck m high blood pressure
höher higher
  höher stellen to turn up (heat, volume)
Höhle f cave
holen to fetch
holländisch Dutch
Holz nt wood (material)
Holzkohle f charcoal
Homöopathie f homeopathy
homosexuell homosexual
Honig m honey
hören to hear
Hörer m receiver (phone)
Hörgerät nt hearing aid
Hörnchen nt croissant

Hose f trousers
Hotel nt hotel
Hotel garni nt bed and breakfast hotel
hübsch pretty
Hubschrauber m helicopter
Hüfte f hip
Hügel m hill
Huhn nt hen
Hühnchen nt chicken
Hummer m lobster
Hund m dog
Hundeleine f dog lead
hundert hundred
Hunger haben to be hungry
Hupe f horn *(of car)*
husten to cough
Husten m cough
Hustenbonbons pl cough sweets
Hustensaft m cough mixture
Hut m hat
Hütte f mountain hut

I

ich I
Idiotenhügel m nursery slope
ihm him
ihnen them
ihr(e) her ; their
Imbiß m snack
Imbißstube f snack bar
immer always
Immunisierung f immunisation
Impfung f vaccination
in in *(place, position)* ; inside ; into
in Ordnung all right *(agreed)*
Infektion f infection
Informationsbüro nt information office
Ingenieur(in) m/f engineer
Inhalationsapparat m inhaler *(for medication)*
Inhalt m contents

inklusive inclusive
Inland nt domestic *(flight, etc)*
Inlandsgespräch(e) nt national call(s)
innen inside
Innenstadt f city centre
innerlich for internal use *(medicine)*
Insekt nt insect
Insektenschutzmittel nt insect repellent
Insel f island
Insulin nt insulin
intelligent intelligent
interessant interesting
Internet nt internet
Internet-Café nt internet café
Internet-Seite f website
Ire/Irin m/f Irishman/woman
irgend jemand someone
irgendwo somewhere
irisch adj Irish
Irland nt Ireland
Irrtum m mistake
Italien nt Italy
Italiener(in) m/f Italian
italienisch adj Italian

J

ja yes
Jacht f yacht
Jachthafen m marina
Jacke f jacket ; cardigan
Jagderlaubnis f hunting permit
jagen to hunt
Jahr nt year
Jahrestag m anniversary
Jahreszeit f season
Jahrgang m vintage
Jahrhundert nt century
jährlich annual ; yearly
Jahrmarkt m fair

JANUAR January

j

je everyone
Jeans pl jeans
jede(r/s) each
jemand somebody ; someone
jene those
jetzt now
Jod nt iodine
joggen to jog
Jogginganzug m tracksuit
Joghurt m or nt yoghurt
Johannisbeere(n) f currant(s)
Journalist(in) m/f journalist
jucken to itch
Jude/Jüdin m/f Jew
Jugendherberge f youth hostel
Jugendliche(r) m/f teenager

JULI July

jung young
Junge m boy
Junggeselle m bachelor

JUNI June

Juwelier m jeweller's

K

Kabel nt cable ; lead (electrical)
Kabelfernsehen nt cable TV
Kabine f cabin ; berth (train, ship)
Kaffee m coffee
Kaffeehaus nt café
Kaffeemaschine f percolator
Kai m quayside
Kakao m cocoa
Kakerlake f cockroach
Kalb nt calf (young cow)
Kalbfleisch nt veal

KALT cold

Kamera f camera
Kameratasche f camera case
Kamillentee m camomile tea
Kamin m fireplace

Kamm m comb ; ridge
kämpfen to fight
Kanada nt Canada
Kanadier(in) m/f Canadian man/
woman
kanadisch adj Canadian
Kanal m canal ; (English) Channel
kandiert glacé
Kaninchen nt rabbit
Kanister m (petrol) can
Kanu nt canoe
Kapelle f chapel ; orchestra
kaputt broken ; out of order
kaputtmachen to break (object)
Kapuze f hood (of jacket)
Karaffe f decanter ; carafe
Karfreitag m Good Friday
Karotten pl carrots
Karte f card ; ticket ; map ; menu
Kartentelefon nt cardphone
Kartoffel(n) f potato(es)
Kartoffelpüree nt mashed potato
Kartoffelsalat m potato salad
Karton m box (cardboard) ; carton
Käse m cheese
Kasino nt casino

KASSE cash desk / pay here

Kasserolle f casserole
Kassette f cassette ; cartridge ;
tape
Kassettenrecorder m cassette
player ; tape recorder
Kassierer(in) m/f cashier
Kastanie f chestnut
Katalog m catalogue
Kater m hangover
katholisch Catholic
Katze f cat
kaufen to buy
Kaufhaus nt department store
Kaugummi m chewing gum
Kaution f deposit
Kehle f throat

Keilriemen m fan belt
kein... no...
keine(r/s) no ; none
Keks(e) m biscuit(s) (sweet)
Keller m cellar
Kellner(in) m/f waiter/waitress
kennen to be acquainted with
Keramik f pottery
Kern m pip
Kerze f candle
Kette f chain
Kfz-Versicherung f car insurance
Kiefer f pine
Kiefer m jaw
Kilo(gramm) nt kilo(gram)
Kilometer m kilometre
Kind(er) nt child(ren)
Kinderbett nt cot
Kindermädchen nt nanny
Kindersitz m child seat (car)
Kinderstuhl m high chair
Kinderteller m child's helping
Kinderwagen m pram
Kinn nt chin
Kino nt cinema
Kiosk m kiosk
Kirche f church
Kirmes f funfair
Kirsche(n) f cherry (cherries)
Kissen nt cushion ; pillow
Kiste f box (wooden)
Klage f complaint
klar clear
Klarer m schnapps
Klärgrube f septic tank
Klasse f class ; grade
Klavier nt piano
Klebeband f adhesive tape
kleben to stick (with glue)
Klebstoff m glue
Kleid nt dress
Kleider pl clothes
Kleiderbügel m coat hanger
Kleiderschrank m wardrobe

klein little (small) ; short
Kleingeld nt change (money)
Klempner(in) m/f plumber
Klettband nt Velcro®
klettern to climb (mountains)
Klimaanlage f air-conditioning
klimatisiert air-conditioned
Klingel f doorbell
klingeln to ring (bell, phone)
Klinik f clinic
Klippe f cliff (along coast)
klopfen to knock (on door)
Kloß m dumpling
Kloster nt monastery ; convent
Kneipe f pub
Knie nt knee
Kniestrümpfe pl pop socks
Knoblauch m garlic
Knöchel m ankle
Knochen m bone
Knödel m dumpling
Knopf m button ; knob (radio, etc)
Knoten m knot
Koch m chef
kochen to boil ; to cook
Kocher m cooker ; stove
Köchin f cook
Kochschinken m cooked ham
Kochtopf m saucepan
Kode m code
Köder m bait (for fishing)
koffeinfreier Kaffee m decaf-
  feinated coffee
Koffer m suitcase ; trunk
Kofferanhänger m luggage tag
Kofferraum m carboot
Kognak m brandy
Kohl m cabbage
Kohle f coal
Kohlrübe f swede
Koje f berth (in ship) ; bunk
Kollege/Kollegin m/f colleague
Köln Cologne
Kölnischwasser nt cologne

k

komisch funny (amusing)
kommen to come
Kommode f chest of drawers
Komödie f comedy
Kompaß m compass
Komponist(in) m/f composer
Kondensmilch f condensed milk
Konditorei f cake shop ; café
Kondom nt condom
Konfektions- ready-made (clothes)
Konferenz f conference
Konfitüre f jam
König m king
Königin f queen
königlich royal
können to be able to ; to know how to
Konsulat nt consulate
Kontaktlinsen pl contact lenses
Kontaktlinsenreiniger m contact lens cleaner
Konto nt bank account
Kontrolle f check ; control
kontrollieren to check (passports, tickets)
Konzert nt concert
Konzertsaal m concert hall
Kopf m head
Kopfhörer pl headphones
Kopfkissen nt pillow
Kopfsalat m lettuce
Kopfschmerzen pl headache
Kopftuch nt scarf (headscarf)
Kopie f copy (duplicate)
kopieren to copy
Korb m basket
Korinthe f currant
Korken m cork (of bottle)
Korkenzieher m corkscrew
Körper m body
Körperpuder m talc
Kortison nt cortisone
Kosmetiksalon m beauty salon
Kosmetiktücher pl paper tissues

kosten to cost
Kosten pl cost (price)
kostenlos free (costing nothing)
köstlich delicious
Kostüm nt suit (woman's)
Krabbe f crab
Kräcker m cracker
Kraftstoff m fuel
Kragen m collar
Krämpfe pl cramps
krank ill ; sick

KRANKENHAUS hospital

Krankenkasse f medical insurance
Krankenwagen m ambulance
Krankheit f disease
Kräuter pl herbs
Kräutertee m herbal tea
Krawatte f tie
Krebs m crab (animal) ; cancer (illness)
Kreditkarte f credit card
Kreisverkehr m roundabout
Kreuz nt cross (also crucifix)
Kreuzfahrt f cruise
Kreuzschraubenzieher m Phillips screwdriver®
Kreuzung f junction ; crossroads
Kreuzworträtsel nt crossword
Krieg m war
Kristall nt crystal
Krone f crown
Krücken pl crutches
Krug m jug
Küche f kitchen ; cuisine
Kuchen m flan ; cake
Küchenbrett nt chopping board
Küchenpapier nt kitchen paper
Kugel f ball ; scoop (of ice cream)
Kugelschreiber m pen ; biro
Kuh f cow
kühl cool
Kühlbox f cool-box (for picnic)
kühlen to chill (wine, food)

Kühler m radiator (of car)
Kühlschrank m fridge
Kümmel m caraway seed ; cumin ; schnapps
Kunde/Kundin m/f client ; customer
Kunst f art
Kunstfaser f man-made fibre
Kunstgewerbearbeiten pl crafts
Kunsthalle f art gallery
Künstler(in) m/f artist
künstlich artificial ; man-made
künstliche Hüfte f hip replacement
Kupfer nt copper
Kupplung f clutch (of car)
Kurierdienst m courier service
Kurort m spa
Kurs m course ; exchange rate
Kurve f curve ; corner ; bend
kurz short ; brief
Kurz(zeit)parkplatz m short-stay car park
kurzsichtig short-sighted
Kurzwarengeschäft nt haberdasher's
Kuß m kiss
küssen to kiss
Küste f coast ; seaside
Küstenwache f coastguard

L

lächeln to smile
Lächeln nt smile
lachen to laugh
Lachs m salmon
Lack m varnish
Laden m shop ; store
Lagerhalle f warehouse
Lakritze f liquorice
Lamm nt lamb
Lampe f lamp
Land nt country (Italy, France, etc) ; land

landen to land
Landkarte f map (of country)
Landschaft f countryside
Landung f landing (of plane)
Landwein m table wine
lang long
Länge f length
Langlauf m cross-country skiing
langsam slow(ly)
langsamer werden to slow down
langweilig boring
Langzeitparkplatz m long-stay car park
Lappen m cloth (rag)
Laptop m laptop
Lärm m noise
lassen to let (allow)
Last f load
Laster m truck
Lastwagen m truck ; lorry
Lätzchen nt bib (baby's)
Lauch m leek
laufen to run
Laugenbrezel f soft pretzel
laut noisy ; loud(ly) ; aloud
läuten to ring (doorbell)
Lautsprecher m loudspeaker
Lautstärke f volume (of sound)
Lawine f avalanche
Lawinengefahr f danger of avalanches
leben to live (exist)
Lebensgefahr f danger to life
Lebensmittel pl groceries
Lebensmittelvergiftung f food poisoning
Lebensversicherung f life insurance
Leber f liver
Lebkuchen m gingerbread
Leck nt leak (of gas, liquid)
Lederwaren pl leather goods
ledig single (not married)
leer empty ; flat (battery) ; blank

Leerlauf *m* neutral *(gear)*

legen to lay

Lehrer(in) *m/f* teacher *(school)* ; instructor

leicht light *(not heavy)* ; easy

Leid *nt* grief
  es tut mir leid (I'm) sorry

leider unfortunately

leihen to rent *(car)* ; to lend

Leihgebühr *f* rental

Leinen *nt* linen *(cloth)*

leise quietly ; soft ; faint
  leiser stellen to turn down *(volume)*

Leiter *f* ladder

Leitung *f* telephone line

Lenker *m* handlebars

Lenkrad *nt* steering wheel

lernen to learn

lesbisch lesbian

lesen to read

letzte(r/s) last ; final

Leuchtturm *m* lighthouse

Leute *pl* people

Licht *nt* light
  das Licht anschalten to switch on lights

Lichtmaschine *f* dynamo

Lichtschalter *m* light switch

Lidschatten *m* eye shadow

liebe(r) dear *(in letter)*

Liebe *f* love

lieben to love

liebenswürdig kind

lieber rather

Lieblings- favourite

Lied *nt* song

Lieferwagen *m* van

Liegestuhl *m* deckchair

Liegewagen *m* couchette

Lift *m* elevator ; lift

Liftpaß *m* lift pass *(on ski slopes)*

Likör *m* liqueur

Limonade *f* lemonade

Limone *f* lime *(fruit)*

Lineal *nt* ruler

Linie *f* line *(row, of railway)*

Linienflug *m* scheduled flight

linke(r/s) left(-hand)

links to the left ; on the left

Linkshänder(in) *m/f* left-handed person

Linse *f* lens

Linsen *pl* lentils

Lippen *pl* lips

Lippenpflegestift *m* lip salve

Lippenstift *m* lipstick

Liste *f* list

Liter *m* litre

Loch *nt* hole

lochen to punch *(ticket, etc)*

locker loose *(screw, tooth)*

Löffel *m* spoon

Loge *f* box *(in theatre)*

Lohn *m* wage

Loipe *f* cross-country ski run

Lokal *nt* pub

Lorbeerblatt *nt* bayleaf

los loose
  was ist los? what's wrong?

Los *nt* lot *(at auction)* ; ticket *(lottery)*

lösen to buy *(ticket)*

löslich soluble

Lounge *f* lounge

Löwe *m* lion

Luft *f* air

Luftfilter *m* air filter

Luftfracht *f* air freight

Luftkissenboot *nt* hovercraft

Luftmatratze *f* air bed/mattress

Luftpost *f* air mail

Luftpumpe *f* pump *(bike/airmattress)*

Lüge *f* lie *(untruth)*

Lunge *f* lung

Lupe *f* magnifying glass

Lutscher *m* lollipop

Luxus *m* luxury

M

machen to make ; to do
Mädchen nt girl
Mädchenname m maiden name
Made f maggot
Magen m stomach
Magenschmerzen pl stomachache
Magentabletten pl indigestion tablets
Magenverstimmung f indigestion
Magermilch f skimmed milk
Magnet m magnet

Mais m sweetcorn
Make-up nt make-up
malen to paint
Malzbier nt malt beer
man one
managen to manage (be in charge)
manchmal sometimes
Mandarine f tangerine
Mandel f almond ; tonsil
Mandelentzündung f tonsillitis
Mangel m flaw
Mann m man ; husband
Männer pl men
männlich masculine ; male
Manschettenknöpfe pl cufflinks
Mantel m coat
Margarine f margarine
marineblau navy blue
mariniert marinated
Marke f brand (of product) ; token (for phone)
Markt m market
Marktplatz m market place
Marmelade f jam
Marmor m marble

Maschine f machine
maschineschreiben to type

Masern pl measles
Maßband nt tape measure
Maße pl measurements
Mast m mast
Material nt material
Matratze f mattress
Mauer f wall
Maus f mouse (animal/computer)
Maut f toll (motorway)
Mayonnaise f mayonnaise
Mechaniker(in) m/f mechanic
Medikament nt drug ; medicine
Medizin f medicine
Meer nt sea
Meeresfrüchte pl seafood
Mehl nt flour
mehr more
Mehrwertsteuer (MWST) f value-added tax
meiden to avoid (person)
Meile f mile
mein my
meiste(n) most
Meisterwerk nt masterpiece
melden to report (tell about)
Melone f melon ; bowler hat
Menge f crowd
Messe f fair (commercial) ; mass (church)
Messegelände nt exhibition centre
messen to measure
Messer nt knife
Messing nt brass
Metall nt metal
Meter m metre
Metro f metro (underground)
Metzgerei f butcher's
mich me (direct object)
Mietauto nt hire car
Miete f rent
mieten to hire ; to rent (house, etc)
Mietgebühr f rental (amount)
Mietvertrag m lease (rental)
Migräne f migraine

m

Mikrowelle f microwave oven
Milch f milk
Milchprodukte pl dairy produce
Milchpulver nt powdered milk
Millimeter m millimetre
Million f million
minderwertig low quality
Mindest- minimum
Mineralwasser nt mineral water
Minimum nt minimum
Minister(in) m/f minister (politics)
Minute(n) f minute(s)
Minze f mint (herb)
mir me (indirect object)
mischen to mix
Mißverständnis nt misunderstanding
mit with
Mitfahrgelegenheit f lift (in car)
Mitglied nt member (of club, etc)
mitnehmen to give a lift to
  zum Mitnehmen take-away (food)
Mittag m midday
Mittagessen nt lunch
Mitte f middle
Mitteilung f message
Mittel nt means
  ein Mittel gegen a remedy for
mittelalterlich medieval
Mittelmeer- Mediterranean
Mitternacht f midnight

MITTWOCH Wednesday

Mixer m blender ; mixer
Möbel pl furniture
Möbelpolitur f furniture polish
Mobiltelefon nt mobile phone
möbliert furnished
Modem nt modem
modern fashionable ; modern
mögen to enjoy (to like)
möglich possible
Mohn m poppy
Möhre(n) f carrot(s)

m

Mole f jetty
Monat m month
monatlich monthly
Mond m moon

MONTAG Monday

Moped nt moped
Morgen m morning ; tomorrow
morgen tomorrow
Morgendämmerung f dawn
Morgenmantel m dressing gown
Moschee f mosque
Moskitonetz nt mosquito net
Motor m motor ; engine
Motorboot nt motor boat
Motorhaube f bonnet (car)
Motorrad nt motorbike
Motte f moth (clothes)
Mountainbike nt mountain bike
Mücke f midge
müde tired
Müll m rubbish
Müllbeutel m bin liner
Mülleimer m bin (dustbin)
Mumps m mumps
München Munich
Mund m mouth
Mundwasser nt mouthwash
Münster nt cathedral
Münze(n) f coin(s)
Münzfernsprecher m payphone
Münztelefon nt payphone
Muscheln pl mussels
Museum nt museum
Musik f music
Muskat m nutmeg
Muskel m muscle
müssen to have to ; to must
mutig brave
Mutter f mother
Mütze f cap (hat)
MWST f VAT

N

nach after ; according to ; to *(with names of places)*
Nachbar(in) *m/f* neighbour
Nachmittag *m* afternoon
nachmittags pm ; in the afternoon
Nachname *m* surname
Nachricht *f* note *(letter)* ; message
Nachrichten *pl* news
Nachspeise *f* dessert ; pudding
nächste(r/s) next
Nacht *f* night
 über Nacht overnight
Nachtdienst *m* night duty *(chemist)*
Nachthemd *nt* nightdress
Nachtisch *m* dessert
Nachtklub *m* night club
nachzahlen to pay extra
nackt nude ; naked ; bare
Nadel *f* needle
Nagel *m* nail *(metal)*
Nagelbürste *f* nailbrush
Nagelfeile *f* nail file
Nagellack *m* nail polish/varnish
Nagellackentferner *m* nail polish remover
Nagelschere *f* nail scissors
Nähe *f* proximity
 in der Nähe nearby
nähen to sew
Name *m* name ; surname
Narkose *f* anaesthetic
Nase *f* nose
naß wet
national national
Nationalität *f* nationality
Natur- natural
Naturlehrpfad *m* nature trail
Naturschutzgebiet *nt* nature reserve
Nebel *m* mist ; fog
neben by *(next to)* ; beside
Nebenstraße *f* minor road

neblig foggy
Neffe *m* nephew
Negativ *nt* negative *(photo)*
nehmen to catch *(bus, train)* ; to take *(remove)*
nein no
Nektarine *f* nectarine
Nelke *f* carnation
nennen to quote *(price)*
Nervenzusammenbruch *m* nervous breakdown
Nest *nt* nest
nett nice *(person)* ; kind
Netto- net *(income, price)*
Netz *nt* net ; network
neu new
neueste(r/s) newest ; latest
Neujahr(stag) *m* New Year's Day
Neuseeland *nt* New Zealand
nicht not ; non-
Nichte *f* niece

NICHTRAUCHER no smoking

nichts nothing
nie never
Niederlande *pl* Netherlands
niedrig low
Niedrigwasser *nt* low tide
niemand no one ; nobody
Niere(n) *f* kidney(s)
niesen to sneeze
nirgends nowhere
noch still *(up to this time)* ; yet
noch ein(e) extra *(more)* ; another
Norden *m* north
Nordirland *nt* Northern Ireland
nördlich north ; northern
Nordsee *f* North Sea
Normal(benzin) *nt* regular *(petrol)*
Normal- standard *(size)*
Notarzt *m* emergency doctor
Notaufnahme *f* accident & emergency dept

NOTAUSGANG emergency exit

n

Notdienstapotheke f on-duty chemist
Notfall m emergency
notieren to make a note of
nötig necessary
Notizblock m note pad
Notruf m emergency number
Notrufsäule f emergency phone (on motorway)
Notsignal nt distress signal
notwendig essential ; necessary

NOVEMBER November

nüchtern sober
Nudeln pl pasta ; noodles
Null f nil ; zero ; nought
numerieren to number
Nummer f number ; act
Nummernschild nt numberplate
nur only
Nürnberg Nuremberg
Nuß (Nüsse) f nut(s)
n **nützlich** useful

O

oben upstairs ; above ; this side up
oben auf on top of...
Oberschenkel m thigh
obligatorisch compulsory
Obst nt fruit
Obstkuchen m fruit tart
oder or
offen open
  offene Weine pl wine served by the glass
öffentlich public
öffnen to open ; to undo
Öffnungszeiten pl business hours
oft often
o **ohne** without
ohnmächtig fainted
ohnmächtig werden to faint
Ohr(en) nt ear(s)
Ohrenschmerzen pl earache

Ohrringe pl earrings
okay OK
ökonomisch economic

OKTOBER October

Öl nt oil
Ölfilter m oil filter
Olive f olive
Olivenöl nt olive oil
Ölstandsanzeiger m oil gauge
Ölwechsel m oil change
Omelett nt omelette
Onkel m uncle
Oper f opera
Operation f operation (surgical)
Optiker m optician's
orange orange (colour)
Orange f orange (fruit)
Orangensaft m orange juice
Orchester nt orchestra
Ordner m file (for papers)
Oregano m oregano
organisch organic
organisieren to organize
Organspenderausweis m donor card
Ort m place
  an Ort und Stelle on the spot
örtlich local
örtliche Betäubung f local anaesthetic
Ortschaft f village ; town
Ortsgespräch nt local call
Ortszeit f local time
Osten m east
Osterei nt Easter egg
Ostermontag m Easter Monday
Ostern nt Easter
Österreich nt Austria
Österreicher(in) m/f Austrian
österreichisch adj Austrian
Ostersonntag m Easter Sunday
östlich eastern
Ozean m ocean

P

Paar nt pair ; couple (persons)
ein paar a couple of (a few)
packen to pack (luggage)
Paket nt parcel ; packet
Palast m palace
Pampelmuse(n) f grapefruit(s)
Panne f breakdown (of car)
Papier(e) nt paper(s)
Papiertaschentücher pl tissues (Kleenex®)
Pappe f cardboard
Paprikaschote f pepper (vegetable)
Parfüm nt perfume
Parfümerie f perfumery
Park m park
parken to park

PARKEN VERBOTEN no parking

Parkett nt stalls (in theatre)
Parkhaus nt multi-storey car park
Parkkralle f wheel clamp
Parkplatz m car park
Parkscheibe f parking disk
Parkschein m parking ticket (to display)
Parkuhr f parking meter
Parkverbot nt no parking zone
Partei f political party
Partner(in) m/f partner (boy/girl-friend)
Party f party (celebration)
Paß m passport ; pass (in mountains)
Paß geschlossen pass closed
Passagier m passenger
passen to fit
passieren to happen

PAßKONTROLLE passport control

Paßnummer f passport number
Patient(in) m/f patient (in hospital)
Pauschalreise f package tour
Pauschaltarif m flat-rate tariff

Pause f pause ; interval
keine Pausen no intervals
Pelz m fur
Pelzmantel m fur coat
Pendelverkehr m shuttle (service)
Penis m penis
Penizillin nt penicillin
Pension f boarding house
pensioniert retired
per via ; by
per Expreß by express mail
per Post by post
perfekt perfect
Periode f period (menstruation)
Perlen pl pearls
perlend sparkling
Person f person
Personal nt staff
Personalausweis m identity card
Personalien pl particulars
persönlich personal(ly)
Perücke f wig
Pessar nt cap (diaphragm)
Petersilie f parsley
Pfannkuchen m pancake
Pfarrer(in) m/f church minister
Pfeffer m pepper (spice)
Pfefferkuchen m gingerbread
Pfefferminzbonbon nt mint (sweet)
Pfefferminztee m mint tea
Pfeife f pipe (smoker's)
Pferd nt horse
Pferderennen nt horse-racing
Pfirsich(e) m peach(es)
Pflanze f plant (green)
Pflaster nt plaster (for cut)
Pflaume(n) f plum(s)
Pforte f gate
Pfund nt pound
Pfund Sterling nt sterling (pound)
Picknick nt picnic
Picknickdecke f picnic rug
Pier m jetty ; pier

p

pikant savoury
Pille f pill
Pilot(in) m/f pilot
Pils/Pilsner nt lager
Pilz(e) m mushroom(s)
Pilzkrankheit f thrush (candida)
Pinzette f tweezers
Pistazie f pistachio
Piste f runway ; ski run
Pizza f pizza
planmäßig scheduled
Planschbecken nt paddling pool
Plastik- plastic (made of)
Plastikbeutel m plastic bag
Platte f plate ; dish ; record
Platz m seat ; space ; square (in town) ; court
Plätzchen nt biscuit(s)
Platzkarte f seat reservation (ticket)
Plombe f filling (in tooth)
plötzlich suddenly
pochiert poached (egg, fish)

p

Polizeirevier nt police station
Polizeiwache f police station
Polizist(in) m/f policeman/woman
Pommes frites pl chips (french fries)
Pony nt pony
Ponyreiten nt pony trekking
Porree m leek
Portier m porter (for door)
Portion f portion
Portrait nt portrait
Portugal nt Portugal
Portugiese/Portugiesin m/f Portuguese
portugiesisch Portuguese adj
Post f post ; post office
Post- postal
Postamt nt post office
Postanweisung f money order
Poster nt poster
Postkarte f postcard

postlagernd poste restante
Postleitzahl f postcode
praktisch handy ; practical
Pralinen pl chocolates
Präservativ nt condom
Praxis f doctor's surgery
Preis m prize ; price
Preisliste f price list
Priester m priest
Prinz m prince
Prinzessin f princess
privat private
Privatstrand m private beach
Privatweg m private road
pro per
  pro Stunde per hour
  pro Kopf per person
  pro Jahr per annum
probieren to taste ; to sample
Problem nt problem
Programm nt programme
Programmierer(in) m/f computer programmer
prost! cheers!
protestantisch Protestant
provisorisch temporary
Prozent nt per cent
prüfen to check (oil, water, etc)
Prüfung f exam (school, university)
Publikum nt audience
Puderzucker m icing sugar
Pullover m sweater ; jumper
Pulver nt powder
  pulverförmig in powder form
Pulverkaffee m instant coffee
pünktlich on schedule ; punctual
Puppe f doll ; puppet
Puppenspiel nt puppet show
pur straight (drink)
Pute f turkey
Pyjama m pyjamas

Q

Qualität f quality

170

Qualitätswein m good quality wine
Qualle f jellyfish
Quantität f quantity
Quarantäne f quarantine
Quelle f spring (of water) ; source
quetschen to squeeze
Quetschung f bruise
Quittung f receipt
Quiz nt quiz show

R

Rabatt m discount
Rad nt wheel ; bicycle
radfahren to cycle
Radfahrer(in) m/f cyclist
Radiergummi m rubber (eraser)
Radieschen pl radishes
Radio nt radio

RADWEG cycle track

Rahmen m frame (picture)
Rand m verge ; border ; edge
Randstein m kerb
Rang m circle (in theatre) ; rank
Rasen m lawn
Rasierapparat m shaver ; razor
Rasiercreme f shaving cream
rasieren to shave
Rasierklinge f razor blade
Rasierschaum m shaving foam
Rasierwasser nt aftershave (lotion)
Rasthof m service area; travel inn
Rastplatz m picnic area
Raststätte f service area
raten to advise
Rathaus nt town hall
Rauch m smoke
rauchen to smoke

RAUCHEN VERBOTEN no smoking

Raucher(in) m/f smoker (person)
rauh rough
Raum m space (room)

rechnen to calculate
Rechnung f bill (account) ; invoice
rechte(r/s) right (not left)
rechts to the right ; on the right
Rechtsanwalt m lawyer ; solicitor
Rechtsanwältin f lawyer ; solicitor
reden to speak
reduzieren to reduce
Reformhaus nt health food shop
Regal nt shelf
Regen m rain
Regenmantel m raincoat
Regenschirm m umbrella
regnen to rain
Reibe f grater (for cheese, etc)
reich rich (person)
Reich nt empire
reichhaltig rich (food)
reif ripe ; mature (cheese)
Reifen m tyre
Reifendruck m tyre pressure
Reifenpanne f flat tyre
Reihe f row (line) ; tier
rein pure
reinigen to clean
Reinigung f dry-cleaner's
Reis m rice
Reise f trip (journey)
  gute Reise! have a good trip!

REISEBÜRO travel agency

Reiseführer m guidebook
Reiseführer(in) m/f tour guide
Reisegruppe f party (of tourists)
Reisekrankheit f travel sickness
reisen to travel
Reisepapiere pl travel documents
Reisepaß m passport
Reisescheck m traveller's cheque
Reiseveranstalter m tour operator
Reiseziel nt destination
Reißverschluß m zip
reiten to ride (horse)
Reiten nt riding

r

Rennbahn f racecourse
rennen to run
Rennen nt race (sport)
Rentner(in) m/f pensioner ; senior citizen
Reparatur f repair
Reparaturwerkstatt f car repairs
reparieren to repair ; to mend
reservieren to book ; to reserve
reserviert reserved
Reservierung f booking (in hotel)
Reservierungen pl reservations
Restaurant nt restaurant
Restgeld nt change (money)
retten to rescue ; to save (person)
Rettungsboot nt lifeboat
Rettungsinsel f life raft
Rettungsring m lifebelt
Rettungsschwimmer(in) m/f lifeguard
Rezept nt prescription ; recipe
R-Gespräch nt reverse charge call

r

Rhein m Rhine
Rheinfahrten pl Rhine cruises
Rheumatismus m rheumatism
Richter(in) m/f judge
richtig correct ; right ; proper
Richtung f direction
riechen to smell
Rinderbraten m roast beef
Rindfleisch nt beef
Ring m ring
Ringstraße f ring road
Riß m tear (in material)
Rock m skirt
Roggenbrot nt rye bread
roh raw
Rohr nt pipe (drain, etc)
Rollo nt blind (for window)

r

Rollschuhe pl roller skates
Rollstuhl m wheelchair
Rolltreppe f escalator
Roman m novel
romanisch Romanesque

Röntgenaufnahme f X-ray
rosa pink
Rose f rose (flower)
Rosenkohl m Brussels sprouts
Rosenmontag m carnival (Monday before Shrove Tuesday)
Roséwein m rosé wine
Rosine(n) f raisin(s)
Rost m rust ; grill
Rost- roast
Rostbraten m roast
rosten to rust
rostfreier Stahl m stainless steel
rostig rusty
Röstkartoffeln pl sautéed potatoes
rot red
rote Bete f beetroot
Röteln pl German measles ; rubella
rote Johannisbeeren pl redcurrants
Rotwein m red wine
Rücken m back (of body, hand)
Rückerstattung f refund
Rückfahrkarte f return ticket
Rückfahrt f return journey
Rückflugticket nt return airticket
Rückgrat nt spine
Rücklicht nt rear light
Rucksack m rucksack
Rückspiegel m rearview mirror
rückwärts backwards
rückwärts fahren to reverse (car)
Rückwärtsgang m reverse (gear)
Ruder nt rudder ; oar
Ruderboot nt rowing boat
rudern to row (boat)
rufen to shout
Rufnummer f telephone number
Ruhe f rest (repose) ; peace (calm)
  Ruhe! be quiet!
ruhen to rest
ruhig calm ; quiet(ly) ; peaceful
Rührei nt scrambled egg

172

Ruine f ruin (castle, etc)
rund round
Rundfahrt f tour ; round trip
Rundreise f round trip
Rundwanderweg m circular trail for ramblers
Rutschbahn f slide (chute)
rutschen to slip
rutschig slippery

S

Saal m hall (room)
Sache f thing
Sachen pl stuff (things) ; belongings
Sackgasse f no through road
Safe m safe (for valuables)
Saft m juice
sagen to say ; to tell (fact, news)
Sahne f cream (dairy)
  mit Sahne with whipped cream
Saison f season
Salat m salad
Salatsoße f salad dressing
Salbe f ointment
Salz nt salt
Salzkartoffeln pl boiled potatoes
Salzwasser nt salt water

SAMSTAG Saturday

Sand m sand
Sandalen pl sandals
Sandstrand m sandy beach
Satellitenfernsehen nt satellite TV
satt full
Sattel m saddle
Satteltaschen pl panniers (for bike)
Satz m set (collection) ; sentence
sauber clean
säubern to clean
sauer sour
Sauerkraut nt sauerkraut
Sauerstoff m oxygen
Sauger m teat (on bottle)

Säule f petrol pump
Saum m hem
Sauna f sauna
Säure f acid
saure Sahne f soured cream
S-Bahn f suburban railway
Schach nt chess
Schaden m damage
schädlich harmful
Schaf nt sheep
Schaffner(in) m/f conductor (bus, train) ; guard
Schale f shell (egg, nut) ; dish
schälen to peel (fruit)
Schallplatte f record (music)
Schalter m switch
Schaltgetriebe nt manual (gear change)
Schaltknüppel m gear lever ; gearshift
Schaltuhr f timer
scharf hot (spicy) ; sharp
Schatten m shade
schätzen to value ; to estimate
Schauer m rain shower
Schaufel und Handfeger dustpan and brush
Schaufenster nt shop window
Schaukel f swing (for children)
Schaum m foam
Schaumbad nt bubble bath
Schaumfestiger m hair mousse
Schaumwein m sparkling wine
Schauspiel nt play
Schauspieler(in) m/f actor/actress
Scheck m cheque
Scheckbuch nt cheque book
Scheckkarte f cheque card
Scheibe f slice
Scheibenputzmittel nt screenwash
Scheibenwischer pl windscreen wipers
Schein(e) m banknote(s) ; certificate(s)
scheinen to shine (sun, etc) ; to

s seem

Scheinwerfer m headlight ; flood-
light ; spotlight
  Scheinwerfer anschalten switch
  on headlights

Schere f scissors *(pair of)*

scherzen to joke

Scheuerlappen m floorcloth

Scheune f barn

Schi- see Ski-

schicken to send

schießen to shoot

Schiff nt ship

Schild nt sign *(notice)* ; label

Schinken m ham

Schirm m umbrella ; screen

Schlachterei f butcher's

schlafen to sleep

Schlafsack m sleeping bag

Schlaftablette f sleeping pill

Schlafwagen m sleeping car *(on
train)*

s **Schlafzimmer** nt bedroom

Schlag m shock *(electric)*

Schlaganfall m stroke *(medical)*

schlagen to hit

Schläger m racket *(tennis, etc)*

Schlagloch nt pothole

Schlagsahne f whipped cream

Schlange f queue ; snake

Schlangenbiß m snake bite

Schlauch m hosepipe ; inner tube

Schlauchboot nt dinghy *(rubber)*

schlecht bad ; badly

Schlepplift m ski tow

schließen to shut ; to close

Schließfach nt locker *(luggage)*

schlimm serious

Schlitten m sleigh ; sledge

Schlittschuh laufen to ice skate

s **Schlittschuh(e)** m ice skate(s)

Schlittschuhbahn f ice rink

Schloß nt castle ; lock *(on door, etc)*

Schluß m end

Schlüssel m key

Schlüsselbein nt collar bone

Schlüsselkarte f cardkey *(for hotel)*

Schlüsselring m keyring

Schlußlichter pl rear lights

SCHLUßVERKAUF sale

schmecken to taste

schmelzen to melt

Schmerz m pain ; ache

schmerzhaft painful

Schmerzmittel nt painkiller

Schmerztablette f paracetamol®

Schmuck m jewellery ; decorations

schmutzig dirty

Schnaps m schnapps ; spirits

schnarchen to snore

Schnee m snow

Schneebrille f snow goggles

Schneeketten pl snow chains

Schneepflug m snowplough

schneiden to cut

schnell fast ; quick

Schnellboot nt speedboat

Schnellimbiß m snack bar

Schnellzug m express *(train)*

Schnittbohnen pl green beans

Schnittlauch m chives

Schnittwunde f cut

Schnorchel m snorkel

Schnuller m dummy *(for baby)*

Schnur f string

Schnurrbart m moustache

Schnürschuhe pl boots *(ankle)*

Schnürsenkel pl shoelaces

Schokolade f chocolate

schön lovely ; fine ; beautiful ;
good *(pleasant)*

Schornstein m chimney

Schotte/Schottin m/f Scot

schottisch Scottish

Schottland nt Scotland

Schrank m cupboard

Schraube f screw

Schraubenmutter f nut *(for bolt)*

Schraubenschlüssel m spanner
Schraubenzieher m screwdriver
schrecklich awful
schreiben to write
Schreibmaschine f typewriter
Schreibtisch m desk
Schreibwarenhandlung f stationer's
schriftlich in writing
Schritt m pace ; step
  Schritt fahren! dead slow
Schublade f drawer
Schuh(e) m shoe(s)
Schuhcreme f shoe polish
Schuhgeschäft nt shoe shop
Schuhputzmittel nt shoe polish
schulden to owe
Schulden pl debts
Schule f school
Schulter f shoulder
Schuppen pl scales (of fish) ; dandruff
Schürze f apron
Schüssel f bowl (for soup, etc)
Schuster m shoe mender's
Schutzhelm m helmet (for bike)
Schutzimpfung f vaccination
schwach weak
Schwager m brother-in-law
Schwägerin f sister-in-law
Schwamm m sponge
schwanger pregnant
schwarz black
Schwarzbrot nt brown bread
schwarze Johannisbeeren pl blackcurrants
Schwarzweißfilm m black and white film
Schwein nt pig
Schweinefleisch nt pork
Schweiß m sweat
Schweiz f Switzerland
Schweizer(in) m/f Swiss
schweizerisch Swiss adj
Schwellung f swelling
schwer heavy

Schwester f sister ; nurse ; nun
Schwiegermutter f mother-in-law
Schwiegersohn m son-in-law
Schwiegertochter f daughter-in-law
Schwiegervater m father-in-law
schwierig hard (difficult)
Schwimmbad nt swimming pool
schwimmen to swim
Schwimmflossen pl flippers
Schwimmweste f life jacket
schwindelig dizzy
schwitzen to sweat
See f sea
See m lake
seekrank seasick
Segel nt sail
Segelboot nt sailing boat
segeln to sail
sehen to see
Sehenswürdigkeit f sight
Sehne f tendon
sehr very
seicht shallow (water)
Seide f silk
Seife f soap
Seil nt rope
Seilbahn f cable railway ; funicular
sein(e) his
sein to be see GRAMMAR
seit since
Seite f page ; side
Seitenspiegel m wing mirror
Seitenstraße f side street
Seitenstreifen m hard shoulder
Sekretär(in) m/f secretary
Sekt m sparkling wine
Sekunde f second (time)
Selbstbedienung f self-service
selten rare (unique)
seltsam strange (odd)
Senf m mustard

SEPTEMBER September

S

servieren to serve *(food)*
Serviette *f* napkin
Servolenkung *f* power steering
Sessel *m* armchair
Sessellift *m* chairlift
setzen to place ; to put
  sich setzen to sit down
  setzen Sie sich bitte please
  take a seat
Sex *m* sex *(intercourse)*
Shampoo *nt* shampoo
Shorts *pl* shorts
sicher sure ; safe ; definite
Sicherheit *f* safety
Sicherheitsgurt *m* seatbelt ;
  safety belt
Sicherheitsnadel *f* safety pin
Sicherung *f* fuse
Sicherungskasten *m* fuse box
sie she ; they
Sie you *(polite sing. and pl.)*
Sieb *nt* sieve ; colander
Silber *nt* silver
Silvester *m* New Year's Eve
singen to sing
Sitz *m* seat
sitzen to sit
Ski(er) *m* ski(s)
  Ski fahren to ski
Skianzug *m* ski suit
Skihose *f* ski pants
Skijacke *f* ski jacket
Skilanglauf *m* cross-country skiing
Skilaufen *nt* skiing
Skilehrer(in) *m/f* ski instructor
Skilift *m* ski lift
Skipaß *m* ski pass
Skipiste *f* ski run
Skistiefel *pl* ski boots
Skistock *m* ski stick/pole
Skiverleih *m* ski hire
Slip *m* knickers ; underpants
Slipeinlage *f* panty liner
Snack *m* snack
Snowboard *nt* snow board

Socken *pl* socks
Soda *nt* soda water
Sodbrennen *nt* heartburn
Sofa *nt* sofa
Sofabett *nt* sofa bed
sofort at once ; immediately
Software *f* computer software
Sohle *f* sole *(of shoe)*
Sohn *m* son
Sojabohnen *pl* soya beans
Sojamilch *f* soya milk
Sommer *m* summer
Sommerfahrplan *m* summer rail-
  way timetable
Sommerferien *pl* summer holidays
Sonder- special
sonn- und feiertags on Sundays
  and public holidays
Sonne *f* sun
Sonnenaufgang *m* sunrise
sonnenbaden to sunbathe
Sonnenbrand *m* sunburn *(painful)*
Sonnenbräune *f* suntan
Sonnenbrille *f* sunglasses
Sonnencreme *f* sunblock
Sonnendach *nt* sunroof *(car)*
Sonnenöl *nt* suntan oil
Sonnenschirm *m* sun umbrella ;
  sunshade
Sonnenstich *m* sunstroke
Sonnenuntergang *m* sunset
sonnig sunny

SONNTAG Sunday

Sonntagsdienst *m* Sunday duty
  (chemist, doctor)
sorgen für to look after ; to take
  care of
Soße *f* dressing *(for food)* ; sauce
Souterrain *nt* basement
Souvenir *nt* souvenir
Spanien *nt* Spain
Spanier(in) *m/f* Spaniard
spanisch Spanish *adj*
Spannung *f* voltage

sparen to save *(money)*
Spargel m asparagus
Sparpreis m economy fare
Spaß m fun ; joke
spät late
Spaten m spade
Spätvorstellung f late show
Spaziergang m stroll ; walk
Speck m bacon
Speise f dish ; food
Speiseeis nt ice cream
Speisekarte f menu
Speisewagen m dining car
Spesen pl expenses
Spezialität f speciality
Spiegel m mirror
Spiegelei nt fried egg
Spiel nt game ; pack *(of cards)*
Spielbank f casino
spielen to gamble ; to play
Spielkarte f card *(playing)*
Spielplatz m playground
Spielzeug nt toy
Spielzeugladen m toy shop
Spielzimmer nt playroom
Spinat m spinach
Spirale f coil *(IUD); spiral*
Spirituosen pl spirits *(alcohol)*
Spitze f lace ; point *(tip)*
Splitter m splinter
Sportartikel pl sports equipment
Sportgeschäft nt sports shop
Sporttauchen nt scuba diving
Sprache f speech ; language
Sprachführer m phrase book
Spraydose f aerosol
sprechen to speak
  sprechen mit to talk to
springen to jump
Spritze f injection ; hypodermic needle
sprudelnd fizzy
Sprudelwasser nt sparkling water
Sprungschanze f ski jump

Spülbecken nt sink *(kitchen)*
spülen to flush toilet ; to rinse
Spülkasten m cistern *(of toilet)*
Spülmittel nt washing-up liquid
Spur f lane *(of motorway/main road)*
Staatsangehörigkeit f nationality
Stachel m sting
Stadion nt stadium
Stadt f town ; city
Stadtführung f guided tour of the town
Stadtmitte f city centre
Stadtplan m map *(of town)*

STADTZENTRUM town/city centre

Stahl m steel
Stand m stall ; taxi rank
ständig permanent(ly) ; continuous(ly)
Standlicht nt sidelight
stark strong
Starthilfekabel nt jump leads
Station f station ; stop ; hospital ward
statt instead of
stattfinden to take place
Statue f statue
Stau m traffic jam
Staub m dust
Staubsauger m vacuum cleaner
Staubtuch nt duster
stechen to bite *(insect)*
Stechmücke f mosquito ; gnat
Steckdose f socket *(electrical)*
Stecker m plug *(electric)*
stehen to stand
stehlen to steal
steil steep
Stein m stone
Stelle f job ; place; point *(in space)*
stellen to set *(alarm)* ; to put
stempeln to stamp *(visa)*
Steppdecke f quilt
sterben to die

S

S

Stereoanlage f stereo
Stern m star
Steuer f tax
Steuerung f controls
Steward/Stewardeß m/f steward/stewardess
Stich m bite (by insect) ; stitch (sewing) ; sting
Stiefel pl boots (long)
Stiefmutter f stepmother
Stiefvater m stepfather
Stil m style
still still (motionless)
stilles Wasser nt still water
Stimme f voice
stimmt so! keep the change!
Stirn f forehead
Stock m cane (walking stick) ; stick ; floor
Stockwerk nt storey
Stoff m cloth (fabric)
Stoppschild nt stop (sign)
Stöpsel m plug (in sink)
stören to disturb (interrupt)

BITTE NICHT STÖREN do not disturb

stornieren to cancel
Stornierung f cancellation
Störung f hold-up ; fault ; disorder (medical)
Stoßdämpfer m shock absorber
stoßen to knock ; to push
Stoßstange f bumper (on car)
Stoßzeit f rush hour
Strafe f punishment ; fine
Strafzettel m parking ticket (fine)
Strand m beach
Strandkorb m wicker beach chair with a hood ; beach hut
Straße f road ; street
  Straße gesperrt road closed
Straßenarbeiten pl roadworks
Straßenbahn f tram
Straßenkarte f road map

Streichhölzer pl matches
Streifenkarte f multiple journey travelcard
Streik m strike (industrial)
streiten to quarrel
Streß m stress
stricken to knit
Strickjacke f cardigan
Stricknadel f knitting needle
Strohhalm m straw (for drinking)
Strom m current ; electricity
Stromanschluß m electric point
Strömung f current (water)
Stromzähler m electricity meter
Strümpfe pl stockings
Strumpfhose f tights
Stück nt bit ; piece ; cut (of meat) ; play (theatre)
Student(in) m/f student m/f
Studentenermäßigung f student discount
Stufe f step (stair)
Stuhl m chair
stumpf blunt (knife, blade)
Stunde f hour ; lesson
Sturm m storm
Sturzhelm m crash helmet
suchen to look for
Süden m south
südlich southern
Summe f sum (total amount)
Sumpf m marsh
Super(benzin) nt four-star petrol
Supermarkt m supermarket
Suppe f soup
Surfbrett nt surfboard
surfen to surf
süß sweet
Süßigkeiten pl sweets
Süßstoff m sweetener ; saccharin
Süßwaren pl confectionery
Synagoge f synagogue
Szene f scene

T

Tabak m tobacco
Tabakwarenhandlung f tobacconist's
Tablett nt tray
Tablette(n) f tablet(s) ; pill(s)
Tachometer nt speedometer
Tafel f table ; board ; bar of chocolate
Tafelwein m table wine
Tag m day
  jeden Tag every day
Tageskarte f day ticket ; menu of the day
Tagespauschale f daily unlimited rate (for rented car)
Tagessuppe f soup of the day
täglich daily
Taille f waist
Tal nt valley
Tampons pl tampons
Tank m fuel/petrol tank
Tankanzeige f fuel gauge
Tankdeckel m petrol cap
Tanksäule f petrol pump
Tankstelle f petrol station
Tanne f fir
Tante f aunt
Tanz m dance
tanzen to dance
Tarif m rate ; tariff
Tasche f pocket ; bag
Taschenbuch nt paperback
Taschendieb m pickpocket
Taschenlampe f torch ; flashlight
Taschenmesser nt penknife
Taschenrechner m calculator
Taschentuch nt handkerchief
Tasse f cup
Taste f button ; key (on keyboard)

TASTE DRÜCKEN push button

taub deaf

Taube f pigeon
tauchen to dive
Tauchen nt diving
Taucheranzug m wetsuit
Taucherbrille f goggles (swimming)
tauschen to exchange
tausend thousand
Taxi nt taxi ; cab
Taxifahrer(in) m/f taxi driver
Taxistand m taxi rank
Tee m tea
Teebeutel m tea bag
Teekanne f teapot
Teelöffel m teaspoon
Teig m pastry
Teil nt part
teilen to divide ; to share
Teilkaskoversicherung f third party, fire and theft
Telefon nt telephone
Telefonauskunft f directory enquiries
Telefonbuch nt phone directory
telefonieren to telephone
Telefonkarte f phonecard
Telefonnummer f phone number
Telefonzelle f phonebox
Telegramm nt telegram
Teller m plate
Tempel m temple
Temperatur f temperature
Tennis nt tennis
Tennisplatz m tennis court
Tennisschläger m tennis racket
Teppich m rug
Teppichboden m fitted carpet
Termin m date ; deadline ; appointment
Terminal nt terminal (airport)
Terminkalender m diary ; Filofax®
Terminplaner m personal organizer
Terrasse f patio ; terrace (of café)
Terrorist(in) m/f terrorist
Tesafilm® m Sellotape®

teuer dear *(expensive)*
Theater *nt* theatre
Theke *f* counter *(in shop, bar, etc)*
Thermometer *nt* thermometer
Thermosflasche *f* flask *(thermos)*
Thunfisch *m* tuna
Thymian *m* thyme
tief deep ; low *(in pitch)*
Tiefkühltruhe *f* deep freeze ; freezer
Tier *nt* animal
Tierarzt/Tierärztin *m/f* vet
Tinte *f* ink
Tintenfisch *m* octopus ; squid
Tisch *m* table
Tischdecke *f* tablecloth
Tischler(in) *m/f* carpenter
Tischtennis *nt* table tennis
Tischwein *m* table wine
Toastbrot *nt* sliced white bread for toasting
Tochter *f* daughter
Toilette *f* toilet ; lavatory
Toilettenartikel *pl* toiletries
Toilettenbürste *f* toilet brush
Toilettenpapier *nt* toilet paper
Tollwut *f* rabies
Tomate *f* tomato
Tomatenpüree *nt* tomato purée
Tomatensaft *m* tomato juice
Tomatensoße *f* tomato sauce
Ton *m* sound ; tone ; clay
Tönung *f* hair dye
Töpferwaren *pl* pottery
Tor *nt* gate ; goal *(sport)*
Törtchen *nt* cake *(small)*
Torte *f* gâteau ; tart
tot dead
töten to kill
Tourist(in) *m/f* tourist
Touristen-Information *f* tourist information
Touristenkarte *f* tourist ticket
Touristenklasse *f* economy class

Touristenroute *f* tourist route
Touristenticket *nt* tourist ticket
tragbar portable
tragen to carry ; to wear
Tragflügelboot *nt* hydrofoil
Trainingsschuhe *pl* trainers
trampen to hitchhike
Trauben *pl* grapes
traurig sad
Treffen *nt* meeting
treffen to meet *(by chance)*
Treppe *f* stairs
Tresor *m* safe
Tretboot *nt* pedalo
trinken to drink
Trinkgeld *nt* tip *(for waiter, etc)*

TRINKWASSER drinking water

trocken dry ; stale *(bread)*
Trockenmilch *f* powdered milk
Trockenobst *nt* dried fruit
trocknen to dry
Truthahn *m* turkey
tschüs cheerio ; bye
T-shirt *nt* T-shirt
Tuch *nt* cloth ; scarf ; towel ; shawl
tun to do ; to put
 das tut nichts that doesn't matter
Tunnel *m* tunnel
Tür *f* door
türkis turquoise *(colour)*
Turm *m* tower
Turnschuhe *pl* gym shoes
typisch typical

U

u.A.w.g. RSVP
U-Bahn *f* metro ; underground
übel sick *(nauseous)*; bad
über over ; above ; about ; via
überall everywhere
überbuchen to overbook

Überfahrt f crossing (sea)
Überfall m mugging
überfällig overdue
überfüllt crowded (train, shop, etc)
übergeben to hand over ; to present (give)
  sich übergeben to vomit
Übergewicht nt excess baggage
überhitzen to overheat
überholen to overtake
Überholverbot nt no overtaking
Übernachtung mit Frühstück bed and breakfast
überprüfen to check (to examine)
Überschwemmung f flash flood
übersetzen to translate
Übersetzung f translation
überweisen to transfer (money)
Überzelt nt fly sheet
Überzieher m overcoat
übrig left over ; extra (spare)
Ufer nt bank (of river) ; shore
Uhr f clock ; watch
Uhrarmband nt watch strap
Uhrmacher m watchmaker's
um around
  um 4 Uhr at 4 o'clock
umdrehen to turn around
umgeben von surrounded by
Umgehungsstraße f ring road; bypass (road)
Umkleidekabine f changing room (at swimming pool, in shop)

UMLEITUNG diversion

Umschlag m envelope
umsonst free (costing nothing)
umsteigen to change
umstoßen to knock over (object)
Umweg m detour
Umwelt f environment
unbefugt unauthorized

UNBEFUGTEN ZUTRITT VERBOTEN no entry to unauthorized persons

unbegrenzt unlimited
und and
Unfall m accident

UNFALLSTATION casualty dept

ungefähr approximately
ungefährlich safe (not dangerous)
ungerade odd (number)
ungewöhnlich unusual
Unglück nt accident
ungültig invalid
ungültig werden to expire (ticket, passport)
Universität f university
unmöglich impossible ; unsafe
uns us
unser(e) our
unsicher uncertain (fact)
unten downstairs ; below
  nach unten downward(s) ; downstairs
unter under(neath)
unter Wasser underwater
unterbrechen to interrupt
Unterbrecher m circuit breaker
Unterbrecherkontakte pl points (in car)
untere(r/s) lower ; bottom
Unterführung f subway ; underpass (for pedestrians)
Unterhemd nt vest
Unterhose f underpants
Unterkunft f accommodation
unterrichten to teach
Unterrichtsstunde f lesson
unterschreiben to sign
Unterschrift f signature
Untersuchung f test ; examination (medical)
Untertasse f saucer
Untertitel pl subtitles
Unterwäsche f underwear ; lingerie
unwohl unwell
Urin m urine

u

u

Urlaub m leave ; holiday
  auf Urlaub on holiday ; on leave
Urlaubsgebiet nt resort (holiday)
Ursprungsland nt country of origin
USA pl USA

V

Vagina f vagina
Vanille f vanilla
Vanilleeis nt vanilla ice cream
Vanillesoße f custard
Vase f vase
Vater m father
Vegetarier(in) m/f vegetarian
vegetarisch vegetarian
Veilchen nt violet (flower)
Ventil nt valve
Ventilator m fan (electric) ; ventilator
Verband m bandage
Verbandskasten m first aid kit
verbinden to connect (join)
Verbindung f connection (train, etc); service (bus, etc); line (phone)
verbleit leaded

VERBOTEN forbidden

Verbrechen nt crime
verbrennen to burn
Verbrennung f burn
verbringen to spend (time)
verderben to go bad (food) ; to spoil
verdienen to deserve ; to earn
verdorben bad (fruit, vegetables)
Verein m society (club)
vereinbaren to agree upon ; to arrange
Vereinbarung f agreement
Vereinigtes Königreich nt United Kingdom
Vereinigte Staaten (von Amerika) pl United States (of America)

Verfallsdatum nt expiry date ; eat-by date
verfault rotten (fruit, etc)
Vergangenheit f past
Vergaser m carburettor
vergeben to forgive
vergessen to forget
vergewaltigen to rape
Vergewaltigung f rape
Vergnügen nt enjoyment ; pleasure
  viel Vergnügen! have a good time!
Vergnügungspark m amusement park
vergoldet gold-plated
Vergrößerung f enlargement
verhaften to arrest
verheiratet married
verhindern to prevent
Verhütungsmittel nt contraceptive
Verkauf m sale
verkaufen to sell
Verkäufer(in) m/f salesman/woman
Verkehr m traffic
Verkehrsbüro nt tourist information
Verkehrspolizist(in) m/f traffic warden
Verkehrszeichen nt road sign
verkehrt wrong
verkehrt herum upside down
Verlängerungskabel nt extension cable
Verleih m rental company ; hire company
verletzen to injure
verletzt injured (person)
Verletzung f injury
verlieren to lose
verlobt engaged (to be married)
Verlobte(r) m/f fiancé(e)
verloren lost (object)
vermeiden to avoid

vermieten to rent ; to let *(room, house)*

Vermieter(in) *m/f* landlord/lady

Vermietung *f* hire

vermißt missing *(person)*

Vermittlung *f* telephone exchange ; operator

verpassen to miss *(plane, train, etc)*

Verrenkung *f* sprain

verschieben to postpone

verschieden different

verschiedene several; different

verschlucken to swallow

verschmutzt polluted

verschreiben to prescribe

verschwinden to disappear

verschwunden missing

versichern to insure

versichert sein to be insured

Versicherung *f* insurance

Versicherungsbescheinigung *f* insurance certificate

versilbert silver-plated

verspätet delayed

Verspätung *f* delay

versprechen to promise

Verstauchung *f* sprain

verstecken to hide

verstehen to understand

verstopft blocked *(pipe)* ; blocked *(road)* ; constipated

versuchen to try

Vertrag *m* contract

Vertreter(in) *m/f* sales rep

Verwandte(r) *m/f* relative

verwenden to use

verwirrt confused

Verzeihung! sorry ; excuse me

verzollen to declare *(customs)*

Video *nt* video

Videokamera *f* video camera

Videokassette *f* video cassette/tape

viel much

viele many

vielleicht perhaps

Viertel *nt* quarter

Viertelstunde *f* quarter of an hour

vierzehn Tage fortnight

Villa *f* villa

violett purple

Virus *nt* virus

Visitenkarte *f* business card

Visum *nt* visa

Vitamin *nt* vitamin

Vogel *m* bird

Volkslied *nt* folk song

Volkstanz *m* folk dance

voll full

Volleyball *m* volleyball

Vollkornbrot *nt* dark rye bread; wholemeal bread

Vollmilchschokolade *f* milk chocolate

Vollnarkose *f* general anaesthetic

Vollpension *f* full board

vollständig whole

volltanken to fill tank *(petrol)*

von from ; of

vor before ; in front of
 vor 4 Jahren 4 years ago

voraus ahead
 im voraus in advance

vorbei past

vorbereiten to prepare

Vorbestellung *f* reservation

Vorder- front

Vorderradantrieb *m* front-wheel drive

Vorfahrt *f* right of way *(on road)*

VORFAHRT BEACHTEN give way

vorgekocht ready-cooked

Vorhang *m* curtain

Vorhängeschloß *nt* padlock

Vorname *m* first name

VORNE EINSTEIGEN enter by front door

Vorschrift *f* regulation *(rule)*

VORSICHT caution

Vorspeise f starter (in meal) ; hors d'œuvre

VORSTELLUNG performance

Vor- und Zuname m first name and surname
Vorverkauf m advance booking
Vorwahl(nummer) f dialling code
vorziehen to prefer
Vulkan m volcano

W

Waage f scales (weighing)
wach awake
Wache f security guard
Wachsbehandlung f waxing (hair removal)
Waffe f gun
Wagen m car ; carriage (railway)
Wagenheber m jack (for car)
Wahl f choice ; election
wählen to dial (number) ; to choose
Wählton m dialling tone
während while ; during
Währung f currency
Wald m wood ; forest
Waldlehrpfad m nature trail
Wales nt Wales
Waliser(in) m/f Welshman/woman
walisisch Welsh
Walnuß(-nüsse) f walnut(s)
wandern to hike
Wanderschuhe pl walking boots
Wanderstock m walking stick
Wanderung f hike
Wanderweg m trail for ramblers
Wange f cheek
wann? when?
Waren pl goods
warm warm
Wärmflasche f hot-water bottle

Warmwasser nt hot water
Warnblinkanlage f hazard warning lights
Warndreieck nt warning triangle
Warnung f warning
Wartehalle f lounge (at airport)
warten (auf) to wait (for)
Wartesaal m waiting room
warum? why?
was? what?
waschbar washable
Waschbecken nt washbasin
Wäsche f linen ; washing (clothes)
Wäscheklammer f clothes peg
Wäscheleine f clothes line
waschen to wash
waschen und fönen wash and blow dry
Wascheraum m laundry room
Wäscherei f laundry
Wäschereiservice m laundry service
Wäschetrockner m tumble dryer
Waschmaschine f washing machine
Waschmittel nt detergent
Waschpulver nt washing powder
Waschsalon m launderette
Wasser nt water
wasserdicht waterproof
Wasserfall m waterfall
Wasserhahn m tap
Wassermelone f water melon
Wassermotorrad nt jet ski
Wasserski fahren to water ski
Wassertreter m pedal boat/pedalo
Watte f cotton wool
Wattebausch m cotton bud
Wechsel m change
Wechselgeld nt change (small coins)
Wechselkurs m exchange rate
wechseln to change (money) ; to give change
Wechselstube f bureau de

change
Weckdienst m early morning call
Wecker m alarm clock
Weckruf m alarm call
weder ... noch neither ... nor
Weg m path ; way ; country lane
wegfahren to leave in vehicle
weggehen to leave on foot
Wegweiser m signpost
Wegwerfwindeln pl disposable nappies
weh tun to ache ; to hurt (be painful)
weiblich female ; feminine
weich soft
weichgekochtes Ei nt soft-boiled egg
Weihnachten nt Christmas
Weihnachtsgeschenk nt Christmas present
Weihnachtskarte f Christmas card
weil because
Wein m wine
Weinberg m vineyard
Weinbrand m brandy
weinen to cry (weep)
Weinhandlung f wine shop
Weinkarte f wine list
Weinkeller m wine cellar
Weinprobe f wine-tasting
Weinstube f wine bar
Weintrauben pl grapes
weiß white
Weißbrot nt white bread
Weißwein m white wine
weit far ; loose (clothing)
weiter farther ; further on
weitermachen to continue
weitsichtig long sighted
Weizen m wheat
welche(r/s) which ; what ; which one
Wellen pl waves (on sea)
Welt f world
Wende f U-turn (in car)

wenden to turn
wenig little
weniger less
wenn if ; when (with present tense)
wer? who?
Werbespot m advert (on TV)
werden to become
Werk nt plant (factory) ; work (of art)
Werkstatt f garage (for repairs)
Werktag m weekday
Werkzeug nt tool
Werkzeugkasten m toolkit
Wert m value
Wertbrief m registered letter
Wertsachen pl valuables
wertvoll valuable
wesentlich essential
Wespe f wasp
wessen? whose?
Weste f waistcoat
Westen m west
westlich western
Wetter nt weather
Wetterbericht m weather forecast
Wettervorhersage f weather forecast
Wettkampf m match (sport)
Whirlpool m jacuzzi
wichtig important
wie like ; how
wieder again
wiederaufladen to recharge (battery)
wiederholen to repeat
wiegen to weigh
Wien Vienna
Wiese f lawn ; meadow
wieviel how much
wie viele how many?
Wild nt game (hunting, meat)
Wildleder nt suede
Wildschwein nt boar
willkommen welcome

185

W

Wimpern pl eyelashes
Wimperntusche f mascara
Wind m wind
Windeln pl nappies ; diapers
windig windy
Windmühle f windmill
Windpocken pl chickenpox
Windschutz m windbreak *(camping)*
Windschutzscheibe f windscreen
windstill calm *(weather)*
Winter m winter
Winterreifen pl snow tyres
wir we
wirksam effective *(remedy, etc)*
Wirt(in) m(f) landlord (-lady)
Wirtschaft f pub ; inn ; economy
wissen to know *(facts)*
Witwe(r) f(m) widow(er)
Witz m joke
wo? where?
Woche f week

W

Wochenende nt weekend
Wochentag m weekday
wöchentlich weekly
woher... where ... from
wohin... where
Wohnadresse f home address
wohnen to stay ; to live *(reside)*
Wohnheim nt hostel
Wohnmobil nt dormobile
Wohnort m home address
Wohnung f flat *(apartment)*
Wohnwagen m caravan
Wohnzimmer nt living room ;
  lounge *(in house)*
wolkig cloudy
Woll- woollen
Wolldecke f blanket
Wolle f wool

W

wollen to want *(wish for)*
Wort nt word
  in Worten in words *(on cheques)*
Wörterbuch nt dictionary
Wunde f wound *(injury)*

Würfel m dice
Wurst f sausage
Würstchenbude f hot-dog stand
würzig spicy
Würzmischung f seasoning

Y

Yachthafen m marina

Z

zäh tough *(meat)*
Zahl f number *(figure)*
zahlen to pay
Zähler m meter
Zahn m tooth
Zahnarzt/Zahnärztin m/f dentist
Zahnbürste f toothbrush
Zahncreme f toothpaste
Zähne pl teeth
Zahnpasta f toothpaste
Zahnschmerzen pl toothache
Zahnseide f dental floss
Zahnstocher m toothpick
Zange f pliers
Zäpfchen nt suppository
z.B. e.g.
Zebrastreifen m zebra crossing
Zehe f toe
Zeichentrickfilm m cartoon
Zeichnung f drawing
zeigen to show
Zeit f time *(of day)*
Zeitkarte f season ticket
Zeitschrift f magazine
Zeitung f newspaper
Zeitungskiosk m newsstand
Zelt nt tent
Zeltboden m groundsheet
zelten to camp
Zentimeter m centimetre
zentral central
Zentralheizung f central heating

Zentralverriegelung f central locking (car)
Zentrum nt centre
zerbrechlich fragile ; breakable
zerrissen torn
Ziege f goat
Ziegel m brick

ZIEHEN pull

Ziel nt destination ; goal ; target
ziemlich quite (rather)
Zigarette(n) f cigarette(s)
Zigarettenpapier nt cigarette papers
Zigarre(n) f cigar(s)
Zimmer nt room (in house, hotel)

ZIMMER FREI vacancies

Zimmermädchen nt chambermaid
Zimmernachweis m accommodation information
Zimmernummer f room number
Zimmerservice m room service
Zirkus m circus
Zitrone f lemon
Zitronentee m lemon tea

ZOLL customs/toll

zollfrei duty-free
Zone f zone
Zoo m zoo
Zopf m plait
zornig angry
zu to ; off (water supply) ; too ; at
zu Hause at home

ZU MIETEN for hire
ZU VERKAUFEN for sale

zubereiten to make a meal
Zucchini pl courgettes
Zucker m sugar
zuckerfrei sugar-free
Zuckerkrankheit f diabetes
zudrehen to turn off (tap)

Zug m train
Zuhause nt home
zuhören to listen
Zukunft f future
Zulassung f log book (car)
Zuname m surname
Zündkerzen pl spark plugs
Zündschlüssel m ignition key
Zündung f ignition
Zunge f tongue
zurück back
zurückfahren to go back (by car)
zurückgeben to give back
zurückgehen to go back (on foot)
zurückkommen to come back
zurücklassen to leave behind
zusammen together
Zusammenstoß m crash (collision)
zusätzlich extra ; additional
zuschauen to watch
Zuschlag m surcharge ; supplement
zuschließen to lock
Zustellung f delivery (of mail)
Zutaten pl ingredients
Zutritt m entry ; admission

ZUTRITT VERBOTEN no entry

zuviel too much
zuviel berechnen to overcharge
zuzüglich extra
zwanglose Kleidung f informal dress
zwei two
Zweigstelle f branch (office)
zweimal twice
zweite(r/s) second
zweite Klasse f second class
Zwiebel f bulb ; onion
Zwillinge pl twins
zwischen between
Zwischenstecker m adaptor
Zyste f cyst

Z

NOUNS

In German all nouns begin with a capital letter. The plural forms vary from noun to noun – there is no universal plural as in English (cat – cats, dog – dogs):

singular	*plural*
Mann	**Männer**
Frau	**Frauen**
Tisch	**Tische**

German nouns are *masculine (m)*, *feminine (f)* or *neuter (nt)*, and this is shown by the words for **the** and **a(n)** used before them:

	masculine	*feminine*	*neuter*
the	**der Mann**	**die Frau**	**das Licht**
a, an	**ein Mann**	**eine Frau**	**ein Licht**

The plural for **the** for all forms is **die**:

        die Männer   **die Frauen**   **die Lichter**

There's no plural for the **ein** form. The plural noun is used on its own.

From the phrases in this book you'll see that the endings for the word for **the** vary according to what part the noun plays in the sentence:

If the noun is the subject of the sentence, i.e. carrying out the action, then it is in the *nominative* case (the one found in dictionaries), e.g. **der Mann steht auf (the man stands up)**. The subject **der Mann** comes before the verb.

If the noun is the direct object of the sentence, i.e. the action of the verb is being carried on the noun, then the noun is in the *accusative* case, e.g. **ich sehe den Mann (I see the man)**. Note how the ending of **der** has changed to **den**. The same applies to **ein**, e.g. **ich sehe einen Mann (I see a man)**.

If you see in front of the English noun **of**, **'s**, or **s'**, then the noun is in the *genitive* case (i.e. it belongs to someone or something), e.g. **das Haus der Frau (the woman's house)**. Note how the ending of **die** (Frau) has changed to **der**. The same applies to **ein**, e.g. **das Haus einer Frau (a woman's house)**.

If you see **to the** or **to a** in front of the English noun, then the noun is in the *dative* case, e.g. **ich gebe es der Frau (I give it to the woman)**. Note how the ending of **die** (Frau) has changed to **der**. The same applies to **ein**, e.g. **ich gebe es einer Frau (I give it to a woman)**.

Other words used before nouns have similar endings to **der** and **ein**. Those like **der** are:

dieser this ; jener that ; jeder each ; welcher which

Those like **ein** are:

mein my ; dein your (familiar sing.) **; Ihr your** (polite sing. and plural) **; sein his ; ihr her ; unser our ; euer your** (familiar plural)**; ihr their**

Here are the cases for **der**:

	masculine	*feminine*	*neuter*	*plural*
Nominative	**der Mann**	**die Frau**	**das Licht**	**die Frauen**
Accusative	**den Mann**	**die Frau**	**das Licht**	**die Frauen**
Genitive	**des Mannes**	**der Frau**	**des Lichtes**	**der Frauen**
Dative	**dem Mann**	**der Frau**	**dem Licht**	**den Frauen**

Here are the cases for **ein**:

	masculine	*feminine*	*neuter*
Nominative	**ein Mann**	**eine Frau**	**ein Licht**
Accusative	**einen Mann**	**eine Frau**	**ein Licht**
Genitive	**eines Mannes**	**einer Frau**	**eines Lichtes**
Dative	**einem Mann**	**einer Frau**	**einem Licht**

The word **kein** (**no**, **not any**) also has the same endings as for **ein**, except that it can be used in the plural:

Nominative **keine Männer**	*Genitive* **keiner Männer**
Accusative **keine Männer**	*Dative* **keinen Männern**

MY, YOUR, HIS, HER

These words all take the same endings as for **ein** and agree with the noun they accompany, i.e. whether *masculine*, *feminine*, etc and according to the noun's function (*nominative*, *accusative*, etc):

mein Mann kommt my husband is coming (nom.)
ich liebe meinen Mann I love my husband (acc.)
das Auto meines Mannes my husband's car (gen.)
ich gebe es meinem Mann I give it to my husband (dat.)
meine Kinder kommen my children are coming (nom. pl.)
ich liebe meine Kinder I love my children (acc. pl.)
die Spielsachen meiner Kinder my children's toys (gen. pl.)
ich gebe es meinen Kindern I give it to my children (dat. pl.)

Other words which take these endings are:

dein your (familiar sing.) **; sein his ; ihr her ; unser our ; euer your** (familiar plural) **; Ihr your** (polite sing. and plural) **; ihr their**

ADJECTIVES

When adjectives are used before a noun, their endings vary like the words for **der** and **ein**, depending on the gender (*masculine*, *feminine* or *neuter*) and whether the noun is plural, and how the noun is used in the sentence (whether it is the subject, object, etc). Here are examples using the adjective **klug – clever**

	masculine	feminine
Nominative	**der kluge Mann**	**die kluge Frau**
	ein kluger Mann	**eine kluge Frau**
Accusative	**den klugen Mann**	**die kluge Frau**
	einen klugen Mann	**eine kluge Frau**
Genitive	**des klugen Mannes**	**der klugen Frau**
	eines klugen Mannes	**einer klugen Frau**
Dative	**dem klugen Mann**	**der klugen Frau**
	einem klugen Mann	**einer klugen Frau**

	neuter	plural
Nominative	**das kluge Kind**	**die klugen Männer**
	ein kluges Kind	**kluge Frauen**
Accusative	**das kluge Kind**	**die klugen Männer**
	ein kluges Kind	**kluge Frauen**
Genitive	**des klugen Kindes**	**der klugen Männer**
	eines klugen Kindes	**kluger Frauen**
Dative	**dem klugen Kind**	**den klugen Männern**
	einem klugen Kind	**klugen Frauen**

When the adjective follows the verb, then there is no agreement:
der Mann ist klug / die Frau ist klug / das Kind ist klug

PRONOUNS

subject		direct object	
I	ich	**me**	mich
you *(familiar sing.)*	du	**you** *(familiar sing.)*	dich
he/it	er	**him/it**	ihn
she/it	sie	**her/it**	sie
it *(neuter)*	es	**it** *(neuter)*	es
we	wir	**us**	uns
you *(familiar plural)*	ihr	**you** *(familiar plural)*	euch
you *(polite sing. & pl.)*	Sie	**you** *(polite sing. & pl.)*	Sie
they *(all genders)*	sie	**them** *(all genders)*	sie

Indirect object pronouns are:

to me mir ; **to you** *(familiar sing.)* **dir** ; **to him/it ihm** ; **to her/it ihr** ; **to it** *(neuter)* **ihm** ; **to us uns** ; **to you** *(familiar plural)* **euch** ; **to you** *(polite sing. and plural)* **Ihnen** ; **to them ihnen**

YOU

There are two ways of addressing people in German: the familiar form – **du** (when talking to just one person you know well), **ihr** (when talking to more than one person you know well), and the polite form – **Sie** (always written with a capital letter), which can be used for one or more people.

VERBS

There are two main types of verb in German – **weak** verbs (which are regular) and **strong** verbs (which are irregular).

	weak	*strong*
	SPIELEN	HELFEN
	to play	**to help**
ich	**spiele**	**helfe**
du	**spielst**	**hilfst**
er/sie/es	**spielt**	**hilft**
wir	**spielen**	**helfen**
ihr	**spielt**	**helft**
Sie	**spielen**	**helfen**
sie	**spielen**	**helfen**

Other examples of **strong** verbs are:

	SEIN	HABEN
	to be	**to have**
ich	**bin**	**habe**
du	**bist**	**hast**
er/sie/es	**ist**	**hat**
wir	**sind**	**haben**
ihr	**seid**	**habt**
Sie	**sind**	**haben**
sie	**sind**	**haben**

To make a verb negative, add **nicht**:

ich verstehe nicht	*I don't understand*
das funktioniert nicht	*it doesn't work*

PAST TENSE

Here are a number of useful past tenses:

ich war	*I was*
wir waren	*we were*
Sie waren	*you were (polite)*
ich hatte	*I had*
wir hatten	*we had*
Sie hatten	*you had (polite)*
ich/er/sie/es spielte	*I/he/she/it played*
Sie/wir/sie spielten	*you/we/they played*
ich/er/sie/es half	*I/he/she/it helped*
Sie/wir/sie halfen	*you/we/they helped*

Another past form corresponds to the English **have ...ed** and uses the verb **haben to have**:

ich habe gespielt	*I have played*
wir haben geholfen	*we have helped*

In German the present tense is very often used where we would use the future tense in English:

ich schicke ein Fax	*I will send a fax*
ich schreibe einen Brief	*I will write a letter*